FOCUS ON GROUP PSYCHOTHERAPY

Clinical Essays

Focus on Group Psychotherapy

Clinical Essays

WITHDRAWN

Saul Scheidlinger

INTERNATIONAL UNIVERSITIES PRESS, INC.
New York

Library of Congress Cataloging in Publication Data

Scheidlinger, Saul, 1918–
    Focus on group psychotherapy.

    Bibliography: p.
    Includes index.
Contents: Who does what to whom in "people-
helping" groups and why? — Group process in group
psychotherapy — The concept of empathy in group
psychotherapy — On the concept of the "mother-
group" — [etc.]
    1. Group psychotherapy—Addresses, essays,
lectures. I. Title. [DNLM: 1. Psychotherapy, Group
—Collected works. WM 430 S318f]
RC488.S28   616.89'152   82-53
ISBN 0-8236-1990-7   AACR2

Manufactured in the United States of America

To my son
David J. Scheidlinger, M.D.

CONTENTS

Part IV
Group Treatment of Adults

Part V
Group Psychotherapy in the 1980's

PREFACE

This volume consists of a selection of contributions to the theory and practice of group psychotherapy. All but two of these essays have already appeared in widely dispersed publications. Their presentation as a unit responds to the expressed wish of students and colleagues to have these papers made more easily accessible.

With its explicit focus on clinical issues in group psychotherapy, this book can serve as a companion piece to my recently published volume, *Psychoanalytic Group Dynamics — Basic Readings* (1980), which was limited specifically to group process theory.

The varied articles in this publication cover a time span of two decades; but their insights constitute, in a sense, a personal account of one group psychotherapist's view of his field during almost four decades. Group psychotherapy is an infinitely more complex discipline today than it was when I conducted my first group as a trainee in 1943. In fact, as the book reveals, its mind–boggling growth has been such as to almost justify the facetious definition of a group therapy expert as someone "who knows less and less about more and more."

I hope that the reader will discern in these contributions my ongoing and earnest desire to clarify through restatement and definition the vague concepts and loose terminology unfortunately characteristic of our field. It should also be apparent that, coincident with my basic allegiance to Freudian theory of personality, I have always relied on eclecticism and on innovation in adapting group treatment methodologies to the realities of patients, whether children, adolescents, or adults. The detailed and lengthy clinical illustrations are intended to close the gap between practice and theory and to allow the reader to draw independent conclusions from the data.

The material in this volume has been grouped into five parts. Part I, hitherto unpublished, maps the clinical group modalities in mental health within the context of the broader realm of "people–

helping" groups. Part II contains five chapters devoted to what is termed "limited-domain theorizing"—each designed to serve as a building block for a future general theory of group psychotherapy. Parts III and IV deal with group practice issues and with treatment models for children, adolescents, and adults. In these contributions, the evolution of orderly and systematic technologies for the group therapy of hard-to-reach, severely deprived patients is a prime consideration. The final section, Part V, written specifically for this book, attempts to predict the directions of group psychotherapy for the 1980's.

Each part opens with editorial discussions aimed at integrating the content and placing it in proper theoretical perspective.

I hope that this book will serve as a source of readings in training programs for group psychotherapists and other professionals working with human groups. Perhaps experienced practitioners will also find that some parts serve as refreshers or stimulants in their quest for a broader scope in group psychotherapy.

Saul Scheidlinger
August 1981

ACKNOWLEDGMENTS

I am greatly indebted to the many people who have served as enablers and as helpers in the development of my ideas about group psychotherapy. In addition to my numerous colleagues and students, my friends Professors Leopold Bellak and Emanuel Hallowitz have been a source of unflinching encouragement and support over many years.

Special thanks are due to the following co-authors of three of the essays in this book for kindly allowing me to reprint our joint work: Marjorie Holden, M.S.W., Marjorie Pyrke, M.S.W., Kenneth Porter, M.D., and Estelle Rauch, M.S.W. I have also acknowledged their specific contributions in the sourcenotes for the appropriate chapters.

I am grateful to the publishers and copyright holders for permission to reproduce previously published pieces, as noted in the sourcenotes.

My appreciation also goes to Drs. Mel Roman and Arthur Waldhorn for their editorial help, which served to enhance the readability of some of the essays.

I am indebted to Evelyn Post for her patience and painstaking efforts in the preparation of successive drafts of the manuscript.

Last but not least, my wife, Rosalyn Tauber Scheidlinger, not only provided the climate necessary for the work on this book, but also most valuable editorial assistance.

Part I

THE CONTEXT OF
GROUP PSYCHOTHERAPY

INTRODUCTION

Chapter 1, which was expressly written for this volume, deals with the urgent need for conceptual and methodological clarity in the broader realm of so-called "people-helping" groups. Despite the expected overlap dictated by the complexity of the task, I am advocating that an overall framework be maintained, wherein clinical group psychotherapy, with its primary focus on the "repair" of personality pathology, be distinguished from "therapeutic" group modalities in mental health as well as from the varied personal growth, training, and support group endeavors in the community.

All of these approaches can have beneficial effects, as they share the utilization of potent motivational forces for human betterment inherent in group involvement; they differ, nevertheless, with respect to such essential features as clientele, basic goals, techniques, and backgrounds of the service providers. More specifically, each group modality employed to promote change in people's behavior is best considered in the context of the following four interrelated variables: (1) the change-agent variable, which includes the latter's training, theoretical persuasion, and objectives for the group; (2) the client variable, which refers to such characteristics as sex, age, sociocultural background, and the expectations in the use of the given group service; (3) the methodology variable, which entails the service provider's preference for specific techniques within the confines of his or her broader assumptions regarding the promotion of desired behavior change in the participants, and (4) the process variable, which reflects the totality of what the service provider believes to be transpiring in the group experience. (What a given change-agent believes to be transpiring is not necessarily the same as what actually transpires as observed by others.)

3

In the proposed definition of clinical group psychotherapy, it is worth noting that the patient is the *individual*—never the group. Next, the therapist is a mental health professional who has received specialized training in this modality for specific populations, i.e., adults, adolescents, or children. (Proficiency in dyadic or family therapy is not sufficient in itself to qualify one for group psychotherapy practice.) Finally, the diagnostic assessment of each patient's problem is only minimally bound to diagnostic labels, and is instead related to the existing strengths and weaknesses in ego functioning.

There is also an implied assumption in the forthcoming chapter that group psychotherapy of various kinds should contain definite indications and contraindications for specific patients, whether utilized exclusively or in combination with other interventions. This area continues to be the subject of much study and further refinements in the field.

While personally adhering to the Freudian psychoanalytic school of thought, I make no claim that, apart from its possibly broader scope as an explanatory system in psychology, it has proven more effective as a group therapy than other models. In fact, my position in the introductory chapter and throughout this volume reflects an underlying belief in the need for a pragmatic orientation—the promotion of objective, interdisciplinary research endeavors aimed at assessing ways in which groups can best be employed in the service of both mental health prevention and therapy.

Chapter 1

WHO DOES WHAT TO WHOM IN "PEOPLE-HELPING" GROUPS AND WHY? THERAPEUTIC GROUP APPROACHES IN COMMUNITY MENTAL HEALTH

The disquieting symptoms of personal and social pathology characteristic of this "age of anxiety" highlight for us the importance of group belonging as a source of sustenance and gratification for the individual. From the standpoint of community mental health theory, an essential component of any person's social and psychological functioning resides in a meaningful reciprocal relationship between the individual and at least one, if not a number of, relatively stable groups. Whether one chooses to conceptualize this primarily in Erikson's terms of individual and group identity, along Freudian lines of identifications and object relationships, or in sociology's framework of individual security and social bonding, the implications are sufficiently clear: When we enhance the stability of family life, of peer groupings, of informal organizations, or of neighborhoods as–a–whole, we are in effect promoting the viability of psychosocial "care-giving" systems — vital agents in the prevention of breakdown and in the maintenance of positive mental health (Caplan, 1974). This is a formidable task in the face of rapid social and cultural changes in today's society with its conflicting standards, massive economic readjustments, and the impersonality of modern life. In depressed urban areas where social disorgani-

5

zation and personal deprivation assume major proportions, this problem becomes a staggering one.

As Americans in increasing numbers began searching in recent years for new group experiences to help them find meaning for their existence, new guidelines for living as well as avenues for self–actualization — an almost chaotic proliferation of psychosocial group modalities came into being. I need only mention as illustrations the myriad of still widely advertised encounter, sensitivity or assertiveness training, self–help, transcendental meditation and other religious groupings (Parloff, 1970).

It is my aim in this introductory chapter to suggest a meaningful differential framework for viewing all of these so–called "people–helping" groups — with particular focus on those employed in the human services' sector which I represent — in the face of an almost complete blurring of boundary lines among them in the marketplace.

As a beginning, I propose that when trying to differentiate between the varied group modalities, we think of them as more or less planned efforts at promoting change in human behavior. Next, while it is not uncommon to have all such beneficial group measures portrayed (Lieberman, 1977) or even labeled as "group therapy" (Mowrer, 1964), I would urge from the outset that we aim at the strictest possible delineation between the varicolored spectrum of group modalities — be they offered in the context of mental health settings or without — and traditional group psychotherapy.

Four Approaches

Much confusion in this realm of "who does what to whom and why" could be avoided if we distinguish at the outset among the following four major, broadly related yet specifically different, categories of "people-helping" groups: Category I, Group Psychotherapy; Category II, "Therapeutic" Groups, addressed to designated clients in mental health settings; Category III, Human

Development and Training Groups; and Category IV, Self-Help and Mutual Help Groups.

Category I: Group Psychotherapy

In attempting this kind of differentiation, I would first define *group psychotherapy* as I once did (Scheidlinger, 1967), as a specific field of clinical practice lodged in the broader realm of the psychotherapies. It refers to a psychosocial process wherein an experienced one-to-one psychotherapist (usually a psychiatrist, psychologist, social worker, or nurse-clinician), with special additional group process training, utilizes the emotional interaction in small, carefully planned groups to "repair" mental ill health, i.e., to effect amelioration of personality dysfunctions in individuals specifically selected for this purpose. A clinical orientation, including a diagnostic assessment of each member's problems and strengths, is part of this picture. The participants are cognizant of the psychotherapeutic purpose and accept the group experience as a means to obtain relief from distress and modify their pathological mode of functioning. (The remaining chapters in this book will be devoted entirely to some of the theoretical and practical aspects of this modality, which is exclusively employed by mental health professionals.)

Category II: "Therapeutic" Groups

Category II refers to mental-health-oriented *"therapeutic"* groups, and comprises all other group approaches utilized by human services' personnel (not necessarily trained professionals), in inpatient or outpatient clinical facilities. These approaches serve most often as an auxiliary or conjoint measure to a primary treatment regimen, and are aimed at some kind of remediation or at the enhancement of optimum functioning in persons designated as psychiatric patients. In hospital settings, examples would be therapeutic community, social rehabilitation, or occupational therapy groups. In outpatient settings there might be waiting list or diagnostic groups, as well as parent counseling groups in child guidance clinics. The para-therapeutic groups for children and adolescents described in Chapter 9 would belong here as well. (Since these groupings are most closely allied with group psychotherapy proper, I will elaborate on them further at a later point in this chapter as well as in Chapter 12.)

Category III: Human Development and Training Groups

My proposed Category III, which combines *human development and training* groups, belongs more in the realm of affective and cognitive education than psychotherapy. It would encompass on one end of a continuum the whole array of personal-expressive, consciousness-raising, and sensitivity groups open to the general public. As noted by Rogers (1967), Moustakas (1967), and more recently by Solomon and Berzon (1972), all of these markedly diverse group undertakings appear to share such basic aims as countering social isolation, making relationships more authentic, spontaneous and meaningful, as well as helping people to become more sensitive to their feelings and bodies.

On the other end of this continuum would fall the multiple training and organizational development enterprises, which have generally emerged in this country under three different auspices. First, there was the Laboratory Method with its T-group theory and practice of the late 1940's, described by Bradford, Gibb, and Benne (1964) and by Golembiewski and Blumberg (1970). There is general agreement among these authors that laboratory training constitutes an educational endeavor with such goals as: (1) enhancing participants' awareness and sensitivity to emotional reactions in themselves and others; (2) learning about the perceptions and consequences of one's behavior on other group members; (3) clarifying personal and social values in a democratic and scientific context; (4) acquiring insights that would link personal values with situational requirements; and (5) achieving behavioral skills required for effective social functioning. An offshoot of this Laboratory Method, which had originally been sponsored by the National Training Laboratories and the National Education Association in Bethel, Maine, is the *self-analytic* group, first introduced at Harvard University and subsequently employed in the human relations departments of other universities. The major aim of these small, nondirective classroom study groups, led by a course instructor, is to analyze group process and structure as well as the emergence of group member roles (Bales, 1950; Gibbard, Hartman, and Mann, 1974). Similar to these self-analytic groups are the so-called Tavistock Study groups originated by A. K. Rice (1965) at the Tavistock Clinic in London, England, and subsequently introduced into this country in the context of Group Relations Conferences by the Washington School of Psychiatry (Rioch, 1970). Based in large measure on the group process theories of Bion (1959), these training conferences stress experiential learning about overt and covert leadership and authority issues in small as well as in large groups.

Category IV: Self-Help Groups

As for Category IV, while *self-help* groups with problem-solving objectives, such as Alcoholics Anonymous, Recovery, Inc., Synanon or even spiritualist healing groups, have been with us for some time, to judge by the literature, they appear to have been "discovered" only recently by the mental health professions. Thus, there are, for example, Caplan and Killilea's (1976) and Dumont's (1974) writings on support systems and self-help treatment programs, as well as a whole issue of the *Journal of Applied Behavioral Science* (Summer–Fall 1976) devoted to the subject.

Self-help groups generally represent voluntary, face-to-face group structures for mutual aid and the accomplishment of a special purpose. They usually comprise peers seeking assistance in satisfying a common need, overcoming a common handicap or life-disrupting problem, and attempting to bring about desired social or personal change. There is a perception afoot here that member needs cannot be adequately met by existing institutions and professions. Once members agree to assume individual responsibility, the group offers them material assistance, emotional support, an ideology, and, above all, a "cause," which together serve to enhance a strong sense of personal identity. In their "peer therapy" mission, self–help groups such as Alcoholics Anonymous generally aim at blocking the relapse process rather than curing the underlying causes of the malady, i.e., alcohol abuse.

Granting that it is often difficult to chart exact boundaries among the above four broad categories of "people–helping" groups, I maintain nevertheless that such an attempt at differentiation by the service providers, albeit with some ambiguities, is preferable to the utter confusion one finds in the realm of the human services as well as in the literature.

In this connection, when encountering any kind of group problem–solving modality in practice or in print, I have found it personally useful to ask the following five questions: (1) Who are the group members and how were they selected? (2) What are the specific aims of a given service provider for each group member and for the group as an entity? (3) What is the practitioner's theory (ideology) regarding the etiology of client problems as well as regarding what transpires in the group process? (4) What are the specific techniques employed? (5) What is the practitioner's professional training and work experience? These guidelines have invariably helped me in placing the given group approach in a meaningful context (not to mention the assessment of the probable competency of the practitioner).

In view of my avowed interest in treatment groups offered under an explicit mental health umbrella, the remainder of my discussion will accordingly be devoted to this more circumscribed theme. (I do not mean to imply here that any one category of human helping groups is superior to any other, but rather that they differ from one another. Only the need of a given client can suggest the optimum modality appropriate for the situation at hand.)

During the 1950's, group psychotherapists were very preoccupied with defending the efficacy of their method vis–à–vis dyadic psychotherapy. The last two decades, in contrast, with group therapy safely ensconced as an accepted modality in mental health, can be characterized by an almost explosive proliferation of specific group therapies, ranging from the psychoanalytic group approach, to experiential, transactional analysis, gestalt, psychodrama and even behavior modification groups. In other words, almost every major "school" of individual therapy (Corsini, 1973) has produced some practitioners who have applied its techniques and theories to group treatment. Any discussion of trends is complicated not only by the voluminous writings, but also by marked discrepancies in frames of reference and standards of reporting, not infrequently by proponents of a similar theoretical viewpoint (Kaplan and Sadock, 1971).

Luckily, an earlier extreme "professional nationalism" has gradually given way, in part at least, to a search for generic conceptual issues that transcend specific theoretical schools of thought. This has been accompanied by a much–needed emphasis on research, including the use of recordings and videotapes, which permit consensual validation of assumed elements in the therapeutic process (Dies, 1979).

When a trained group therapist of any theoretical persuasion has placed a patient in his or her group, one is nowadays quite safe in assuming that the following two questions had been posed beforehand: (1) Is this patient most likely to benefit from the contemplated kind of group therapy when contrasted with or combined with dyadic therapy, family therapy, and/or drug therapy? (2) Given the unquestioned desirability of group therapy for this patient, is the particular group under consideration a suitable one? This second question pertains to what is termed "balancing" a group, with reference to such criteria as age, sex, ethnic, socioeconomic and educational backgrounds, as well as the specific nature of the pathology. For example, having one man in a group comprising women only would not be advisable. Also, placing a withdrawn and constricted individual in a group of impulsive personalities would be as questionable as having a group containing withdrawn and constricted individuals only (Freedman and Sweet, 1954).

Most group psychotherapists are likely to see prospective group patients at least a few times individually. The purpose here is to prepare them for the new procedures as well as for the inevitable initial strains involved in joining a group. It is also helpful as a means of establishing at least a minimal working alliance with the therapist. Since it is still impossible nowadays to predict with accuracy how a given group experience will turn out, there is usually an implied, if not an explicit, agreement that the first few sessions in the group be viewed as a trial period by both the group member and therapist (Rabin, 1970). (As will be seen later in Chapter 11, some group therapists use combined individual and group sessions almost routinely, especially where character reconstruction and deep-seated insight are aimed for.)

Among the many unresolved conceptual issues in the field of group psychotherapy is the relative importance of group processes versus individual personality transactions. While almost always initially depicted as the treatment of *individuals in a group,* there are still a few noted authorities, such as Slavson (1964) and Wolf and Schwartz (1962), who question the importance of group-as-a-whole phenomena in group therapy, and stress instead the primacy of concepts based on the individual patient and on interpersonal transactions. This is in contrast to some British group therapists such as Bion (1959) or Ezriel (1950), who, with their exclusive preoccupation with group events at the expense of individual personality factors, have gone to the other extreme. I have aired these topics recently in a broader context (Scheidlinger, 1980), in addition to my discussion of them in the narrower, reprinted critique of Bion's (1959) theories in Chapter 2 of this book.

It is worth noting here that within the dominant psychoanalytic camp of group psychotherapists to which I generally adhere, there are two major subschools. The first, comprising such writers as Slavson (1964), Glatzer (1962), and Durkin (1964), relies on the classical Freudian model that calls for the analysis of transference and resistance and for "working through" (i.e., the degree to which a patient's ego can be helped over layers of resistance to master unconscious motivational content). The second is represented by Yalom (1970, 1975), who is a follower of the so-called "Sullivanian School." Yalom discounts the importance of the Freudian "transference neurosis," of planned therapeutic regression leading to genetic insight, and of covert group–as–a–whole manifestations.

A very popular extension and adaptation of the psychodynamic orientation within group psychotherapy is transactional analysis (Goulding, 1972). The treatment here attempts to identify the covert gratifications — the "payoffs" of the "games" which people play with one another (Berne, 1966). The task of the therapist and group is to recognize the momentary ego states (parent, child, adult) which characterize each individual's interactions. There is also a call for identifying the particular "game" played as well as the unconscious life plan which the patient appears to have chosen in early childhood. This life plan resides in the enduring position of whether the self and others are "okay" or "not okay." Therapeutic change is predicated on the patient's evolving ability to planfully shift his "real self" from one ego state to another.

The remainder of this chapter will deal with the variegated spectrum of "therapeutic" group influence measures that belong in my earlier mentioned Category II and which are outside of the more strictly clinical range of group psychotherapy.

Not unlike the realm of group psychotherapy (Category I), these varied "therapeutic" group modalities employed in clinical psychiatric settings are so different and wide–ranging as to almost defy any lucid description and classification. Their number and diversity are enough to confuse, if not to frighten the uninitiated, since they encompass many methodologies used by many practitioners. The difficulty in understanding this broad array of group practices is compounded by the fact that a single approach such as social rehabilitation groups for psychiatric patients, for example, might be used today in clinical or nonclinical, residential or out-patient settings, and be conducted by psychiatrists, psychologists, social workers, nurses, occupational therapists, or even nonprofessional workers! And yet, as I have noted elsewhere (Scheidlinger, 1968a), the need for arriving at some kind of conceptual clarity and order is essential in this field, which is already beset by professional role conflicts and confused terminology that encompass such rubrics as group therapy, group education, social group work, art therapy, recreational therapy, occupational therapy, and the like.

MAJOR GROUP INFLUENCE FOCI

The five guideposts mentioned earlier in this chapter, as a means of comprehending the way a given group practitioner is planning to utilize the well-known motivational forces for change and growth in small groups, can serve as a first step in this direction. In addition, I have found it useful to classify "therapeutic" group influence attempts other than group psyhotherapy according to their major focus: (1) *Activity–Catharsis–Mastery;* (2) *Cognitive–Informational;* (3) *Interpersonal–Socialization;* and (4) *Relationship–Experiential.* (Group psychotherapy might be characterized in such a scheme as comprising a fifth category, an *Uncovering–Introspective* one.)

While no single classification can be expected to resolve the confusion in such a complex field, the one proposed here has a few advantages. First, it is addressed to a given group influence model instead of to the practitioner and to his or her orientation. Second, it is not directly dependent on the nature and degree of personality pathology of the group members, but on their particular momentary need for intervention. Third, in the context of mental health or even learning theory, it permits one to ascertain, if only hypothetically, which of the group members' needs or ego functions (Bellak, Hurvich, and Gediman, 1973) are likely to be engaged by a given modality directly, and which more tangentially. Finally, as one moves from the first focus to the last, allowance is made for stimulation of increasing "depth" levels of group interaction, which are discussed in the next chapter of this volume.

Activity-Catharsis-Mastery Focus. Within the suggested framework, it can readily be seen how manual activity or work groups that foster reaching out, touching, and exploration of materials address themselves to broadly similar needs. Included here are group programs for patients with severe ego pathology in which the movement from self-absorption to even a rudimentary interest in some outside object represents a step forward. Occupational, art, and dance "therapies" that provide opportunities for catharsis, channeling of tension, and ego mastery belong here as well. Additional ego benefits inherent in these approaches pertain to reality testing and enhancing the self-concept.

Cognitive-Informational Focus. This category comprises, on the one hand, group educational models such as family life education that emphasize the imparting of new facts and new attitudes and, on the other hand, programs that attempt to teach new occupational or recreational skills (Fidler and Fidler, 1963). Both of these modalities are intended to engage those functions that are relatively undisturbed by conflict (autonomous ego functions).

Interpersonal-Socialization Focus. The third category consists of group approaches that are designed to meet people's needs for security, a sense of belonging, and companionship. Traditional social group work as practiced in leisure time or so-called "character-building" institutions would be a case in point (Hartford, 1972). The aim here with youths, for example, is to enhance socialization, offer support at the usual points of developmental crisis, maximize individual capacities, and encourage responsible community roles. In clinical settings this kind of approach would be exemplified by patient government groups, sewing clubs, informal lounge and game room programs, or certain kinds of orientation groups (Rostov, 1965). In this category, there would be a planful and direct emphasis on strengthening such ego functions as the capacity for forming mature object relations, fostering catharsis and sublimation, and facilitating appropriate adaptive and defensive patterns (Fleischl, 1962).

Relationship–Experiential Focus. This appears in a number of intervention methods which, while generally removed from group psychotherapy proper, nevertheless often possess a definite diagnostic and treatment intent for each individual member. Included here would be therapeutic community sessions, patient social clubs, social rehabilitation and halfway house programs, as well as social group work in psychiatric or medical settings. The latter might address itself to larger milieu groupings or to small groups, whether of the activity or discussion type. An illustration that comes to mind is a special therapeutic community unit for chronic schizophrenic patients aimed at establishing "an environment with interpersonal relationships expressing humane concern, reducing the isolation of the psychotic and restoring the reality of a voice in one's affairs" (Hoover, Raulinaitis, and Spaner, 1965, p. 29). In this program, through the contact of each person with other individuals and a meaningful group, with staff members wearing civilian clothing and pitching in whenever a job needed to be done, an unusual democratic climate that stressed individual and social responsibility was evolved.

In ego psychological terms, the major emphasis is on the therapeutic value of group membership, on an enhanced ego identity accruing from being part of an effective and cohesive group. In such group approaches, ego strengthening also can occur through symbolic gratifications of earlier unmet needs and through a re-experiencing of emotional relationships in a new setting with new members.

The term "therapeutic community," first used by Main (1946) in conjunction with the resocialization of British psychiatric war casualties, has since been depicted in a great variety of fashions. In the words of Wilmer (1981), it has ". . . been used as a battle cry, a charm and a password" (p. 95), and in my experience tends to be most frequently confused with group psychotherapy. A thoughtful overview of the initial ideological fervor and more recent realizations of the limitations of the therapeutic community approach was also offered by Mandelbrote (1979).

It must be reemphasized here that no classification scheme can be expected to cover all eventualities and provide a perfect fit for every group intervention modality. Furthermore, exact demarcation lines are often difficult, if not impossible, to draw between certain educational or supportive and group treatment endeavors. In this connection, a review of the literature on the group treatment of psychotics leads to the impression that its goals and techniques would generally place it into the relationship–experiential category, even though the authors may have employed the term "group psychotherapy" to depict it.

We have to content ourselves with a minimum of guideposts along a continuum of group influence models that range from the least intensive educational efforts, on the one end, to the most depth–focused psychoanalytic endeavors, on the other. When patient needs are assessed in the framework of a comprehensive mental health facility, any one such group modality can constitute the most desirable and effective treatment choice for a given patient at a given time. As Campbell (1965) has noted, there is no better place to force a therapist to relinquish his unrealistic "drive to be the omnipotent healer" (p. 124) than the community mental health center. Here the chronic nature of many of the problems encountered, the limitations of available techniques, and the staggering needs for service, coupled with perennial staff shortages, force one to be flexible. Such flexibility may refer to the setting of realistic treatment goals, the choice of the most desirable treatment modality, and of the most appropriate helper.

Recognition of the proven potency of the varied "therapeutic" group approaches (Category II) in counteracting noxious emotional strains and enhancing people's positive mental health and rehabilitation, need not lead to an obliteration of the distinction between them and traditional group psychotherapy (Category I). One could argue, to the contrary, that a comprehensive view of all treatment modalities in the framework of planned intervention measures to restore adaptive social functioning only heightens the need for concise diagnostic assessment and treatment methods. This has been demonstrated in relation to crisis intervention and short-term psychotherapy, in which an orderly and integrated series of concepts and methodology are considered even more necessary than in long-term treatment (Bellak and Small, 1965). The greater the need for flexibility in goals and innovation in methodology encountered in the context of a community mental health center, for example, with its mandate to provide all of the required mental health services (outpatient and inpatient, direct and indirect) to a given neighborhood, the greater the necessity for conceptual and methodological clarity and order.

In sum, I have presented a broad overview of a variety of group approaches designed to help people. In the face of a thriving increase in the use of such approaches under mental health auspices, I have stressed the need for conceptual and methodological clarity on the part of service providers. A classification system for the various group intervention measures is suggested which is linked to the aims of the practitioner, to client needs, and to the technologies employed to promote change.

Broader issues regarding clinical group psychotherapy and "therapeutic" group approaches in mental health have been subjected to particular scrutiny, as an introduction to the more detailed discussion of selected group psychotherapy theories and practice models constituting the remainder of this book.

The federally funded community mental health center movement, which began in the sixties, was a major sponsor of the varied, mushrooming therapeutic group intervention measures discussed in this chapter. It is my belief that, irrespective of this movement's cloudy future under the new national administration, the planful use of the small group in the context of therapy, education, and personal growth is bound to escalate in the face of the ever increasing need for human services in urban America, especially among the less affluent and the poor.

Part II

THEORETICAL PERSPECTIVES

INTRODUCTION

The five contributions in the second part of this book are devoted to group psychotherapy theory. They all reflect my sobering awareness that the desired theoretical advances in this field have been hampered by a number of difficulties. To begin with, there is the fact that such theorizing must entail the integration of two disparate, yet related conceptual systems, each complex in its own right: (1) the small group process system, pertaining to the question of "what makes groups tick," and applicable to all groups; and (2) the group psychotherapy process system, a clinical intervention modality aimed at the amelioration of personality pathology. The understanding and management of the last-named group psychotherapy process is complicated by the co-presence of three interdependent factors: individual personalities; interpersonal transactions; and group-as-a-whole manifestations. To compound the problem, as I noted in Chapter 1 of this volume, these three factors operate on at least two "depth" levels: a contemporaneous dynamic and a genetic-regressive level.

The above circumstances account for my belief that an acceptable, global psychoanalytic group process theory (Scheidlinger, 1980) or group psychotherapy theory (see also Chapter 12 of this volume) is not in the cards, in the near future at least. The limited-domain kind of theorizing that encompasses specific concepts and phenomena, and which is exemplified here, will hopefully yield immediate leads for the improvement of aspects of clinical practice — and ultimately perhaps, general theories.

The primary thrust of Chapter 2 resides in its comprehensive critique of the theoretical model of W. R. Bion, a uniquely influential, yet insufficiently understood and rarely criticized British psychoanalyst. I am cognizant, in this connection, that the historical part of this presentation, which deals with the relationship between the group dynamics field and group psychotherapy in the 1950's, is somewhat outdated. I hope that it will interest the reader nevertheless, insofar as this heyday of American group dynamics research and practice can be considered historically in the framework of today's realization that the earlier enthusiastic expectations have fallen far short of fulfillment (Goodstein and Dovico, 1979). The subsequent, broader theoretical issues posed by me, including suggestions for collaborative group psychotherapy research by group clinicians and social psychologists, continue to be relevant to the present.

Chapter 3 deals with the concept of empathy. The idea for it was sparked by my work in an urban slum neighborhood, where there were understandable problems in reaching the many socially and emotionally disadvantaged patients through traditional psychotherapy. Not unlike Kohut's (1977) patients, who had suffered from narcissistic difficulties due in large measure to a lack of empathic mothering in their childhoods, our group patients required a corrective emotional experience in which far-reaching empathic communications were specifically fostered. My own view of the process of empathy in group psychotherapy, with its close link to identification, is somewhat different from the central position which Kohut (1977) had accorded to his "empathic, introspective-observational stance" in dyadic psychoanalysis.

As was true with Chapter 3, the impetus for Chapter 4 on the concept of the "mother–group," emerged from clinical observations in therapy groups for socially and emotionally deprived adults. The patients' perceptions of the group entity in a benign maternal vein tended to go hand–in–hand with markedly ambivalent transferences toward the therapist. I viewed these perceptions of a "mother–group" as primitive kinds of object relationships (identifications), rather than as developmentally more advanced transferences. I also hypothesized that the earliest phases in therapy groups were not only characterized by such primitive identifications, but by other primary–process manifestations (i.e., oral fantasies) as well. As therapy proceeds, the more advanced transferences, including oedipal fantasies, and real object ties gain in ascendancy.

Chapter 5 aims to bridge the concept of leadership as developed in the three related disciplines of social psychology, analytic group psychology, and group psychotherapy. Conceptual clarity is sought through proposed working definitions of "group," "group leader," and "group psychotherapist." In this regard, the group dynamic leadership functions aimed primarily at meeting group maintenance needs are distinguished from the clinical–therapeutic functions of the group therapist. In this comparison the necessary fusion of the creative–artistic and professional–scientific aspects in the group therapist's role is highlighted. The surprising conclusion that over 3000 publications on the subject have failed to produce an integrated understanding of leadership was mitigated in part by the fact that empirical observations yielded some circumscribed findings relevant to leadership practice.

The last chapter of this section (Chapter 6), devoted to the subject of scapegoating, covers an old and popularly used concept. Nevertheless, it appears to have eluded the proper attention of group therapy writers, who have dealt with it in an overly general and inconclusive fashion. I have accordingly attempted to depict the complex process of scapegoating in therapy groups, in both phenomenological and psychodynamic terms. The clinical illustrations portray scapegoating episodes as group defensive manifestations utilizing the mechanism of either projection or projective identification, and include suggestions for the therapeutic management of this vexing group phenomenon.

Chapter 2

GROUP PROCESS IN GROUP PSYCHOTHERAPY: TRENDS IN THE INTEGRATION OF INDIVIDUAL AND GROUP PSYCHOLOGY

The intensified quest that began in the 1950's for a better understanding of the nature of small groups is well known. It has captured the interest of students from a number of related behavioral sciences, especially social psychology, sociology, and anthropology. Also involved in the subject of group dynamics have been practitioners from a variety of professional fields including educators, social group workers, and institutional, guidance, and community organization personnel. All of these professional groups have been concerned with the utilization of the motivational potential for behavioral change that resides in face–to–face groups. In contrast to these disciplines, the rapidly growing field of group psychotherapy, though directly involved with small groups, has shown a marked neglect of group psychological phenomena.

This chapter, which deals with the problem of integrating the fields of individual and group psychology in group psychotherapy, was primarily influenced by two developments. First of all, there was the growing, though still reluctant, admission among some leading American psychoanalytic group therapists that group dynamics contributions might prove useful to their field. This was illustrated in the special issue on "Group Dynamics and Group Psychotherapy" published by the *International Journal of Group*

Reprinted, in part, from *American Journal of Psychotherapy*, 14:104–120, 346–363, 1960, by permission.

25

Psychotherapy (1957). Second, there appeared in print over a period of five years some major group psychological theories developed abroad by a British group psychoanalyst, W. R. Bion (1952). To my surprise, though at first almost completely ignored by American group therapists, these theories have gained considerable recognition among American students of group dynamics.

GROUP DYNAMICS AND PSYCHOANALYTIC GROUP PSYCHOTHERAPY

Any discussion of the relationship between the fields of group dynamics and group psychotherapy must include their differing backgrounds and foci of interest. Group dynamics, in the sense of a systematic approach to small group behavior, received its major impetus through the pioneering work of Kurt Lewin and his co-workers (1939). In Lewin's conceptualizations regarding groups, both the differences and interdependence between properties of individual members and the broader group were central. He believed further that since a group comprises a field of forces in a state of quasi–equilibrium, any change in one subpart immediately produces changes in all the other subparts. Lewin stressed not only the interrelatedness between the person and the environment, but also the importance of characterizing the properties and forces at work in the group situation — the social field. One of his greatest contributions was to demonstrate ways in which groups could be studied through experimental methods. His investigations of group atmospheres and leadership (Lewin, Lippitt, and White, 1939) or of group decision and change (Lewin, 1947) still remain classics in social psychology. Lewin's concepts and research approach have been developed further by his colleagues and students, especially at the Research Center for Group Dynamics in Michigan. Most of this work has focused on the various properties of groups and how they influence the attitudes and behavior of the group members. The publications on cohesiveness (Festinger, Schacter, and Back, 1950); and on pressures toward conformity (Back, 1951; Festinger,

1951) are outstanding examples. Although the term "group dynamics" is often associated exclusively with the theoretical standpoint of Lewin, there have also been conceptual and research approaches from other social psychologists such as Cattell (1951) and Stogdill (1950), and from sociologists, including Bales (1950). Two separate volumes, one edited by social psychologists (Cartwright and Zander, 1953), the other by sociologists (Hare, Borgatta, and Bales, 1955), have outlined various major theoretical orientations with a preliminary attempt to view them together as a meaningful whole.

Group psychotherapy has at times been defined in the loosest terms, encompassing many kinds of groups with mental hygiene or educational objectives. In line with my discussion in Chapter 1, it will be viewed here strictly as a field of clinical practice, a specific approach within the wider realm of psychotherapy.

Group psychotherapy had its beginnings in the United States at the turn of the century, under medical auspices. Originally, it involved attempts to apply educational methods in groups of patients with tuberculosis and, subsequently, schizophrenic patients. The earliest groups with a clear treatment orientation for nonpsychotic adults were those of Schilder (1936), Wender (1936), Slavson, (1950), Moreno (1945), and Lowrey (1944). The history of group psychotherapy has been adequately covered in the literature (Kaplan and Sadock, 1972), and needs no repetition. It is noteworthy, however, that group psychotherapy received its particular impetus for growth during and following World War II. Major factors were the government's interest in problems of civilian and army morale, as well as the need for the most expeditious treatment of the numerous neurospychiatric casualties.

As might be expected with such a new and rapidly expanding field, the practice of group psychotherapy outstripped its theoretical and conceptual clarity. Since group psychotherapy with very few exceptions has evolved from the general field of psychotherapy, its concepts and techniques naturally reflect this fact. First of all, as noted in Chapter 1, there is a primary emphasis on curing individual mental illness. Furthermore, in accordance with general clinical practice, although a patient comes with isolated complaints, some comprehensive appraisal of his whole personality is involved. Closely linked to this kind of study is an attempt to arrive at specific goals, techniques, and levels of treatment. In some instances, a thoroughgoing reorganization of personality is the aim; in others, the goal is more limited, involving the modification of selected areas of conflict and defensive patterns. In such planning, group therapy's limitations for various types of patients, age groups, and even points in treatment, are all important considerations. Other obvious factors are the facilities of the particular clinical setting, the training of the therapists, and above all, their theoretical orientation.

Group therapists with a psychoanalytic orientation (who, incidentally, are in a majority at the present time) attempt to explain the therapeutic process in accordance with psychoanalytic theory. Among the group therapists who follow the classical Freudian orientation are Slavson (1950), Berman (1950), Wolf (1950), Grotjahn (1953), Loeser and Bry (1953), Fried (1955), and Durkin (1964). The well-known Freudian emphasis on psychosexual growth levels and on the interplay of biological and genetic concepts is reflected in their contributions. Psychopathology, in its broadest sense, is viewed as the emergence in the patient's life of earlier, irrational, and undifferentiated response patterns with which he is unable to cope, and which promote pathological defense reactions and undue anxiety. The adherents of Horney's system in the field of group therapy, such as Rose (1953), view the neurotic personality as being torn between its innate, creative, and humanizing self (the real self) and its compulsive striving for perfection (the idealized image). There is also the conflict between one's need for satisfaction and security and the inconsistent, hypocritical reality of today's society. Instead of achieving self–realization, the individual's energies are used up in these conflicts with accompanying pathological "character dynamisms" and distorted hierarchies of values. Powdermaker and Frank (1953), and more recently Yalom (1975), are exponents of Sullivan's theories as applied to group psychotherapy. Focus here is on interpersonal relationships as primary factors in personality development and in pathogenesis. There is essential agreement with the Freudians regarding the significance of childhood experiences. Unconscious mental phenomena are recognized, although there are no precise formulations of various degrees of repression or of how interpersonal difficulties are related to individual personality organization and pathology. The orthodox concepts of psychosexual phases and zones are supplanted by tenets of social interrelationships from earliest childhood.

Despite the above conceptual differences regarding the exact causes of personality pathology, most group therapists with a psychoanalytic orientation would probably agree on the following generic, interrelated elements as characteristic of *all* psychotherapy: (1) relationship, (2) emotional support, (3) catharsis, (4) reality testing, (5) insight, and (6) reorganization of defense patterns. These same cardinal factors are believed to operate in group psychotherapy, albeit varying in quality and quantity because of the existence of a complex group situation with its multipersonal character.

The earliest writings on group psychotherapy theory tended to deal almost exclusively with individual behavior or with the therapeutic process. Consideration of the dynamic aspects of the group-as-a-whole, which are probably basically the same for all face-to-face groups, were largely neglected. In the case of some group therapists adhering to Freudian concepts of psychopathology, they even ignored Freud's own postulates of group psychology, or those of his followers. Where such references did appear, they were frequently characterized by considerable ambiguity (Scheidlinger, 1952b). Among the factors responsible for this lag in the needed emphasis on group processes are the relative newness of group therapy as a treatment approach; the fact that group therapists are mostly clinicians and practitioners lacking in familiarity with social psychological theory or research; therapists' preoccupation with concepts of individual personality and psychopathology; the limited range and clarity of the existing psychoanalytic concepts of group behavior; the relatively late interest within Freudian theory in problems of ego psychology, especially the individual's conscious ego patterns oriented toward the environment.

From what has been said so far, it is not difficult to understand why there has been, until recently, a minimum of mutual influence between group dynamics and analytic group psychotherapy. Aside from the difference in their major work orientation — experimental research and scientific methodology in the former, and the clinical therapeutic task in the latter — there has also been the matter of conceptual emphasis. The group dynamics literature suggests a primary preoccupation with group properties, group tasks, and performance, with "manifest" behavior and observable effects accruing through the group process. With it is a trend toward systematic, carefully controlled, quantitative investigations. This stands in contrast to the psychoanalytic theories, which stress detailed individual personality assessment, especially of irrational, unconscious layers. Similarly, the psychoanalytic concepts of group behavior aim at an explanation of the deeper, primarily unconscious forces and motivations which underlie such readily observed group phenomena as cohesiveness, leadership, and emotional contagion. Unlike the concepts of group dynamics, the psychoanalytic concepts, especially those of group behavior, have by-and-large not been verified as yet by objective, scientific methods.

The Need for Conceptual Clarification and Integration

In connection with my earlier inquiry into Freudian group psychology (Scheidlinger, 1952b), I outlined the group-relevant psychoanalytic propositions with emphasis on the following issues: (1) the meaning of behavior, (2) the development of social attitudes and the capacity for group ties, (3) group emotional processes, (4) the role of the leader, and (5) the interaction of individual personality and group factors. The need for further clarification of these propositions emerged distinctly. At the same time, I thought that some of these notions could, despite their limitations, be employed as hypotheses in studying man's behavior in groups. I suggested, furthermore, that in the much desired interdisciplinary investigations of group phenomena, the integration of concepts and techniques of Freudian group psychotherapy and Lewinian group dynamics should prove especially fruitful. That is, despite the broader conceptual affinity between these two systems, already noted by Brown (1936), a significant distinction resides in Lewin's emphasis on explaining individual or group behavior as a function of the momentary social field. Freud's psychological approach, in contrast, while underplaying the present interaction between the personality and the environment — the social reality — is primarily oriented in "depth." Its foci of inquiry are the genetic propositions closely linked to inner motivations and their historical origins — the repressed, unconscious memories and the unconscious aspects of ego defenses. If employed together with other disciplines, the two orientations could thus complement each other. Lewinian "field theory" could contribute its group dynamics concepts and rich methodological experience, while the Freudians would add regard for "depth factors" in individual and group behavior. (Such collaborative efforts would also serve to dispel the still frequent misconceptions about the various theories.)

The subsequent group psychotherapy literature (two years following the above discussion) continued to ignore the field of group dynamics, with one major exception — a volume by Bach (1954) describing a group treatment approach which attempted to integrate the prevalent psychoanalytic view of group therapy with Lewinian group dynamics theory. Besides transference, countertransference, and resistance, which involve primarily unconscious processes, Bach stressed the importance of utilizing such typical "group situational" concepts as cohesiveness, group moods, group role, group pressures, and tensions. It is noteworthy, however, that in his translations of the group dynamics notions to the operations of group psychotherapy, Bach found it necessary to lean heavily on such neo-Freudian formulations as those of Sullivan (1953) or of Ruesch and Bateson (1951). These formulations are also oriented primarily toward the contemporaneous interaction between the organism and the environment. Despite the occasional utilization of such Freudian concepts as oedipal conflict in his discussion of psychopathology, he dismissed all of the major Freudian group–relevant hypotheses as being too historical, and as overemphasizing regression and primitivity. In trying to bridge the gap between individual and group psychology theories, a similar preference for Sullivan's postulates of interpersonal relations was also revealed in some social psychological publications (Shepard and Bennis, 1956).

The question arises here whether this is only due to the acknowledged limitations of Freudian social theory, or, in addition, as Hall and Lindzey (1954) suggested, to a relative ignorance and considerable misunderstanding of it among social psychologists. There is perhaps good reason to assume that the biological, "instinct" taint of Freudianism had discouraged greater application of its propositions to group dynamics theory. In this context the instinct-based formulations of Bion and the reactions to them assume particular significance. (See Chapter 12 of this volume for an updated discussion of some of these issues.)

BION ON PSYCHOANALYTIC GROUP PSYCHOLOGY

Bion's complicated and comprehensive theoretical outline of what he termed "group dynamics" was based on his work with therapy groups in England. In seven consecutive contributions developed over a span of three years (Bion, 1948–1951), and in two later papers (1952, 1955), he postulated the existence of certain complex psychological processes present in all groups.

These processes entail a rational, conscious level and an emotional, completely irrational one. Thus, the "work group" refers to the task and reality–oriented aspect of a group's activity in which the members planfully cooperate. This activity is occasionally aided, but most generally interfered with, by powerful, unconscious emotional forces—three "basic assumptions"—which are held in common by the whole group. Each of these "assumptions" represents an emotional state with a central theme regarding the group's aims, including the construct of a leader. The "dependent basic assumption" is related to a perception of a leader who will sustain, feed, and protect. The "basic assumption of pairing" contains the idea that the group has come together for purposes of procreation, with which are associated feelings of messianic hope and guilt. The leader here, the fantasied product of sexual contact, appears as an unborn genius. Finally, there is the "basic assumption of fight-flight," with a leader who initiates such feelings.

Bion underscored the "instantaneous, inevitable, and instinctive" character of the "basic assumption" mental activity, which is anchored in man's innermost core as a group animal. At any particular point, a given group's "work" functions (which, according to Bion, correspond to the characteristics ascribed by Freud to the ego) are pervaded by phenomena of only a single "basic assumption." The latter in time gives way to another of the two remaining "basic assumptions" that then operate together with the "work group" functions. The two inactive "basic assumptions" reside in a "protomental system in which physical and mental activity is undifferentiated and which lies outside the field ordinarily considered profitable for psychologic investigations" (Bion, 1952, p. 236). The emotions associated with each "basic assumption," such as anxiety, fear, love, or hate, are viewed as having a unique quality. While any member (aside from the "work group" leader) can be identified as the leader in line with the emotional content of the given "basic assumption," such an identification could at times refer (as Freud also suggested) to an idea, such as the history of the group or the group "bible."

The "work group" stresses self-understanding, the power of reason, and the need for growth. "Basic assumption" activity, on the other hand, is opposed to individual development, does not recognize the concept of time, and is incapable of symbol formation. When time awareness seems required, it usually brings forth among the group members feelings of persecution. The moment a group begins to act on a "basic assumption," it evokes a reverse need for reality contact with its associated regard for truth. "Work group" functions thus are brought into play.

Bion went into some detail in relating specific group phenomena — recordkeeping, attacks on outside groups, schisms, emergence of dual leadership, forming of a committee — to his schema, but space does not permit me to elaborate on these.

Bion is rather critical of Freud's (1921) "superficial" study of group psychology without actual observation of groups. He insists also that Freud was wrong in implying that group psychology comes into being with the aggregation of a number of people. For "no individual, however isolated in time and space, should be regarded as outside a group or lacking in active manifestations of group psychology" (Bion, 1952, p. 239). Furthermore, "All the functions of the basic assumption group are in full activity before even the group comes together in a room, although their observation may be difficult, and continue after the group has dispersed" (Bion, 1952, p. 241). A group is assembled only for practical reasons so that its characteristics can be demonstrated through the interpretations by the analyst.

In discussing McDougall's (1920) and Freud's (1921) ideas, Bion stressed how his own formulations related to theirs. He accorded some value to Freud's description of the "two specialized work groups," an army and a church, which deal in Bion's terminology with "fight-flight" and "dependency" "basic assumption" phenomena. He added what he considered an important example omitted by Freud — the aristocracy — a "specialized work group" preoccupied with breeding and thus related to the "basic assumption" of "pairing." In discussing group cohesion, Bion accepted Freud's hypothesis of libidinal ties for only the "pairing" type of group manifestations, suggesting that in the remaining two kinds of groups the bond has a different quality. He was quite emphatic, however, in denying the suggestion that the leader's ideas and personality influence a group. Quite to the contrary, according to him, the leader and the group members are at the mercy of "basic assumption" forces.

Bion revived the still unresolved controversy of the origin of gregariousness in humans. He took strong issue with Freud's suggestion that social tendencies could be viewed as a product of early family experiences, thus constituting an essentially learned set of responses. He repeatedly stressed the inborn character of man as a "herd animal," and his concepts here are strongly reminiscent of such early "social instinct" theorists as Trotter (1916) or McDougall (1920).

A unique aspect of Bion's theoretical scheme resides in its connection with psychoanalytic conceptions developed in England by Melanie Klein. Among these are some that are considered by psychoanalysts to be rather controversial in nature. In brief, Melanie Klein postulated the existence of powerful emotional conflicts in the earliest months of the infant's life, characterized by "psychotic" anxieties which underlie the later classic Freudian infantile neurosis. The psychic mechanisms of introjection and projection were assumed to operate in the first four months, when the infant in its "paranoid–schizoid position" has introjected part–objects, the mother's breasts. Splitting processes (e.g., differentiation between a "good" and "bad" breast) and persecutory anxieties (fear of bad breast) are a part of this picture. In the "depressive position," which follows and achieves its climax at six months, the infant was believed to show evidence of anxiety over the loss of the "good" internalized part–objects, and then, whole objects. Ambivalent feelings toward the internalized and the real external mother occur after the first half-year. These go hand–in–hand with genital and oedipal kinds of strivings, including the wish to receive and have a child. It is important to note that Melanie Klein believed the young infant's inborn, unconscious fantasies contain symbolic equations of breast, feces, penis, and child.

In Melanie Klein's system, object relationships exist within the personality as well as between the personality and external objects. The inner fantasy world with its internalized objects is believed to be of primary importance, and the mastery of external reality is dependent on the mastery of this inner world. There also is emphasis on inborn destructive impulses, with a related assumption that anxiety is experienced from birth on, and is ultimately bound up with the threats emanating from these impulses.

It would be outside the scope of this chapter to elaborate further on the theories of Melanie Klein or to take part in the controversy these have evoked. The pros and cons on the subject have been covered rather fully in the psychoanalytic literature in England as well as in the United States (Klein, Heimann, and Money-Kyrle, 1955; Zetzel, 1956; Bibring, 1947). For our purposes, it is important to note that Bion saw his description of group events as being related to her theories; however, except for occasional bibliographical references to the papers of Klein and her followers, Bion failed to demonstrate this in any detail. As a matter of fact, in his earliest papers, where he was developing his ideas, I could find no mention of Melanie Klein or of her work. This might explain why the first references in the United States to Bion's group dynamics contributions did not mention his link to this British school of thought. Nevertheless, a more painstaking study of his conceptualizations and his very occasional use of such typical Kleinian terms as "persecution by internal objects" in these papers suggests that he was already influenced by these theories. This was later confirmed by his open discussion in the summary part of his paper that appeared in 1952. In the same publication, he again spoke briefly in the Kleinian vein about the objects of the patient's projective identifications. Thus, ". . . aggressiveness, and other instinctual derivatives are externalized onto the basic assumption leader." In turn, guilt is aroused because of "being in possession of the group which is equated with the breast. . ." (1952, p. 245).

In his later contribution in 1955 Bion went even further, claiming that "basic assumption" phenomena could be understood only in terms of "psychotic" mechanisms. They contained features corresponding to "primitive part–object" relationships and associated "psychotic" anxieties. It is noteworthy that the earlier notion of the group representing the mother's breast now became expanded by the idea of its being equated with primitive fantasies about the content of the mother's body (see also Chapter 4 of this volume). There also was an illustration of a neurotic patient's statement, in a therapy group, that she feared choking when eating in a restaurant and was particularly embarrassed at the presence of an attractive woman at her table. The therapeutic interpretations offered by Bion related to the group interactions evoked by this comment, with the patient being the receptor of "projective identifications." Specifically, he thought that the woman perceived the group "as a single object. . . that had been split up into pieces (the individual members of the group) by her eating. . ." with associated feelings of guilt. As to the group's apparent aloofness to the woman's remark, Bion explained it in terms of "splitting and projecting" mechanisms. The group members achieved this ". . . by splitting off good parts of their personality and placing them in the analyst" (p. 246), thus freeing themselves from any sense of responsibility toward the woman. In line with Kleinian views on schizoid mechanisms, Bion concluded that such a "loss of individual distinctiveness" in a group is identical with psychotic depersonalization.

In general, all "basic assumption" phenomena were thus seen by Bion as defensive reactions against "psychotic" anxiety.

Some Critical Observations Regarding Bion's Approach

It is noteworthy, first of all, that although Bion himself is essentially a follower of the orthodox Freudian position on personality theory (as modified by Melanie Klein), he is highly critical of Freud's group psychology. He maintained that in contrast to his own direct observations of real groups in action, Freud derived his group psychological notions from the two–person psychoanalytic situation with its exclusive emphasis on the individual. In juxtaposing his own theories with those of Freudian group psychology, Bion limited himself exclusively to Freud's small treatise *Group Psychology and the Analysis of the Ego*, which first appeared in 1921. Con-

sidering the state of social psychology of the time, it apparently did
not occur to him that Freud was considerably ahead of his contem-
poraries in explicitly denying any real dichotomy between individual and group psychology. Furthermore, Freud himself admitted
in his introduction that "anyone who compares the narrow dimensions of this little book with the extent of group psychology will at
once be able to guess that only a few points chosen from the whole
material are to be dealt with here" (pp. 70–71). It is therefore surprising that in his discussions Bion ignored all of Freud's later writings that dealt, for instance, with aggression in groups and between
groups. He also made no reference whatever to the related contributions of other later American psychoanalytic authors in the
sphere of group psychology, such as Redl (1942) or Erikson (1959).
This is the more regrettable in that these authors had dealt with
questions similar to those raised by Bion. Neither of them would,
to my knowledge, basically challenge what to Bion seemed like a
new discovery — that the explanation of certain phenomena must
be sought in the matrix of the group and not in the individual
group members.

It is of interest that in his later writings (1955), Bion's view of
Freud's group theories was considerably less critical than before. In
contrast to his earlier position, he now emphasized agreement with
Freud that there was no need to postulate the existence of a herd instinct. What is even more important, having initially opposed the
very idea, he acknowledged that a description of the group as a
repetition of family group patterns and of neurotic mechanisms
was applicable to less disturbed groups. His position now was that
Freud's discovery of the family group as the prototype of all groups
was incomplete and superficial, needing supplementation rather
than correction. Without elaborating on it, the final view allowed,
roughly speaking, for two regressive levels of psychological manifestations in all groups: Freud's level of "neurotic" family patterns
and their associated stresses, as well as Bion's more "primitive" level
of part-object relationships and their related "psychotic" anxieties.
Since the latter ". . . contain the ultimate sources of all group be-

havior," they must be brought into the open, no matter how disguised, and worked through if "any real therapy" is to result (Bion, 1955, p. 475). He offered the above illustration of a psychoneurotic woman's comment in a group whose "manner and intonation" suggested to him that it dealt with "psychotic" perceptions and anxieties. He had no doubt that in individual analysis this same comment of hers, now accompanied by a different "manner and intonation" would have evoked an interpretation from him "appropriate to a neurotic disability" (1955, p. 472). There is thus a definite implication here, in contradiction to the belief of many group therapists, that group treatment is a "deeper" form of therapy than individual psychoanalysis.

In the above–noted paper Bion failed to explain his use of the term "neurotic," which he ascribed to Freud's group psychology, in juxtaposition to his more "primitive" level of group dynamic manifestations. I can only speculate that he meant to convey the idea that Freudian group theory was more limited, referring only to conflicts stemming from genital and oedipal stages of psychosexual development. Such a view fails to differentiate between the concept of libido, as Freud used it, and genitality. The notion is furthermore implied that neuroses in the Freudian scheme do not include pregenital etiological elements. It also entails a misunderstanding of Freud's view of object ties and identifications in groups as not necessarily "neurotic," and as derived from aim–inhibited, neutralized libidinal and aggressive drives. These include some preoedipal and even pregenital types of ego identification which were discussed by me elsewhere, in connection with their counteracting individual narcissism (Scheidlinger, 1955).

As a matter of fact, contrary to Bion's view, if I were asked to link Freud's model of psychological group formation with one of Bion's "basic assumptions," I would have chosen the "dependent" basic assumption rather than the "pairing" one. Freud's writing on group psychology was primarily stimulated by crowd phenomena and their regressive aspects. He was deeply impressed by the extreme dependence and submissiveness of the individual in relation to the crowd leader. He even compared the tie between the group member and the leader to the highly dependent relationship between subject and hypnotist. To my mind, there is more emphasis on dependence and submissiveness than on direct sexuality with the theme of birth in Freud's (1921) small volume.

In the absence of any clarification of this by Bion, one might assume that the frequent interchangeable use of the terms "primitive" and "psychotic" in connection with his group psychology (contrasted by him with Freud's "neurotic" level), refers to a kind of reactivated fixation level with its attendant conflicts. These are characterized by the earlier-mentioned two psychic positions — paranoid-schizoid and depressive — postulated by the Kleinians as part-and-parcel of all infants' development.

This problem of loose usage of terminology plagues all of Bion's writings about groups, for instance, such concepts as crucial to his theory as the "basic assumptions." At some points he speaks of these as "mental activity," at others as "groups," and not infrequently as "cultures," "levels," and "emotional drives." Understanding of his material is further complicated by the absence of detailed descriptions of the groups he worked with, of the meeting places and, above all, of the individual group members, their backgrounds, personalities, and degrees of pathology. It would indeed be difficult for a group therapist to comprehend case illustrations drawn from group sessions without some, if only minimal, data regarding the genetic and dynamic elements of the personalities of the individual patients.

There is also the matter of the vague, often bordering on the mystic, description of his concepts. Let us look, for example, at the assertion that ". . . basic assumption mental activity requires no training, experience or mental development. It is instantaneous, inevitable and instinctive" (1952, p. 235). A statement formulated in this fashion, to me at least, raises more questions than it possibly answers. It seems not unlike Melanie Klein's controversial idea of nonverbal, inborn unconscious fantasies attributed to the infant from the beginning of life. In another context I have already suggested that some of Bion's concepts also were akin to the "group mind" fallacy (Scheidlinger, 1952). His postulate of "a group mentality as a pool to which the anonymous contributions are made, and through which the impulses and desires implicit in these contributions are gratified" could be a case in point (Bion, 1948, p. 492). This group mentality was viewed by him as uniform, in contrast to the diverse mentalities of the individual group members who influenced its formation.

Turning to the manner in which Bion offered evidence for his theories, the discussions seemed more convincing when illustrated by actual events from small groups. This was weakened, of course, by the earlier-noted failure to delineate his population, the group setting or the individual personalities. Nevertheless, the actual phenomena described had a definite air of plausibility, partly because they appeared to square, to an extent at least, with similar observations reported in the group therapy literature and which I had also experienced in my own work. He was least convincing when he discussed small, face-to-face groups interchangeably with large groups and societies, or when he tried to apply his theories to data from mythology, a field in which he seemed well versed. I also saw little plausibility in his statement that individual psychoanalysis was a group manifestation—a "pairing basic assumption" phenomenon, with the Messiah in a central position. Bion chided Freud for having failed to recognize this and for having made a mistake which should be obvious on purely theological grounds (1952, p. 242)—that the commander-in-chief of a church is not Christ the Messiah, but rather, the Deity.

There were other points, too, where he veered to almost dogmatic assertions of fact, without any apparent evidence. One example is the statement "Every human group instantaneously understands every other human group, no matter how diverse its culture, language, and tradition, on the level of the basic assumptions" (1955, p. 474). He even went so far as to suggest that his theories might aid in the study of world economics, i.e., the value of money in different countries. There were occasions when postulations of Melanie Klein from the development of individuals were carried over in toto to support an idea about groups. Thus, in line with the Kleinian ideas of symbol formation, he asserted that only the "work group" is capable of understanding symbols. In contrast, "In the basic assumption group, the individual is the totem animal. He is not identified with it, or equated with it, he is it." Furthermore, rational discussions in "basic assumption" groups cannot be taken at face value, but rather as identical "with the bizarre verbalizations of the psychotic" (1952, p. 245).

Since Bion offered a particularly strong and detailed refutation of Freud's idea of the nature of group panic, it might be of interest to outline the content and manner of his argumentation on this topic. To begin with, he refers to his own experience in military and civilian panics as confirming his, rather than Freud's, views; however, he fails to describe these experiences. Subsequently, he quotes a very general passage from McDougall's outdated volume *The Group Mind* (1920), about the spread of primary emotions other than fear through a crowd, together with a footnote about the spread of anger through a crowd. From this, he claimed that "McDougall has thus brought very close together, though without making the connection, anger and fear, and thus supports my view that panic is an aspect of F. (fight–flight basic assumption) and that there is no essential difference between panic and flight and uncontrolled attack" (1952, p. 243). Furthermore, according to Bion, insofar as panic is a "basic assumption" phenomenon, it always involves a situation which "might as easily have given rise to rage," and where the fear or rage call for immediate discharge. Frustration tolerance is not possible since it involves time, which is not a dimension of "basic assumption" manifestations. Under such conditions, he further believed that the group will follow any leader who would license either panic flight or attack, and in fact these actions could occur successively. He also thought that the group's degree of organization was not important here, unless that organization ("work group" function) was concerned with the external event which gave rise to the panic or rage.

From the mythological conception of the Greek god Pan, Bion deduced further that panic was already viewed in antiquity as a phenomenon where fear possessed all group members instantaneously. Such fear is felt by the individual group member as something induced, not through an external stimulus, but by an "internal object," in the Kleinian sense of the term. Although Bion failed to explain or describe specific instances of military panic, he asserted vehemently that such panic was not related to the external danger and that it did not involve a loss of group cohesion. He saw panic, instead, as a manifestation of the earlier-mentioned "fight-flight basic assumption," involving regressive psychological mechanisms induced from within the group. He later expatiated on this, suggesting that panic was a consequence of the group members' threatened perception of their individual distinctiveness. It is noteworthy here that, in regard to group cohesion, Bion had asserted that Freud's idea of libidinal ties did not hold for the "dependency" or "fight-flight basic assumption" forces. He never himself explained his ideas of group cohesion for these kinds of group manifestations.

I have presented Bion's discourse on the elements and causes of panic — a not too uncommon group phenomenon — to illustrate the manner in which he utilized his theories to explain group events. Whether and how his argumentation is plausible, I will leave to the reader to decide. However, since Freud there has been a great deal written by both psychoanalysts and social psychologists on this subject of panic. There is a volume by Meerloo (1950), partly based on war experiences, a series of papers on leadership and danger (Quarantelli, 1954), as well as many social psychology texts. As far as I could ascertain, not only did most of these publications not bear out Bion's ideas on the subject, but they more or less went along with Freud's general emphasis on the absence of libidinal group cohesion and of trusted leadership in panic states.

With regard to the contributions from social psychology, including some research findings, there is almost uniform agreement that panic is a flight reaction away from a perceived danger. Not a single investigator noted anything that would even approach

Bion's idea of the link–up between panic flight and panic attack, or that a new type of group cohesion with a "fight–flight" leader emerges. As to military panic, Quarantelli (1954) noted that it is possible only when a breakdown of the normal military group solidarity has occurred. His analysis of the data gathered by the Disaster Team of the National Opinion Research Center suggested that panic flight always represented highly individualistic behavior where preexisting social relationships and group action patterns became disregarded.

Bion and Other Psychoanalytic Views of Group Behavior

In comparing the contributions of Bion more generally to contemporary psychoanalytic theories of group psychology, a few noteworthy observations emerge. There is, first of all, a reaffirmation of Freud's earlier idea that all group behavior has similar underlying dynamics which encompass unconscious psychological phenomena. As in Freud's (1921) and Redl's (1942) conceptualizations, Bion links group formations to types of leadership. However, the group regression, he proposes, is a "deeper" one than heretofore assumed, related to Kleinian ideas of depersonalization, "part–object relationships," and "psychotic" anxiety. In fact, he sees the group as a fantasy in the minds of the members, maintained merely as a defense against "psychotic" anxiety.

Aside from the controversial nature of some of the Kleinian postulates, I think that Bion's material reflects an overemphasis on the pathological "primitive threats" and on group interpersonal reactions as defenses. As a matter of fact, his description of "basic assumption" mental activity is an almost exact replica of Freud's portrayal of the "primary process." Such overemphasis on "primary process" is promoted at the expense of the well-known reality-favoring and growth–promoting elements in groups (especially face–to–face groups) (Scheidlinger, 1952). It also makes insufficient allowance for the possible healthy, nonconflictual, ego–autonomous aspects of individual functioning in a group. In touching on the idea of the loss of individual identity involved in group belonging, Bion links this automatically to "psychotic" depersonalization. It is as though he does not recognize ego functions as intervening between the emerging impulsive derivatives and actual behavior. No attention is given to individual variance in susceptibility to the regressive pull of the group, in line with personality and situational factors. What about the opposite of the "automaton" leader—the mature leader and his possible resistance to even the most powerful regressive group stimulation?

The broader notions of dependency, pairing, and fight or flight as emotional forces inherent in Bion's three "basic assumptions" are not new to group psychology. Freud's (1921) treatise on this subject by itself, however, deals with only one model of group formation, i.e., related to cohesiveness through aim–inhibited libidinal ties or common interests. Not having as yet formulated his theory of aggression, Freud apparently used the term "libido" to encompass aggressive energy as well. To that extent Bion's postulate of a group formation model built around aggression (fight–flight basic assumption) represents a step forward. Freud himself tried to include the role of aggression in group life in some of his later writings. It became more clearly delineated in subsequent contributions on small groups, especially Redl's (1942) work.

Concerning the latter's approach, it should be remembered that some of his concepts, such as "primary" and "secondary" group emotions or "emotional contagion," are not too dissimilar from Bion's. As a matter of fact, considerably earlier Redl had undertaken a task almost identical to Bion's—to supplement Freud's rather limited constructs on group psychology. He, too, enumerated a broader variety of models for psychological group formation, each involving a specific type of leader or "central person." In addition, Redl's (1942) notion of emotional contagion is not unlike Bion's concept of valency. (The latter had defined valency as the capacity for instantaneous, involuntary combining of people for the purpose of sharing and acting on a "basic assumption.")

A major weakness in Bion's contributions obtains from his perpetuation of a problem inherent in almost all writings on psychoanalytic group psychology — the failure to distinguish conceptually, and even clinically, between fantasied and reality–based processes. There is also neglect of external, environmental factors in influencing group development. Bion's "work group" aspects that reflect ego functions are touched on most sketchily, leaving out many elements considered significant in group behavior, such as social role, climate, or structure. For instance, he does not even mention individual roles evolved through the group interaction. There is also the questionable implication that all such ego activities are conscious and rational, while "basic assumption" phenomena are unconscious and irrational. There is insufficient clarity as well about crucial processes identified in group psychotherapy, such as transferences as distinct from identifications and object ties, with all of these lumped under Melanie Klein's concept of projective identifications. As to other kinds of identification, especially among the group members, these are hardly mentioned. This is particularly surprising insofar as Bion accepted Freud's model of group formation for his "pairing basic assumption," which clearly involves identification among the group members. He also did not touch on identifications with the group as an entity, despite his almost exclusive preoccupation with phenomena encompassing the whole group.

A fundamental problem also lies in Bion's distinct failure to adequately relate group concepts or phenomena to the personalities of the group members. The only two concepts of his that could be utilized for such a linkage between the individual and the group are those of cooperation and of valency, ascribed to "work group" and "basic assumption" group operations, respectively. While hardly touching on the meaning of cooperation, his earlier–noted definition of valency contains two related elements involving the individual's capacity for involuntary combination with others: (1) for producing, sharing, or maintaining a given "basic assumption's" emotional state; (2) for acting out (i.e., fighting, fleeing, loving) the conflicts or tensions stimulated by the "basic assumption." These processes are presented with much less clarity than Redl's (1942) similar concept of "emotional contagion." They also fail to deal with the following essential questions: (1) What, if any, is the relationship between a person's valency pattern and his unique personality structure? (2) How would Bion account for the known differences in people's predispositions for initiating or falling in with dependent, aggressive, or loving kinds of behavior? (3) Under what circumstances is a person's "fight–flight" type of behavior, for example, an expression of this kind of a hitherto inhibited need, or of a defense against a still more inadmissible need, perhaps for dependency or sexual love? (4) Given similar etiological needs among a group of people, would there not be differences in the ways these needs emerge in actual behavior? In brief, without a detailed assessment of individuals' genetic and dynamic personality elements, of their impulsive strivings, and of their adaptive and defensive patterns in dealing with inner and environmental tensions, any deeper portrayal of group behavior remains incomplete.

By neglecting to deal with these aspects, the impression is thus conveyed that in group therapy, for instance, it is the group and not the individual that is being treated. This impression was enhanced especially when Bion described the "basic assumption" forces in terms similar to those used by Freud to portray the id, while the "work group" was openly equated to the functions of the ego. (I must add, however, that this type of misleading terminology — for instance, "group ego" or "group unconscious" — has also been employed by some American writers.) Bion appears to seek explanatory concepts for group behavior which belie the tenet that basically psychological processes operate in individuals only. As I have noted elsewhere, a group can be perceived as a whole and reacted to as a whole. A group, in addition, possesses observable characteristics — group properties — and thus comprises a social and psychological reality (Scheidlinger, 1952, 1980).

I would grant that the unconscious group manifestations so ingeniously described by Bion could occur, and that they deserve further evaluation and study. All such manifestations, however, are the product of the individuals' social and emotional interaction. In the strictest sense, it is necessary to emphasize that "basic assumption" activity deals with feelings of individuals. Thus, it is the individual who is dependent, who hates, or flees, or loves. More precisely, it is the individual who initiates feelings or acts that could be explained in terms of "dependency," "fight–flight," or "pairing." It is not necessary in my view to seek an answer to Bion's "seeming paradox" that a group is more than the sum of its members, which relates to the ambiguous concept of the human being as a group animal. This could be more simply explained in Lewin's (1947) experimentally supported concepts of a "mutual field" and of relations between parts and a whole in an ordered system.

BION'S INFLUENCE ON GROUP PSYCHOTHERAPY

As I have noted earlier, Bion's writings had rarely been reflected in the American group psychotherapy literature prior to 1960. This is especially surprising when one keeps in mind that his first paper on group psychology had been published as early as 1948, in which he spoke primarily in the role of a psychiatrist and group therapist.

The only American group therapist who explicitly reacted early to Bion's material was Bach (1954). He asserted that Bion's "speculative description" of group processes contained some observations which overlapped his own, and that Bion's "basic assumption" phenomena could be applied to Bach's outline of seven developmental phases for therapy groups. He also borrowed Bion's term "work group" as connoting what takes place in analytically oriented psychotherapy. He was critical, however, of Bion's laissez–faire type of leadership and his "defaulting in the job of leading," which could give rise to the "primitive group emotional trends" Bion described.

Powdermaker and Frank (1953) only briefly mentioned Bion in their volume. They declared themselves stimulated by his descriptions of the group process, but avoided giving it the prominence he had.

It is noteworthy that in a broader sense the actual group behavior patterns described by Bion—the emotional forces, the reality-geared group developments and their associated leadership types —have been at least partially confirmed in the observations of others. Some of this material has emerged in connection with the delineation of common emotional "themes" and tensions in the course of group therapy interactions. As a matter of fact, the portrayals by some psychoanalytic practitioners of their groups of psychotic patients are most strongly reminiscent of Bion's material. A clear example was Abrahams' (1958) presentation of a group experience with eight female borderline schizophrenic patients. The author spoke of an early dependency phase in which the leader was perceived as a "saving, magical, omnipotent father–mother figure." The emotional interaction occurred primarily on a nonverbal level with the emergence of unconscious pregenital impulses and fantasies. Near the eighth session the first strong expressions of hostility occurred with concomitant new subgroupings; this cut through the earlier esprit de corps that had built around the nonquestioning dependency on the "magical–helper" leader. (Even this brief summary of a long and detailed paper suggests its similarity to Bion's "dependency" and "fight–flight basic assumption" phenomena.)

Some support for Bion's observations regarding the utilization of group dynamic elements in the service of resistance could also be found in the literature. Especially mentioned have been instances of patients substituting a seriously disturbed indigenous leader for the therapist, resorting to the creation of a group history, and forming committees. Furthermore, Bion's justified emphasis on nonverbal forces in the therapeutic group process has also begun to draw serious consideration from other group therapists.

However, I have not found any confirmation in my own observations or in the literature that the "work group basic assumption" forces occurred in the sequence or manner so painstakingly outlined by him. As to Bion's assertions regarding the relationship between his work and the concepts of Melanie Klein, this had not even been mentioned by American group therapists. Bach (1954), for example, did not question Bion's way of evolving his conceptual system nor its theoretical sources. This could have occurred because Bach had based his comments on Bion's earliest seven papers where, as I have noted, the latter's theoretical leanings were less apparent.

The fact that certain patterns resembling those described by Bion have been observed in therapy groups for psychotics gives at least partial support to his observation that "the more disturbed the group, the more easily discernible are these fantasies and mechanisms" (1955, p. 958).

Bion in American Group Dynamics Literature

In turning to Bion's influence on group dynamics literature, I will limit myself to instances in which there was explicit reference to his contributions. A brief comment appeared in Cartwright and Zander's (1953) volume. The authors spoke of Bion's observations on the existence of covert group goals as thus supporting the intuitive notion of a "hidden agenda" (p. 308). Subsequently, Thelen (1954) wrote favorably of Bion's concept of a "subconscious group mentality" as explaining certain group events, especially periods of nonproductivity. He thought that Bion's formulation of "basic assumption" and "work group" activity was similar to his own ideas of the relationship between emotionality and work in influencing group functioning. A group's "hidden agenda" was seen as related to Bion's observations of the group–as–a–whole appearing to have "a secret task into which its energy is flowing" (Thelen, 1954, p. 270). In this discussion of what he termed "subjective reality in groups," Thelen equated the concepts of "group unconscious," "collective unconscious," and "group mentality."

In an interesting attempt to associate predisposing member personality orientations to group compatibility and productivity, Schutz (1955) based some of his theoretical assumptions on Bion's ideas. What is noteworthy here is that he utilized a group concept of Bion's (dependent basic assumption) together with Fromm's notion of "authoritarianism" to connote a basic individual personality characteristic, i.e., power orientation. In theorizing about group processes in human relations training groups, Shepard and Bennis (1956) postulated the existence of "announced" and "hidden interselves" occurring at different phases of the training period. Similar to the earlier–mentioned "hidden agenda," the authors believed them to correspond "quite closely with Bion's modalities" (p. 409).

It can be seen from the above that, to say the least, Bion's material has had some impact on the thinking of group dynamicists. To my knowledge, however, neither his theoretical approach nor his conceptualizations have been subjected to any critical analysis. No one has questioned his ways of gathering data; in the past this occurred with some justification as group therapy practitioners offered subjective descriptions of their experiences without the benefit of separate, objective observers. Could this easy acceptance be due to the fact that Bion's formulations, with their almost exclusive emphasis on group phenomena, approximated the prevailing interests of students of group dynamics? In addition, might there have been the matter of the auspices under which Bion's work was conducted — the Tavistock Institute of Human Relations in England, which has had close ties with the Research Center for Group Dynamics in the United States? Bion's first and major papers appeared in *Human Relations,* which is jointly published by these two institutions.

It should be noted here that Bion was also influenced by the British psychoanalyst Rickman, who followed Lewin's orientation and viewed psychoanalysis as "an historical, dynamic and not a genetic method" (Fairbairn, 1952, p. 127). Interestingly enough, Ezriel (1950), another British analyst, who specifically promoted such an ahistorical, "here and now" approach to group psychotherapy, and who had personally participated in one of Bion's groups, characterized the latter's basic group–relevant concepts as "overly superficial and inadequate to explain the complexity that can be observed in therapeutic groups."[1]

The fact that Bion's theories, despite their limitations, have found fertile ground in the field of group dynamics suggests that they contain much that is valuable, and that the time might well be at hand for more concentrated efforts toward an effective integration of psychoanalytic and group dynamic concepts. I am reminded here of a prediction by Sanford (1953) that the approach to group therapy based on Melanie Klein's theories ". . . is destined soon to become in the United States, as it is now in Great Britain, highly influential, as well as controversial" (p. 318).

SOME THOUGHTS FOR THE FUTURE

The ultimate goal of achieving a conceptual integration between individual and group psychological processes in group psychotherapy has been hampered by the onesidedness of the prevalent empirical and theoretical orientations. There are, on the one hand, such American authorities in the realm of group treatment as Slavson (1964) and Schwartz and Wolf (1957), who have ignored or underplayed the role of group dynamic elements in group psychotherapy. On the other hand, Bion, with his exclusive preoccupation with group phenomena at the expense of individual personality factors, has gone to the other extreme.

What we need to begin with is a recognition that in any small group, a therapy group being no exception, there is a continuous interplay between individual and group psychological processes. To put it differently, every item of such group behavior could be viewed as the behavior of individual personalities in a special process of social and emotional interaction. There are thus two interrelated sets of factors: (1) individual personalities with their genetic and dynamic properties, their motivational and defensive–adaptive patterns, some conscious and some unconscious; and (2) group dynamic elements such as climate, goals, structure, or code,

[1] Personal communication, 1956.

which emerge as the product of the interactions within the group, which can occur on conscious as well as unconscious levels. In terms of the discussion earlier in this chapter, group dynamics contributions have tended to stress the conscious, overt level of these elements, while Freud's and Bion's ideas are focused almost exclusively on the unconscious, covert level. A given group's functioning can at any point be affected primarily by the individual or by the group dynamic set of factors, or as happens most frequently, by a mixture of both.

From the point of view of a group's development, the network of interpersonal relations emerges as the interplay of positive forces tending to strengthen group cohesion, and negative ones, centrifugal in nature. In psychoanalytic terms the "positive" forces comprise identifications, libidinal object ties, and transferences. The opposing forces range from slight antipathies to isolation, hatred, and aggression. They include defensive identifications promoted by fear, as well as negative transferences (Scheidlinger, 1952).

Conceptual models such as Bion's, or the one offered more recently by Bennis (1958), in which groups are viewed as "organisms," almost like minds apart from these of the individual personalities, carry the flavor of the now generally discarded idea of a "group mind." Bennis even went so far as to postulate a genetic theory of group development whereby the group organism, like an individual organism, develops in terms of Freudian oral, anal, and genital psychosexual stages.

Bion's earlier-cited observations that touch on the deepest, primitive, regressive forces in group life reaffirm the importance of allowing for different "depth" levels in the study of groups. As I have noted (Scheidlinger, 1968b) the interaction process in the group psychotherapy experience can be described in terms of two major levels: (1) a dynamic-contemporaneous level, and (2) a genetic-regressive one. The former comprises the more readily observed momentary expressions of conscious needs and ego-adaptive patterns, group roles, network of attractions and repulsions, as well as group structure. The behavior here is primarily reactive to realistic group-situational factors, bringing into play the more external aspects of personality. The genetic-regressive level pertains to unconscious and preconscious motivations, defensive patterns, and conflicts — to such typical clinical phenomena as transference, countertransference, resistance, identification, or projection. The more regressive the group climate, in the sense that the personality defenses have been loosened with accompanying freer expressions of repressed emotionality, the more readily the genetic-regressive level of phenomena is apt to be in ascendancy. It must be underscored that these hypothesized two levels of group interaction are necessarily very closely interrelated. They each contain group- and individual-relevant tension and anxiety states of various depths and intensities. In both levels, the perceptions, verbalizations, and activities of individual group members occur in relation to other individuals, subgroupings as well as the group as an entity. In contrast to Bion's dichotomy of "work group" (rational) and "basic assumption" (emotional) modalities that correspond to the psychoanalytic "secondary" and "primary process" functioning, the above-noted levels have no rigid boundaries. Both could contain personality elements of emotional expression or of adaptive work and growth orientation. The genetic-regressive level in particular, though weighted with the reliving of childhood experiences, can include phenomena akin to the Freudian secondary process, which is characterized by readily available neutralized impulses (libido or aggression) and some reality orientation. In addition, despite the accessibility of preconscious or unconscious elements, there is a place for nonpathological areas of ego functioning in line with the concept of "regression in the service of the ego." This concept has been defined as a process wherein a person can undergo a controlled, temporary and partial regression that facilitates anxiety-free adaptation for purposes of creative expression, interpersonal relation, and work (Schafer, 1958).

In variance with Bion's view, aggressive manifestations can on this level (genetic-regressive) occur hand-in-hand with other emotional expressions, i.e., love or dependency. As a matter of fact, there is clinical support for the notion that hostile behavior could readily represent a facade, a defensive reaction to deeper emotional needs such as sexual ones, for instance. More direct expression of the latter need may then encompass too much anxiety for a given patient or group of patients.

The dynamic–contemporaneous and genetic–regressive interactions could perhaps best be studied within the framework of the process of perception. Let us look at the example of a patient who has just agreed to join a therapy group. In connection with the inevitable doubts and fears about this new experience, related conscious and unconscious memory percepts are apt to be revived. On a conscious level, a variety of antecedent or concurrent group experiences are recalled in an attempt to integrate the strange with the familiar. If not simultaneously, then soon thereafter, with the actual impact of the group process, deep, long–forgotten attitudes and levels of relatedness toward the patient's own family and childhood groups become reactivated. On one plane, the anxious patient perceives the tangible social reality of a number of people, each with his or her complex behavior patterns, as well as broader factors pertaining to the group–as–a–whole. These are communicated to him through verbal or nonverbal channels. On another plane, deep fears of rejection, hurt, exposure, or injury could come to the fore. Whether and how the patient participates depends not only on the quality of these kinds of perceptions, but also on the strength of the individual's desire for this group experience and on the capacities and patterns for interpersonal relating.

When a patient has chosen to continue voluntarily in a group, one could assume that the psychological gratifications accruing from this have outweighed the tensions and frustrations. To put it differently, in line with an earlier speculation of mine, the individual has perceived somewhere in the group certain common qualities, certain points of anchorage for his need to belong, to be fed, to enter a state of psychological unity with others. The establishment of this kind of a sense of unity with the group or with some aspect of it constitutes a recapitulation of an earlier primitive identification, particularly the one mentioned by Freud when the ego has as yet not been completely differentiated from the id. While derived from narcissism, such an identification is seen as a step forward in emotional development, involving a sense of oneness with another being. These kinds of transitory identifications with the group as an entity could be the basis for the sense of support and belonging which helps the patient to weather the later inevitable conflicts and tensions.

Thus, each group member could perceive each other member and the leader on a continuum — from the way they are in " reality," to the most fantasied distortions in line with inner motivations, disturbances in ego functions, and group situational pressures. (This has been portrayed quite clearly in projective tests by Bellak [1954].) Another patient can at one time represent a peer, a realistic object of sympathy, of empathy, or of dislike. This same patient could in a deeper sense be viewed as a loved or hated transference object (sibling or parent) from any previous moment in the life history. Similarly, the group–as–a–whole or even a single group property, i.e, the momentary group climate, could be perceived on many levels from reality — a peer group, through the family group, to the deepest symbolic ideations. Perhaps, as I have suggested above, the group entity could also be perceived in fantasy as the pre-oedipal mother, or even as Bion thought, as the mother's breast! (See Chapter 4 of this volume.) Such notions need to be investigated further, possibly from the broader angle of the relative influence on group functioning of internal personality stimuli projected outward, an aspect which Bion considered so basic to his theory. In this connection, the role of group situational factors along with intervening individual ego processes must be considered in dealing with the problem of activation and expression of such stimuli from the intrapsychic frame.

Group psychotherapy has often been depicted as necessarily more geared toward the social reality than individual psychoanalytic treatment. There has also been recognition of the supportive and emotionally corrective value accruing from this reality–based social interaction. Nevertheless, in theorizing about it, psychoanalytic group practitioners tend to explain patient behavior almost exclusively in terms of the deeper, intrapsychic level. It is as though, with their planful emphasis on a permissive climate with a minimum of structure to facilitate the reactivation of unconscious fantasies and reaction patterns, there is an assumption that the reality-geared perceptions and interactions become nonexistent. This is contrary to systematic observations of even the most unstructured therapy groups (Talland, 1957). As I have noted earlier, even Bion, with his emphasis on an extremely permissive group climate and the deepest levels of group interaction, allowed for a reality-anchored aspect of group ("work group") functioning. Without both aspects — the dynamic-contemporaneous level of social reality, and the deeper, genetic-regressive level of interactions — any understanding of group psychotherapy remains incomplete.

In most small group settings, the average individual's conduct can be understood and predicted with considerable accuracy without resort to deeper, internal motivations and response patterns. This is due to the fact that such behavior tends to be governed primarily by the outer, more readily accessible, more controlled and more rational aspects of the personality. However, when faced with responses to marked tensions or highly irrational group actions, complete understanding appears impossible without resort to unconscious motivations and regressive mechanisms. The same would hold true for much of the demeanor of markedly disturbed individuals in nonpathological groups. The momentary, observable aspects of behavior are then insufficient to explain what has occurred or to predict future conduct. It is no accident that the need for explanatory concepts that deal with the covert elements of individual and group psychological patterns has been felt most keenly by practitioners in group psychotherapy, or in group process training. In both settings, regressive, subsurface personality and group dynamic elements involving the expression of hitherto inaccessible aggressive and libidinal tendencies, together with associated defensive patterns against anxiety or guilt, are bound to emerge.

It is my belief that in trying to bridge the gap between individual and group psychology there is an urgent need for the further objective and methodical clarification of concepts which are relevant to an understanding of group behavior. There is much talk nowadays about the importance of research in group psychotherapy; yet such research is apt to be of limited value without a comprehensive conceptual scheme. As Lewin once put it, ". . . there is nothing so practical as a good theory." In this connection there is the twofold problem of not only a meaningful elucidation of what is meant by certain concepts of group behavior, but also how these concepts could be translated into operational terms for systematic observation and measurement. For this purpose, a series of direct, controlled observations of therapy groups is most desirable. To avoid some of the pitfalls noted in Bion's approach, it is probable that such work could not be carried on by individual group therapists working alone — no matter how gifted. For in group behavior we are dealing with phenomena of marked complexity, complicated even further in a therapy group with its regressive climate, its relative lack of organizational structure or predefined roles, and a membership characterized by personal pathology and varied therapeutic dynamisms. There is a serious question whether, without the help of independent observers or of audiovisual records, it is humanly possible for a group therapist alone to recapture enough of what transpires in a given group session, the exact "what" and "how" of the occurrences.

As I have stated in another context (1952), further progress in the formulation of theory and in research can be greatly enhanced through a collaborative effort of specialists in a number of related disciplines, such as psychoanalysis, group psychotherapy, and social psychology. The objection that current research tools and methodology are not capable of eliciting everything that transpires in a group, particularly with respect to the unconscious and latent phenomena at work, should not discourage us from learning as much as we can. In gathering data, a number of instruments would probably have to be combined. The modified Interaction

Process Analysis method of Bales (1950) has already begun to be used with some success for the observation of therapy groups (Munzer and Greenwald, 1957). In addition, the utilization of sound recordings and possibly even films would be most valuable. The material depicting the observable facets of the group interaction could then be related to the clinical data on individual patients, which would be comprised of the motivational sources, and the current and past defensive and adaptive patterns as gathered through interviews, observations, and available projective techniques, including dreams and free-associative productions. Sociometric measures could serve as an additional means to assess group interaction elements (Borgatta, 1954).

The scientific accuracy would be enhanced if the collaborating experts along with independent teams of researchers could make predictions about long-range as well as short-term phases of a given group's development. In addition, it might be necessary to elicit the reactions of the group members to the group phenomena under scrutiny, and to check these against the observations and inferences in the data. If at all possible, such reactions of the patients should include, in line with our earlier discussion, their unconscious perception of these group elements. Spontaneous or suggested dreams about the group as an entity might, for example, offer one avenue for studying this deeper, intrapsychic level of group phenomena. The frequently used personality questionnaires for assessing the patient's feelings about themselves and others in the group are only of limited usefulness in this connection.

In line with Bion's idea that the more pathological the group composition, the more apparent the regressive level of "psychotic" anxieties and defenses, it might be of interest to compare the group psychological manifestations in groups of patients with different types of pathology. Lastly, there have been some precise, albeit preliminary, investigations which attempt to combine elements from the dynamic-contemporaneous and genetic-regressive levels in the group process (Lippitt, Polansky, Redl, and Rosen, 1952). Part of this work has focused on phenomena very similar, if not identical, to the theoretic postulates of Bion. Such continued systematic observations and research together with conceptual refinements, especially within a multidisciplinary framework, should bring us closer to the much desired fuller understanding of "what makes groups tick."

Chapter 3

THE CONCEPT OF EMPATHY IN GROUP PSYCHOTHERAPY

My interest in the concept of empathy stems from two disparate, but not altogether unrelated sources. In the first place, it springs from a preoccupation with issues of psychoanalytic group psychology, especially with identification and its role in group formation and maintenance (Scheidlinger, 1952); beginning with Freud's little volume on group psychology (Freud, 1921), whenever empathy is mentioned it is always linked in some way with identification. The second source of my interest is a practical one. It relates to the challenge inherent in offering desperately needed mental health services to the disadvantaged dwellers of urban slum neighborhoods. One major problem here lies in the issue of empathy, in the practitioner's grasping fully the culture of what Harrington (1962) has termed "the other America." It is my strong impression, if not bias, that the newer treatment approaches such as family and group therapies, which emphasize mutual participation and empathic communication, represent a step in the right direction.

To arrive at the exact meaning of empathy is not a simple task. There is little about it in the clinical literature generally, and in the group therapy literature specifically. Whenever empathy is mentioned, it tends to be lumped together with related interpersonal processes under the broader headings of sympathy or identification.

Reprinted from *International Journal of Group Psychotherapy,* 16:413–424, 1966 by permission.

Scheler (1954), a German sociologist, presented the most comprehensive phenomenological list of eight different forms of what he termed "sympathetic orientation" or "fellow feeling." The first three represent a primitive kind of pseudosympathy in which the emphasis is on the subject's *own* feeling rather than on any concern *with or for* other people. These are as follows: (1) *Einfuhlung* refers to empathy in the sense of an instantaneous community of feeling along with a reflex motoric mimicry, such as crying when someone else is crying. In the group therapy setting, an example would be the vicarious catharsis wherein one or more patients experience emotional release through another patient's actions or verbalizations. (2) *Miteinanderfuhlung* involves a circumstance in which two or more people react simultaneously and in a similar manner to the same stimulus, but a sense of communality or solidarity is absent. In a treatment group, this could refer to a spectator–like reaction of individuals to a specific event. (3) *Gefuhlansteckung* represents the well–known phenomenon of emotional contagion, which tends to be especially intensified in larger groups. Freud (1921) referred to something in us ". . . which when we become aware of signs of an emotion in someone else, tends to make us fall into the same emotion" (p. 13).

The following "higher" forms of sympathy or "fellow feeling," in which there is a definite focus on the subject's feeling *with or for others,* were further noted by Scheler: (4) *Mitgefuhl* deals with a common feeling of sorrow or pain on the part of two or more people, with awareness that they all suffer. A family's, or for that matter a treatment group's, reaction of mourning over the loss of the leader would be illustrative here. (5) *Einsfuhlung* refers to a feeling at one with another object, be it an individual or a group. It is close to the notion of identification with others on the basis of a common emotional tie, aim, or quality, which underlies the Freudian view of group formation. (6) *Nachfuhlung* is the understanding of how another person feels. It is almost identical in meaning to Freud's (1921) definition of empathy (for which he incidentally used the term *Einfuhlung* in the sense of "feeling into") as a process

". . . which plays the largest part in our understanding of what is inherently foreign to our ego in other people" (p. 66). At a later point I shall give further consideration to empathy together with its dynamic, genetic, and adaptive implications. Scheler's final two categories, (7) *Menschenliebe* and (8) *Akosmistische Person und Gottesliebe*, refer to sentiments of love and respect for mankind and to a mystical sympathy of a religious nature. One might note here that the concept of empathy transcends the fields of psychology and psychopathology, leading into the realms of creativity, aesthetics, and ethics. These last-named three, however, remain necessarily outside the scope of this discussion.

What about some more current views of empathy as applied to psychology? English and English (1958) defined empathy as "apprehension of the state of mind of another person without feeling (as in sympathy) what the other feels. While the empathic process is primarily intellectual, emotion is not precluded but it is not the same emotion as that of the person with whom one empathizes. . . . The attitude in empathy is one of acceptance and understanding, of an implicit 'I see how you feel'" (p. 178). A number of writers have used the terms "empathy" and "sympathy" interchangeably. The emphasis seems to be on the fact that, while empathy, in line with the above definition, precludes a taking over of the object's feelings, there is nevertheless a sympathetic, accepting attitude inherent in the perception of the object. While some authors have emphasized the spontaneous and intuitive element in empathy, Stewart (1956) saw it as a deliberate effort to identify and establish a mutual base for understanding with reference to the object's similar experience, accompanied by growing insight into both oneself and the other person.

In my own view, empathy refers to a process which can be either spontaneous or deliberate. It is not primarily intellectual insofar as it is closely linked to intuition, to a perception, or more specifically, to a communication, which can occur on the unconscious or preconscious level. Its most essential distinguishing feature, when compared to the other kinds of "fellow feelings" or identifications listed by Scheler, lies in the fact that in empathy the *subject's ego boundaries and coherence of self are maintained.* As will be discussed later, it is a kind of identification containing elements of projection and introjection which occur within the context of ego control. In line with the psychoanalytic concept of "regression in the service of the ego," this kind of self–autonomy and identity can be preserved even in the face of the emergence of "primary process" derivatives in the empathizer's conscious experience. Schafer (1958) defined regression in the service of the ego as

> a partial, temporary, controlled lowering of the level of psychic functioning to promote adaptations. . . by maintaining, restoring or improving inner balance and organization, interpersonal relations and work. It is a process which increases the individual's access to preconscious and unconscious contents, without a thoroughgoing sexualization or aggressivization of major ego functions, and there-fore without disruptive anxiety and guilt [p. 122].

It is noteworthy that there is a difference of opinion whether the capacity for empathy is innate or learned. Furthermore, there is the interesting question whether man can fully enter into internal states in other people which are alien to him. Can a man, or a childless woman for that matter, truly empathize with a woman's experience of giving birth?

When it comes to a consideration of the developmental aspects of empathy, most of us would probably agree with Ferreira (1961) who said: ". . . empathy, that mysterious ability to feel with people, is a phenomenon that exists from the youngest days and that most likely goes back historically to the earliest situation of being with mother" (p. 10). In his studies of the development of object relation-ships, Spitz (1963) underlined the importance of reciprocity in early mother–child communications. He emphasized in this connection the existence of a kind of preverbal ". . . dialogue which could be thought of as a precursor of conversation. . ." (p. 156). Erikson (1959) repeatedly indicated that empathic communication was closely related to his concept of mutuality, to the coordination be-tween the developing personality and the significant caretaking persons in the social environment. "Only the experience of such mutuality," he said, "provides a safe pole of self–feeling from which the child can reach out for the other pole: his first love 'objects'" (p. 39).

When we move to a discussion of empathy in individual psychotherapy,[1] we are in reality, as Ruesch and Bateson (1951) have observed, dealing with an interpersonal network of communications. The patient enters the therapeutic situation with a variety of overt and covert expectations, feelings, and attitudes that he communicates to the therapist through verbal and nonverbal channels. The latter, in turn, not only has certain expectations about the patient, but he also more or less deliberately communicates certain attitudes and ideas. Even in the context of the classical Freudian analysis with its well–known "basic rule" and the "mirror" role of the analyst, the latter inevitably communicates nonverbal messages regarding himself as a real person, regarding his preconscious processes, and regarding the broader climate of the treatment setting (Berger, 1964). In this connection Fenichel (1945) emphasized the way in which the analyst oscillates between a position of experiencing and that of observing and conceptualizing. One might say, in addition, that in order to empathize with and to respond appropriately to the patient's communications from the different depth (regressive) levels, the therapist himself regresses "in the service of the ego," as part of the therapeutic process. According to Katz (1963), as part of this regression, the therapist becomes capable of expanding his ego boundaries, of bringing into play a number of aspects of his personality. This would fit in with our earlier discussion of the nature of empathy as an interpersonal process and as a form of adaptation. A therapist's empathic communications would thus be different from an overidentification with a patient or from countertransference reactions generally, in which case the

---

[1] The major interest in this paper is with empathy as an element in psychotherapy. Thus, such issues as empathic deficiency as an index of psychopathology or as a diagnostic criterion will not concern us here.

therapist's own unconscious content is reactivated outside of his ego's control functions.

Greenson (1959) discussed the role of empathy in helping the psychoanalyst assess the analysand's ego strength. He viewed it as especially useful in the comprehension of the subtler emotions that are not fully conscious.

According to Fenichel (1945), empathy consists of two inter-related acts: (1) an identification with the other person, and (2) an awareness of one's own feelings after the identification, and, in this way, an awareness of the object's feelings.

From what has been said heretofore, we can see that, in em-pathy, the therapist not only identifies with the patient insofar as he *experiences* what the patient feels, but also *incorporates* the patient's feelings as if they were his (the therapist's) own. This is followed by an element of detachment required for an objective analysis of what he has perceived. Theodor Reik (1949), who referred to this empathic communication as "listening with the third ear," depicted how the therapist

> can vibrate unconsciously in the rhythm of the other person's im-pulse and yet be capable of grasping it as something outside himself and comprehending it psychologically, sharing the other's experi-ence and yet remaining above the struggle [p. 125].

In this connection, those of us engaged in the training of ther-apists, for individual or for group treatment, must bear in mind the following kinds of questions: (1) To what extent are extreme differences in trainees' initial capacity for empathy a function of something innate or a product of personality development? (2) Can the ability to identify with some kinds of patients and not with others (the first step in empathy in Fenichel's sense), be completely changed by a thorough training analysis? It is my impression that some research data would be valuable in this sphere. What we now have is a general, more or less intuitive knowledge that a given therapist, no matter how well trained or experienced, will relate well to one kind of patient or group and very poorly indeed to another.

Before proceeding to a consideration of the place of empathy in group psychotherapy, it is necessary to be reminded that the basic therapeutic dynamics in individual and in group psychotherapy are the same. What makes group psychotherapy unique, however, is the broader and more complex network of interrelationships involving not only other group members, but also the group as a whole. From the point of view of the helping process, group psychotherapy can be said to contain a supportive and experiential aspect, on the one hand, and, on the other hand, conceptualization and insight. While analytic group psychotherapy, as contrasted with other group treatment approaches, stresses this last–named aspect with its aim of personality reorganization, most group therapists agree about the importance of creating a supportive emotional climate, at least during the initial phase.

As described by Semrad, Kanter, Shapiro, and Arsenian (1963), the early phase of a group is characterized by a variety of tensions and anxieties related to the "vicissitudes of presence and contact." The expressions of regressive dependency and of counteractive aggression are often so marked that the therapist has to make sure that the supportive elements in the group outweigh the disruptive, centrifugal forces. While the therapist undoubtedly is instrumental in the fostering of an underlying atmosphere of acceptance and permissiveness, the vital role of the other group members as active helpers (not only as objects for transference reactions) is not sufficiently emphasized in the literature. It is as though the idea of a lay person, and a patient at that, in a therapeutic role toward other patients would somehow lower the image of group psychotherapy as a professional endeavor. And yet, as Foulkes and Anthony (1957) have shown, the therapeutic functions of the other group members can be observed readily enough. While these authors have not explicitly used the term "empathy," their vivid description of the interpersonal reactions in an analytic therapy group leaves no doubt that they are depicting the phenomenon of an empathic communication. They refer to two levels of such communication in a group: (1) an ordinary language level approximating the "secondary process," and (2) an unconscious level of symbolism related to "primary process" phenomena. In their words: ". . . there is always, to be sure, an unconscious understanding present upon which we build" (p. 259). This ties in with the above depiction of empathy as an overt or a covert process, with the addition that the regression is "in the service of the ego." So much for the role of the group therapist and of the other group members in empathic communication.

What about the group-as-a-whole in this connection? In a previous paper (Scheidlinger, 1964), I examined the subject of an individual's identification with the group entity. This kind of identification was viewed as adaptive in purpose, in line with Freud's notion of shared qualities, interests, or ideals being capable of precipitating group formation. Identification with the group entity was assumed to entail two related elements. The first involves a perception of the group "Gestalt" on a variety of levels, ranging from that of the group as an instrument for need satisfaction, to the deepest ideations, as, for example, a symbolic mother, i.e., mother-group, mother-land, mother-earth (see also Chapter 4 of this volume). The second element refers to a self-involvement, to a relinquishing of an aspect of personal identity to the group, with the effect that the individual reacts to the attributes of the group as if these were his own.

In the course of thinking about this subject, I reviewed some group records drawn from discussion groups for markedly deprived women diagnosed as severe character disorders and borderline psychotics. I was struck by the fact that, with these women at least, the aspect of "being understood" was especially emphasized when they talked about the treatment's value to them. They meant by this, being understood, not by the therapist per se nor by their peers, but by the group (see Chapter 10 of this volume).

The following is an excerpt from an early meeting of such a group:

Mrs. Bell had announced at the beginning of the session that she didn't feel the group had brought up anything for discussion that was helpful to her, so the best thing was simply to drop out. (It was clear to the woman therapist that Mrs. Bell's anger was primarily meant for her. The patient was struggling with her strong wishes for exclusive possession of the therapist and the related rivalry with and resentment toward the other group members.) The other women, taken aback by the criticism, soon began to defend the group, which they only now learned had not been useful to Mrs. Bell. Mrs. Kent became the spokesman for the others, saying: "But you are not telling us what you want help with; you have to let us know what you are thinking." Others spoke up in a similar vein, but Mrs. Bell, glorying in the attention she had managed to draw upon herself, simply shook her head, saying, although with little conviction, that she didn't want to continue. Mrs. Kent reported: "But then you will never know whether you have given the group a chance to help you. You will simply feel that the group didn't help you; but it would be your fault then." Mrs. Harris, who had been silent, now spoke up, her voice choked with emotion. (Apparently the discussion was perceived by her as a threat against the continuation of the group.) "I never had an opportunity in a group like this; it is a great opening for me." She was astonished that people were able to come together and say what they felt. She had never experienced before being really listened to, and she was grateful to the group for this. She went on to enlarge on this theme, and the other women seemed to hang on her every word. She concluded thus: "I used to feel so self-conscious whenever I opened my mouth, but now I have lots to say. I used to think I couldn't say anything but now I am beginning to be more confident that I can explain how I feel in the group, and this makes me feel better."

It would be difficult to find a clearer example of the linkage between the process of group identification and empathy. One could hypothesize, then, that when there is identification on the basis of some common quality or interest in a small group, with its resulting increase in cohesiveness, empathic communication is facilitated. In terms of the earlier-noted two aspects of identification with the group entity, a *perception* by an individual of a group situation which contains a climate of acceptance and empathic communication will facilitate the other aspect, that of self-commitment, the "giving up" of part of one's identity. This kind of involvement can, of course, serve irrational or regressive purposes as well as those of adaptation and growth.

In returning to the matter of a relationship between group identification and empathy, it is noteworthy that Freud (1921), in a footnote to his discussion of group psychology, suggested such a connection. He wrote, "A path leads from identification by way of imitation to empathy, that is, to the comprehension of the mechanism by means of which we are enabled to take up any attitude at all towards another mental life" (p. 110). A perusal of the group therapy literature depicting actual group process offers many illustrations in which the sharing of similar feelings promotes mutual identifications, imitations, expressions of empathy, and desires to be helpful.

Perhaps the best examples in a pure-culture form, so to speak, of the linkage of processes of group identification and empathy are offered by the many self-help organizations, of which Alcoholics Anonymous and Synanon are the most well known. In his study of Alcoholics Anonymous, Stewart (1956) suggested that there is initially a deliberate identification among the members on the basis of their common problem — alcoholism — and their common ideal — sobriety. This is followed by mutual imitation of one another and by empathic communications in a group climate of hope and inspiration, often bordering on the religious. An interesting side aspect of Stewart's observations refers to what Riessman (1965) termed "the helper-therapy principle," i.e., helping oneself in the process of helping others. To quote Stewart ". . . instead of criticizing or judging, the recovered man uses this means to knowledge of the other to know himself better, to strengthen his sobriety, and reciprocally to introduce the 'know-how' of sobriety to the active addict" (p. 74). The work of such self-help organizations is, of course, outside the realm of group psychotherapy; however, some of their processes are very relevant for study. In fact, when considered within the broader spectrum of social psychiatry or of community mental health, they cannot and must not be ignored (see also Chapter 1 of this volume).

This brings us to a consideration of some implications for the mental health practitioner of the concepts of group identification and empathy. I referred earlier to the staggering problem of the masses who live in crowded urban communities characterized by the most extreme economic, social, and psychological pathology. Although the field of community psychiatry is growing rapidly, it is still in its infancy. The most promising advances have been made in the sphere of hospital treatment, the use of day–care centers, "halfway" houses, and rehabilitation workshops. When it comes to specific treatment modalities in outpatient settings, all we have to date are preliminary impressions and experimental programs.

What are some of these impressions? To begin with, there appears to be a marked barrier, as previously indicated, to free communication between the typical mental health practitioner and the urban poor. The reasons for this are complex, of course, but issues related to a lack of basic trust or a lack of possibilities for mutual understanding and empathy undoubtedly play a major role. In trying to develop treatment and rehabilitation facilities, it has become all too clear that the traditional concepts and techniques of individual and group therapy — based, after all, on working with the more advantaged social and economic classes — are not applicable. Among other factors, it has been noted that lower–class clients do not have the motivation for getting involved in a treatment relationship, especially with a middle–class therapist. In fact, the people who most need treatment frequently have to be sought out, "reached out to" in their natural habitat, or made to "get therapy" through court order. Once placed in a treatment situation, there is the problem of the lack of verbal facility, interest in, or capacity to deal with conceptual explanations or interpretations. Frequently, it is also difficult for such patients to focus on their own feelings and to understand references to their inner motivational sources.

On the positive side of this discouraging picture is the more hopeful impression that these patients desire and respond to supportive, directive, structured, and problem–centered treatment

methods. They are especially responsive to family and group approaches, as noted earlier with reference to individuals with severe
ego pathology. In my own work with group therapy of emotionally
and socially deprived clients, a methodology which relies primarily
on elements of reliving and experiencing appeared to be most
promising. It is here that meaningful emotional attachments to
peers, and above all to the group entity on a variety of levels, play a
major role. In other words, when strong group identification and
empathic communication were consciously and deliberately fostered, especially in the early phase of the experience, effective treatment could proceed. In the final stages of such groups, a more
focused orientation on self–awareness and introspection became
possible. However, this required a continuation of the highly supportive group climate, which was utilized to cushion the associated
anxieties and resistances (see also Chapter 10 of this volume).

In addition to the reasons mentioned above, the choice of the
small group as a treatment modality for the population under discussion is related to the fact that, in the face of threat and danger,
the need for association with others increases. This theme was
developed by Lindt and Pennal (1962), and even subjected to
research scrutiny (Mulder and Stemerding, 1963). In a broader
sense, this relationship between external danger and the need to
seek the company of others might be conceptualized in terms of
Erikson's twin concepts of ego and group identity. It is as though,
in the face of a threat to a person's ego identity, the support of significant groups is sought. On one level, this may represent the search
for a protecting, empathic human environment. On a deeper symbolic level, in line with man's universal need to belong, to establish
a state of psychological unity with others, it might represent a wish
to restore the earliest empathic tie to the mother. Peck (1963) has
been one of the foremost proponents of the application and modification of group therapy concepts and methodology to community
mental health. We may well agree with his observation that "the
small group is an excellent vantage point from which both to study
these phenomena. . .[i.e., the nature of mental health and the

processes by which it is maintained and impaired] and to intervene in a useful fashion, and thus . . . group therapists already engaged in work in the mental health field are in a unique position to contribute to mental health in both theory and practice" (p. 289).

In summary, I have explored the concept of empathy in a phenomenological sense as related to the broader realm of interpersonal feelings. I defined empathy as an adaptive process on two major depth levels; I considered its genetic factors and discussed its function in individual and group psychotherapy. Group identification and empathic group communication were viewed as intimately related processes. Some implications of these concepts for the development of group treatment modalities to help the urban poor were assessed.

On the basis of the above, I can only conclude that the concept of empathy, though common in popular usage, remains far from being truly understood. Sparsely covered in the literature of group psychotherapy, it undoubtedly deserves further study and practical application.

Chapter 4

ON THE CONCEPT OF THE "MOTHER-GROUP"

There have been increasing references in the group process and group psychotherapy literature to observations that, on the deepest levels, group members perceive the group-as-a-whole as a maternal image. This chapter scrutinizes the historical roots of the concept of a "mother-group" and the varied usages of the term by students of group behavior. I then relate this notion to the better-known concepts of group identification and transference.

The earliest reference[1] to the group entity as a parental symbol appeared in a paper by Money-Kyrle (1950), in which he postulated three kinds of unconscious perceptions by members of groups: (1) the "good parents," *particularly the mother,* representing the norms and ideals of the group; (2) the "bad parents" in the role of persecutors against whom the group values have to be defended; and (3) the "good parents," especially the father, who in his role as the mother's defender reappears as the group leader. While Money-Kyrle referred to larger societal groupings, Schindler (1951, 1952, 1966) was the first group therapist to speak of the group as a mother symbol. He differentiated between transferences to the therapist as a father, the group members as siblings, and the group entity as mother, on the one hand, and the "group personality"

Reprinted from *International Journal of Group Psychotherapy,* 24:417–428, 1974, by permission.

[1] I am not including here the much earlier appearance of such terms as "mother earth" or "mother country" in folklore and mythology.

along the tripartite model of id, ego, and superego, on the other hand. Bion (1959) made repeated brief references in his writings to the group's unconsciously being perceived at times as a "part-object," such as the mother's breast or other body parts, in line with Melanie Klein's conceptualizations. In a similar vein, I hypothesized that the group members' identification with the group–as–a–whole represents a covert wish to restore an earlier state of unconflicted well–being inherent in the child's exclusive union with the mother (Scheidlinger, 1964).

Interestingly. S. R. Slavson's first and only mention of this theme occurred in 1964, when he briefly stated: "It has been shown that the group serves *in loco maternis*. The leader usually represents symbolically, the father figure, while the group represents the complementary figure of the mother" (p. 27). Similarly, Foulkes and Anthony (1964) asserted at that same time that ". . . on different levels the group can symbolize a variety of objects or persons, e.g., the body. . . the inside of the mother, the womb. It frequently, possibly universally, represents the 'Image of the Mother' hence the term 'matrix'" (p. 115). In the same year, Durkin (1964) postulated two separate transference manifestations in therapy groups:

> (1) the idea of a group—i.e., a large totality of unknown power— conjures up the harsh, pre–oedipal mother image reactivating the individual's narcissistic fear of her; and (2) the individual perceives the group accordingly in distorted fashion, and behaves toward it in a way that resembles his mode of reacting to his mother. While the group member thus is afraid of the group as a whole, the therapist, in turn, is perceived in the image of the good all–giving omnipotent mother [p. 329].

Basing his observations on T–groups and on self–analytic classroom groups, Slater (1966) discussed at some length the group members' perceptions of the group–as–a–whole in a maternal vein. According to him, this "mother–group" was at times perceived as ". . . a source of succorance and comfort, even a refuge" (p. 187). At other times, this mother image was a frightening one involving primitive fantasies ". . . of being swallowed and enveloped." The "group revolt" against the leader, which was depicted as occurring in the early phase of T–groups, was connected, on the one hand, with the members' trying to get the loving indulgent "mother–group" away from the depriving paternal figure; on the other hand, this dethroning of the leader was also associated with a ". . . dramatic heightening of sexual interest" among the group members. Still more recently, Grotjahn (1972) asserted that "as a general rule, the group is a truly good and strong mother, not only in fantasies of transference but also in the reality of the group process" (p. 318). Ruiz (1972) described the early phase of a T–group in which the anxiety experienced by the participants appeared to be perceived as a threat to the idealized image of an unconflicted, nurturing "mother–group."

The most comprehensive discussion in the literature to date on this theme of the "mother–group" was that by Gibbard and Hartman (1973), who, following Slater (1966), asserted that the group members' "affective response to the unconscious perception of the group–as–mother is profoundly ambivalent. The positive side of the ambivalence is the wellspring for what we [the authors] have called the utopian fantasy" (p. 127). This fantasy "offers some assurance that the more frightening, enveloping or destructive aspects of the group–as–mother will be held in check and that a host of oedipal feelings, libidinal and aggressive, will not become fully conscious and gain direct expression in the group. The essence of the utopian fantasy is that the good can be split off from the bad and that this separation can be maintained" (p. 126). (I shall return to some of the significant theoretical issues posed by Gibbard and Hartman at a later point.)

One might note here that, from the viewpoint of group therapy's history, the "mother–group" concept has begun to be discussed in the literature relatively late. The reasons for this are probably twofold: (1) The early psychoanalytic models of group formation, such as those postulated by Freud (1921) and Redl (1942), placed emphasis on the major role of a paternal "central person" in group psychology; and (2) the recently growing emphasis on early object relations in psychoanalytic theory has affirmed the great significance of early mothering in personality development and in psychopathology. This stress has tended to focus the attention of individual and group therapists on the reactivation of early object relations vis-à-vis the mother in the therapeutic process as well. An illustration of this trend is Stone's (1961) depiction of the classical psychoanalytic situation as representing on the unconscious level ". . . the superimposed series of basic separation experiences in the child's relation to his mother" (p. 35). More specifically, Stone viewed the analyst as representing what he termed "the mother of separation," as contrasted with the mother image associated with intimate bodily care.

In a previous publication of mine (Scheidlinger, 1964) which dealt with the individual group members' identification with the group-as-a-whole, I defined identification (as distinct from transference and real object relations) as an endopsychic process calling for a degree of individual involvement with a perceived object or its symbolic representation. I hypothesized further that identification with the group entity entails the following two related elements: (1) ascribing to the group an emotional meaning, i.e., as an instrument for need satisfaction or, on a genetically "deeper" level, as a mother symbol; (2) a self-involvement in the group, a "giving up" of an aspect of personal identity—from the *I* to the *We*—which can serve irrational purposes as well as those of adaptation or growth. I finally wondered whether, in a broader sense, the universal human need to belong, to establish a state of psychological unity with others, does not represent a covert wish to restore an earlier state of unconflicted well-being inherent in the infant's exclusive union with the mother, which serves to counteract a fundamental fear of abandonment and of aloneness in all of us. Continued observations of relevant aspects of group behavior since that time have strengthened my belief in the basic plausibility of the above hypotheses, and have also led me in search of additional data from current object-relations theory for their further elaboration.

Perhaps because of the impetus from the so-called "British School," recent psychoanalytic writings in America about early object relations have multiplied, and have dwelled on aspects of this crucial phase of development in considerably greater detail than did Freud. Although Melanie Klein asserted that in the first three months of life the infant's ego is capable of perceiving and integrating parts of the first object, i.e., the mother's breast, others have seriously questioned whether an infant conceivably possesses the perceptual capacity to accomplish this. Jacobson (1964) insists that for the baby to be able to relate psychologically to something external to himself which satisfies his bodily needs, he has to have passed through at least a rudimentary phase of ego development. This involves ". . . the laying down of memory traces, the organization of experiential states and the beginning ability perceptually to differentiate between the self and the object" (p. 34). Using Freud's better-known terminology, the infant's transition from primary to secondary narcissism calls for some degree of reality-geared representations of self and maternal object, and a perception of the latter as the source of tension relief and need gratification. Only with this rudimentary recognition is the infant believed to experience anxiety in the absence of the mothering figure (Edgecumbe and Burgner, 1972). In this connection, Anna Freud (1965) postulated a separate stage of a *need-satisfying relationship* which falls developmentally between the phase of *primary narcissism* and that of *object constancy.* This stage of a *need-satisfying relationship* is still characterized by the baby's unique egocentricity coupled with a symbiotic perception of the mother as a gratifier of needs; nevertheless, it represents an advance from primary narcissism, in which a primitive state of experiential pleasure is assumed to prevail devoid of any differentiation whatsoever between self and object representations. According to Jacobson (1964), there is an ongoing conflict in the child between the wish to maintain this dependent, need-satisfying style of relating, and opposing forces striving for independent ego functioning, which is believed to continue till the onset of the oedipal period.

In general, then, the term *"need-satisfying* relationship" refers to a specific mode of relating in which the maternal object's need-satisfying functions are paramount. Furthermore, the maternal object is perceived as separate from the self only at 'moments of need; at other times, from the infant's subjective point of view, the object is believed to cease to exist as "somewhere out there." There is broad consensus in the literature that this phase of the need-satisfying relationship lasts from age three months until about 18 months. Gradually, this stage is believed to be supplanted by the psychologically more advanced stage of *object constancy*, in which concern for the mothering figure as an object takes precedence over her mere need–gratifying functions.

I would like to be more specific about the earlier hypothesis of group identification as a covert wish to restore a state of uncon-flicted well–being. The group members' covert wish very likely refers to a yearning for a return to the need–gratifying relationship that I have just outlined. In this context I wish to emphasize that the symbolic "mother–group" is accordingly perceived in purely positive, nonconflictual terms.

Guntrip (1961) related this phase of the child's positive early relationship to the mystic's experience of unity with the Deity, to Plato's "Idea of the Good," as well as to Freud's notion of an oceanic feeling, ". . . an indissoluble connection, of belonging inseparably to the external world as a whole" (p. 361). Guntrip felt, as I do, that this ". . . sense of identity or unity must be the basis of all kinds of feelings of oneness in both personal and communal living" (p. 362).

As I have noted elsewhere, the regressive emotional pulls that characterize the early group formative stages in unstructured groups tend to loosen the individual's self boundaries and reacti-vate primitive wishes and modes of early object relations, including identifications. Such regressive patterns are not necessarily patho-logical; even in the most mature personalities the infantile, need-satisfying modes of relating persist, and are subject to reactivation at moments of threat and anxiety. Greenacre (1972) asserted in this connection that ". . . the introjective–projective reaction leading ultimately to individuation, characteristic of the early stages of life, is never lost and may be revived with special strength in any situation of stress sufficient to cause a feeling of helplessness" (p. 147). Similarly, Schafer (1958) states that in the realm of primary process emotionality (which, as I have stated, characterizes the anxiety-laden period of group formation) ". . . the 'lost' object is not someone who will, it is hoped, return in the future: he is someone who still exists, though he is out of sight, touch, hearing, behind a wall, shattered, and so forth" (p. 222).

Already mentioned as the most extensive discussion of the concept of the "mother–group" in the literature to date, the work by Gibbard and Hartman (1973) was based on observations drawn from "self–analytic" classroom groups of college students. These authors not only found that the group entity was perceived by its members in a maternal vein, but that this shared unconscious fantasy comprised a splitting of "good" and "bad" mother images. The "good" mother entailed nurturant and protective aspects; the "bad" mother, abandoning and destructive ones. The group members employed splitting ". . . to avoid both a state in which 'good' and 'bad' cannot be differentiated and a state in which both are experienced at the same time (genuine ambivalence)" (p. 127). These authors stressed, furthermore, that the utopian perception of the group as a benevolent maternal figure was a manifestation of defensiveness against dealing with painful intragroup conflicts. More specifically, according to Gibbard and Hartman, ". . . the 'good' group functions as a defense both against the primitive, 'bad' engulfing and/or sadistic group (mother) and the fully heterosexual, oedipal group (which is no longer so clearly equated with the mother)" (p. 129).

I welcome Gibbard and Hartman's (1973) path of inquiry into the broader realm of group psychological regression and specifically into that of the relatively neglected concept of the "mother–group." Although, as they have noted, there is much congruence between my earlier hypotheses regarding identification with the group-as–a–whole (Scheidlinger, 1964) and their recent observations, I nevertheless would like to raise some questions here from the framework of group psychotherapy. To begin with, apart from

Durkin's (1964) hypothesized split transference in which the group is perceived by the patients as a threatening preoedipal mother figure, with the therapist becoming the "good, all-giving omnipotent mother," I could find no reference in the group therapy literature to the kind of "bad" mother perception of the group entity that is stressed by Gibbard and Hartman (1973). As is evident from my earlier review of the relevant literature, most other group therapists refer to the group entity as being perceived in a benign maternal vein, on the one hand, with the *therapist* becoming the feared parental transference figure, on the other. Similarly, fears of abandonment by and fusion with the group have been touched on only rarely in the American literature, referring to individual patients characterized by ego pathology, in whom concern with self-object boundaries is marked.

It should be noted in contrast that Bion (1959) and other British followers of Melanie Klein, such as Jaques (1970), have repeatedly written about group members' fears of engulfment by the group, to the point of claiming that individual group belonging always entails a defense against loss of identity stemming from primitive "psychotic" anxieties. (Jaques, to my knowledge, however, never referred to the group as a maternal image, while Bion made occasional references to a perception of the group entity as parts of the mother's body, in line with Kleinian postulates of part-objects.)

A number of possibilities suggest themselves as explanations here. It could be that the phenomena described by Gibbard and Hartman (1973) are in some way unique to short-term analytic classroom groups with their "normal" constituency, assigned readings, examination, and final grades. These groups are undoubtedly different in character from long-term psychotherapy groups with their composition of designated patients and their explicit goals of "repairing" identified personality pathology. (In this connection, I was puzzled by the authors' occasional references to "working through" of conflicts or "exploring in depth" the defensive nature of fantasies; to me at least these suggest an undesirable blurring of the aims of education and therapy, which I discussed in Chapter 1.)

There is also the question of whether the verbal and nonverbal behaviors noted in these classroom groups during their early periods of "manifest utopianism" might be subject to different theoretical explanations by others. Conversely, it is possible too, of course, that therapy groups would abound in the very same manifestations described by Gibbard and Hartman, were it not for conscious or unconscious interferences with their open expression. For instance, in the understandable desire to prevent an unduly high anxiety level, especially in the groups' initial phase, group therapists might well be unwittingly discouraging the emergence of negative feelings toward the group entity. This would serve to reinforce the very mechanisms of repression and denial which Gibbard and Hartman postulated.

To answer such questions we obviously need carefully controlled observations of the relevant phases of group processes in therapy and other small groups, preferably by trained observers other than the therapists. These would not only serve to test the different hypotheses regarding the nature of individual and collective perceptions of the group entity in a maternal or perhaps other vein, but would also help to differentiate between the nature of these group manifestations in self-analytic and T-groups, on the one hand, and "true" therapy groups, on the other.

Pending such observations, I prefer to maintain the earlier stated, more parsimonious hypotheses regarding the perception of the group entity. In brief, according to these, the initial phase of unstructured therapy groups is characterized by nonpathological, regressive perceptions and relationships of all aspects of the group situation: of the leader, of the other group members, and of the group-as-a-whole. From a genetic, developmental viewpoint, these perceptions and relationships represent a reactivation, in the face of the individual and collective stresses and anxieties induced by group formation, of early patterns and especially of primitive identifications, including the search for the kind of nonconflictual, need-gratifying relationship to the mother which I previously discussed.

While the group entity is accordingly perceived in a positive and benign image, the group leader and other members almost immediately become the objects of a gamut of partially ambivalent, but largely hostile and fearful attitudes. As noted by Ruiz (1972) with reference to T-groups, and by Arsenian, Semrad, and Shapiro (1962) regarding therapy groups, when negative feelings thus aroused threaten the group's cohesiveness and basically positive climate, there is a tendency to displace these feelings onto the leader, thus preserving the group's supportive character. While any perception or behavioral item can admittedly serve defensive purposes, I would like to await further evidence before accepting Gibbard and Hartman's conclusions of the regularity with which the members' perceptions of the benign "mother-group" represent an unwillingness "to come to grips with intragroup conflicts and other painful realities of group life" (p. 129). It is also possible that this very perception is progressively utilized by both the members and the therapist in the service of the "therapeutic alliance" or for group maintenance and cohesiveness; thus intragroup conflicts and personal problems can be analyzed at an anxiety level that is not too threatening to the equilibrium of individual patients or the group entity.

The complex theoretical issues posed by attempts to scrutinize the conscious and unconscious aspects of concepts such as the "mother-group" reaffirm the urgent need to descriptively differentiate in group psychology between individual and collective phenomena, as well as between identifications and transferences, on the one hand, and reality-geared perceptions, on the other. I would accordingly question the generally loose application of the term "transference" to either an individual or to a shared perception of the group entity in a maternal vein. For, in my view, transference as a concept pertains to an apperception in relation to a *person,* and moreover, to a repetition in the present of a relatively advanced past relationship, where there has been some degree of differentiation between the self and the object. The perceptions and object relations in the earliest phase of group formation, including the perception of the "mother–group," are better connoted as various kinds of identifications which, in the psychoanalytic hierarchy of object relations, precede real object ties. This is congruent with Kaplan and Roman's (1963) views on group development in therapy groups. Interestingly, too, Abraham (1973) recently claimed to have *experimental* support for her contention that there are many more primitive kinds of object relations than transferences at work in therapy groups.

It should be noted here that, in the strictest sense of the word, "identification" or "transference" represents an explanatory construct. Each pertains to inferred processes which can be utilized to explain certain kinds of social behavior. Furthermore, in scrutinizing any item of an individual's conduct in a group, one must try to differentiate, as Couch (1961) has suggested, among (1) underlying needs, (2) concealment defenses, (3) apperception of interpersonal forces, and (4) reaction to the behavioral press of overt acts of others. In this connection, group therapists must also differentiate between direct expressions of a genuine need, i.e, for a mothering relationship, and defensive exaggerations or minimization of needs. There is also the issue of distinguishing such needs from shared fantasies which might be employed as a means of gratifying them.

In addition to the prevalence of multiple individual and group identifications, the *"early dependency phase"* in a therapy group (Scheidlinger, 1968b) is characterized by poor reality perceptions and much magical thought, including oral fantasies. This phase is supplanted by a more advanced one in which transferences and real object ties predominate, with realistic perceptions including sexual and aggressive expressions.

I would concur with the many writers who have pointed to a probable link between our "age of anxiety" and the unsurpassed recent popularity of varied experiential growth groups. The latter are sought out in people's search for intimacy, for enhanced self–esteem and sense of identity, and perhaps, on a deeper level, for support from a benign "mother–group." In this connection, in writing about our new human problems related to the unprecedented rate of societal change, Toffler (1970) envisioned "stability zones," "love networks," and time–limited supportive groups for people under-going adaptational crises, in order for them to experience, if only briefly, identification with others as well as the support of a benign group entity (see also Chapter 1).

One might be justified in claiming, then, that when the small group is viewed as a helping system, not only do its members need the leader–worker and each other but also the group–as–a–group! Furthermore, in this context the crucial question is *not* how the leader–worker perceives the situation, but how the group member does. These aspects have remained neglected for too long.

Summary

In summary, the concept of the "mother–group" has been sub-jected to special scrutiny. A historical review of the literature reveals increasing references during the last decade to group mem-bers' perceptions of the group entity in a maternal vein.

A previously stated hypothesis of mine, which related individ-ual members' identification with the group–as–a–whole to an un-conscious wish to restore an earlier state of unconflicted union with the mother, has been developed in greater detail and tied more specifically to a yearning for a return to the child's purely positive "need–gratifying relationship." Anna Freud has postulated this as occurring developmentally between the phases of "primary narcis-sism" and "object constancy."

In contradistinction to some writers' views of the early phase of group development as regularly containing simultaneous percep-tions of a threatening "mother–group" image, it was suggested that, it is more likely that the leader and the other group members, rather than the group–as–a–whole, are the objects of such early fearful and hostile feelings. This hypothesis awaits further objective observations of therapy groups.

In order to attain the much–desired theoretical clarity in the

group process field generally and in group psychotherapy specifically, the need for attempting to differentiate between individual
and collective phenomena, on the one hand, and among identifications, transferences, and reality-geared perceptions, on the other
hand, is reaffirmed.

A possible link is suggested between the recent mushrooming
in this age of anxiety of various kinds of experiential "growth"
groups, and people's need for enhanced self-esteem and support
from a benign "mother-group."

Chapter 5

THE PSYCHOLOGY OF LEADERSHIP REVISITED: AN OVERVIEW

In this overview, I have elected to cover the theme of leadership as it appears in three distinct, yet definitely related, fields of inquiry: social psychology, psychoanalytic theory, and group psychotherapy.

To begin with, while dictionaries and history books tend to speak of leaders, social psychologists rightly prefer to use the term "leadership" to connote a reciprocal voluntary influence process by one individual upon others within the context of a group situation. However, just as there is no agreement as to what constitutes a group, there is also no generally accepted definition of leadership. I have personally found useful two parallel definitions of group and leadership, which seem most applicable to the group therapy situation. The first is Cattell's (1951) depiction of a group as an instrument of individual need satisfaction. To quote him: A group is "... an aggregate of organisms in which the existence of all is utilized for the satisfaction of some needs of each" (p. 169). The definition of leadership I prefer is by Pigors (1935), who viewed it as a personality–environment relation wherein a person is so located that his/her "will, feeling and insight direct and control others in the pursuit of a common cause" (p. 12).

While these definitions are sufficiently broad to pertain to small as well as to large groups, in this discussion I will limit myself to the subject of leadership in small, face-to-face groups. References to

Reprinted, in part, from *Group*, 4:5-17, 1980, by permission.

large groups will be utilized only when they are illustrative of significant theoretical positions, as for example, when Freud (1921) discussed army and church groups in his major contribution to group psychology.

THE CONCEPT OF LEADERSHIP IN SOCIAL PSYCHOLOGY

The social psychology literature on leadership is mindboggling, comprising many seemingly unrelated, contradictory, fragmentary, both ambitious and trivial contributions to theory and research. As Bennis (1959) put it: "Of all the hazy and confounding areas in social psychology, leadership theory undoubtedly contends for top nomination. . . the problem is not that there is little evidence, but that the mountain of evidence which is available appears to be so contradictory" (p. 259). In a recent comprehensive review and analysis of more than 3,000 books and articles, Stogdill (1974) concluded that "the endless accumulation of empirical data has not produced an integrated understanding of leadership" (p. vii).

It should be noted, however, that while social psychology literature at present has no global answers to the essence of leadership, it does contain many useful, limited-domain theories and research observations with direct relevance to people-helping groups. What is especially noteworthy is the uncontestable finding that, contrary to folklore and human wishes, leadership connotes a very complex set of functions which occur in every group and involve a combination of personal, environmental, and situational variables. In this connection, the most widely held theory of leadership is Gibb's (1958) interaction theory which entails the following variables: (1) the personality of the leader; (2) the followers and their attitudes, needs, and problems; (3) the group itself as regards both (a) its structure of interpersonal relations and (b) its syntality (group-as-a-group characteristics); and (4) the situation, as determined by the physical setting, the nature of the task, etc. Most significantly for group therapists' purposes as change agents, Gibb wrote that "any satisfactory theory must recognize that it is not these variables per se that enter into the leadership relation, but rather the perception of the leader by himself and by others, the leader's perception of those others and the shared perception by the leader and others of the group and situation" (p. 108).

There are also other theories of leadership worth noting here: the "great man" theory assumes that leaders possess superior qualities differentiating them from their followers (Jennings, 1943); environmental theories view the emergence of leaders as essentially a function of the occasion, wherein they become the instrument to solve a group's momentary problems (Murphy, 1941); and *interaction–expectation* theories consider leadership as based on the initiation of group interaction (Homans, 1950), on the eliciting and maintenance of group structure in interaction and expectation (Stogdill, 1959), or on the leader's ability to reinforce the behavior of group members by offering rewards or punishments (Bass, 1960).

Beginning with the classical study of Lewin, Lippitt, and White (1939) on autocratic, democratic and laissez-faire leadership patterns and group climates, there has been much work on the relationship of leadership styles to leadership effectiveness. Of special interest to mental health workers should be the many contributions which helped to delineate the characteristics of democratic versus charismatic leadership. As compared with charismatic leadership, democratic leadership was usually depicted as delegating authority rather than summoning and controlling, as coordinating rather than canalizing, as accepting different inputs for change rather than demanding adaptation, as being reality–oriented rather than ideology–oriented and, finally, as favoring decision making by consensus rather than relying on personal appeal and on power.

Social psychological observations tend to support the basic human dilemma inherent in all leadership, namely that it is impossible to be a leader and always be liked, and that, similarly, it is impossible to be a group member without resenting the leader, on occasion at least.

There is considerable evidence that people who are judged successful leaders tend to be those who are empathetic and who can help the group members achieve their goals (Mann, 1959). Furthermore, superior performance and high group morale appear to be correlated with a leadership style which combines a caring stance with emphasis on group discipline and task performance. Needless to say, these findings were derived from specific group situations where a "human relations" kind of approach was operable. As Strauss noted (1970), "no one form of leadership is universally appropriate for all personalities, cultures and technologies" (p. 156).

While searching for some clues to future trends in the social psychology of leadership, I fortunately came across the proceedings of a recent conference entitled "Leadership—Where Else Can We Go?" (McCall and Lombardo, 1978). A major theme of this conference was the assertion that "we need to rediscover the phenomena of leadership; the pursuit of rigor and precision has led to an overemphasis on technique at the expense of knowing what is going on in a direct, human way" (p. xii). In short, what was advocated was that future researchers of leadership adopt the methods of anthropologists and become "unstatistical naturalists," observing leaders at work to pick up the nuances and subtleties of these complex processes. For someone who had been criticized almost three decades ago for suggesting that Lewinian group dynamics, with its stress on mere momentary conscious interaction, acquired supplementation by considering Freudian unconscious motivations (Scheidlinger, 1952), it was a pleasant surprise to read of the desirability of a "hero–learning manager" who, instead of using "conscious, rational thinking," relies on "the unconscious, the irrational and the humorous to gain new meaning and perspective" (p. 142). Or, "Leaders like skilled craftsmen work by 'feel.' While complex cognitive maps are probably essential for effective leadership, they may be subconscious or disorganized—and therefore not measurable by conventional tests. . . leadership remains more of a performing art than a science" (p. 157).

With these calls for inclusion of psychodynamic themes in the study of leadership, I cannot think of a better transition point for a consideration of psychoanalytic contributions to this subject.

The Concept of Leadership in Psychoanalytic Theory

I have already referred to Freud's treatise on group psychology (1921), which depicted group formative processes as entailing ego identifications among the group members (siblings) subsequent to a common libidinal tie to the father–leader primarily via incorporation of the latter's image into the superego. We must be mindful here of the fact that Freud's admittedly loose ideas regarding leadership and groups, enunciated in 1921, were stimulated by his having encountered Le Bon's (1903) and McDougall's (1920) writings on crowds. He saw in them prime examples of unconsciously motivated behavior as well as an opportunity to further his contemporary inquiry into the character of the ego ideal, which he subsequently termed "superego." In Freud's scheme, the role of the leader is primary since, as in the case of the loss of an army's commander, group panic and dissolution ensue if no substitute leader is found. He likened the individual member's relation to the leader to the hypnotic situation with its extremes of suggestibility and dependency.

Redl (1942) attempted to supplement Freud's view of leadership in group formation. Reserving the term "leader" for only one of 10 different kinds of group situations, he posited the concept of a central person around whom group–formative processes occur. Redl described the following three types of relationships between the group members and the central person: (1) the central person as an object of identification on the basis of the group members' love or fear; (2) the central person as an object of the group members' love and/or aggressive drives; and (3) the central person as the group members' ego support.

The identification with the central person in Redl's first category of group relationships can vary. The central person can become a model to be admired: "they [the group members] place him. . . in what is usually called their ego ideal" (p. 157). Identification could also be involved in which standards of conduct of the loved parental figure become internalized: "they incorporate the superego–conscience of the central person" (p. 577). Another form of identification can occur on the basis of fear of the central person as an aggressor.

In the second category, neither identification nor incorporation of standards has occurred. The group members choose the central person as an object of their love or as an object of aggression. The third category refers to the use of the central person by the group members, primarily as a means of resolving some of their own conflicts.

Both Freud and Redl thought that on occasion an idea or symbolic abstraction could substitute for the leader. At other times, an ideal or even a secondary leader could coexist with a leader. While various facets of Freud's group psychology, among them especially his idea of a primal horde patricide perpetuated in a phylogenetic memory, have been subjected to much criticism, his notion of individuals' identification with the leader has been almost universally accepted as a basic element in understanding group belonging and cohesiveness.

Psychoanalytic writers have frequently extended Freud's notions of group leadership to the tendency of people under stress to regress to childhood states of dependency and submission to authority figures. Thus, Fenichel (1945) stated: "The formula if you obey, you will be protected is the one all gods have in common with all earthly authorities" (p. 491). In a historical study of dictatorships, Bychowski (1948) noted how, in times of general misfortune, of social and economic upheavals, many people become attuned to an all–powerful leader (parent) who will guide and "save" them. More recently, Janis (1963) studied the behavior of groups, such as soldiers in battle under conditions of external danger. He noted a marked rise in dependency reactions, which he hypothesized as being related to a reactivation of separation anxiety. Under these conditions the military leaders came to represent the fathers of the past, while the fellow–soldiers were reacted to as brothers.

Kris and Leites (1947) rightly cautioned against undue generalizations regarding individuals' propensity to submit to authoritarian leadership. For even in the face of conditions most favorable to submission to a leader, there are always personalities which retain various degrees of personal identity and independence. Kris (1943) discussed the differences in individuals' relations to the leader in their group participation in primarily totalitarian, as opposed to democratic groups. In the former kind of group, individual differences tend to lose their importance and the group's reaction to the leader appears to occur in unison. In a democratic group, each member perceives the leader's message and responds to it in a personalized fashion according to individual experience. From individualized reactions there may gradually evolve individualized evaluations, leading to the readier possibility of disagreement and criticisms of the leader.

As I noted in the previous chapter, Money–Kyrle (1950), an early British follower of Melanie Klein, objected to Freud's portrayal of the group leader only as a father–figure. He suggested that, since both parents are part of a child's object representations, the mother could also be perceived in a leadership role. In line with Kleinian theory, he asserted that parental representations could appear as "good" or "bad" according to a particular individual's childhood experiences.

Since Bion (1948–1951) presented his first writings on this subject as contributions to psychoanalytic group psychology in juxtaposition to Freud's, he deserves mention in this section. He differentiated between four different kinds of leadership: First there is the work–group leader who always operates on the manifest, reality-geared level and who fosters the group's task orientation. In addition, there are the three basic assumption leaders who are a part of each of the fantasied basic assumption "cultures": dependency, fight–flight, and pairing. The latter three leadership roles are most frequently assumed by persons other than the manifest work–group leader.

In a recent publication, Kernberg (1979) scrutinized the complex issue of regression in organizational leadership as exemplified by a psychiatric hospital. He stressed the importance of distinguishing organizational problems derived from personality deficiencies of the leader–administrator from problems related primarily to the organization's task assignment or group processes (i.e., morale). With respect to the latter, he relied almost exclusively on Bion's conceptualizations. Kernberg believes that a functional task orientation is preferable to a political "democratization" of organizational decision making via group consensus. As for personality features in the leader, he delineated the special problems inherent in schizoid, obsessive, paranoid, and narcissistic character structures. In choosing an effective organizational leader, Kernberg stressed the need to assess the candidate's creativity, self–esteem derived from his profession, ability to identify with organizational goals, and willingness to fight for convictions. A major criterion was the candidate's genuine investment in growth and development of other people. Kernberg's observations are congruent with an earlier summary of the psychoanalytic considerations in distinguishing between mature and immature leaders (Scheidlinger, 1952). To begin with, there is Freud's (1931) delineation of "libidinal types"; the "narcissistic" type (in the sense of healthy narcissism) tends to be independent, with a relative absence of internal conflict, and prefers to "give" rather than "take" emotionally. In Freud's words, "People of this type impress others as being 'personalities'; it is on them that their fellowmen are especially likely to lean; they readily assume the role of leader, give a fresh stimulus to cultural development and break down existing conditions."

In addition to Bychowski's (1948) study of dictators, Alexander (1942) and Erikson (1948), among others, have contrasted the characteristics of mature and immature leadership. They found that, in general, in addition to a possibly inborn ability to command attention shared by all leaders, mature leadership calls for personalities who are sensitive to the needs of people, are able and willing to give of themselves emotionally, and are relatively free from unconscious, irrational conflicts. Included is the supposition that such leaders will manage to fill their personal needs, such as for love or power, as well as the group's objectives, without fostering immature and regressive processes in individuals or in the collectivity.

While immature leadership, in the long run, will tend to foster regressive behavior in the group members, it can also succeed in evoking efficient and rapid means to achieve group objectives. This is one reason why people often acquiesce in such leadership for a long time, despite their ambivalence. Redl (1942) observed that indigenous "central persons" with considerable personality pathology frequently served as helpful instruments for the relief of emotional conflicts in less disturbed members of the group.

Needless to say, a full understanding of immature and mature leadership involves not only the study of a given leader's personality structure with its pathological and healthy components, but also how these operate in dynamic interaction with each group member, with subgroups and with the group–as–a–whole. Jennings' (1943) investigation of sociometric leadership choices in a girl's institution is of interest in this connection. Her findings suggest that the chosen leaders tended to be sensitive to both the needs of the group and of individuals. They initiated creative improvements in the group setting, while keeping their personal problems to themselves. They were concerned for the group's cohesiveness and very at ease in establishing rapport with others.

At a recent panel on the "Psychoanalytic Knowledge of Group Processes" (Moore, 1979), all participants decried the fact that it took the American Psychoanalytic Association 22 years to repeat an earlier panel held on this same subject (Semrad, 1958). One of the observations at the panel was that in organizations, individuals tend to identify more with a group culture than with a leader. Another observation referred to a tendency for groups to evidence shared unconscious fantasies. Group leaders not only evoke unconscious wishes but can also utilize these for the gratification of their own or the group's purposes. Generally speaking, there was much reliance in this panel on Bion's (1959) formulations, with special application to large group processes.

In a recent contribution, Saravay (1975) suggested a structural model of group psychology aimed at correcting what he believed were contradictory theoretical elements inherent in Freud's group psychological formulations. Saravay utilized object relations concepts to hypothesize that in group formation there is not only an oedipal level of regression at work, but a preoedipal one as well — an oral-regressive level built around a shared wish to be sustained by a "mother-leader" (as well as the more advanced oedipal ties of Freud's group psychology). In applying these concepts to the group treatment setting, Saravay (1978) subsequently suggested that group development recapitulates the Freudian oral to genital psychosexual stages. In such development, the therapist's interpretations of the relevant transference phases produces redifferentiation of each member's group-related ego and superego structures.

Kohut (1977), who is widely known for his new contributions to the study and treatment of narcissistic personalities, has begun to apply his theories to the field of group psychology. Analogous to his concept that the preoedipal parents are experienced as "selfobjects," Kohut (1976) posited the concept of a "group-self" which he viewed as being more primitive than Erikson's (1959) group identity. He saw this group-self as comprising the group members' shared "grandiose selves" in addition to their shared incorporation of the group leader's ego ideal, as discussed by Freud. As for leadership, Kohut examined the nature of charismatic leaders who use their followers primarily for the narcissistic sustenance of their own shattered self-esteem. He also elaborated on the way the idealization of a leader can serve to defend the group members against narcissistic tensions, such as jealousy, hate, and shame. Paralleling my earlier differentiation between mature and immature leadership, Kohut stressed the mature leader's empathic understanding of the needs and feelings of others. Since group processes, according to Kohut, tend to be activated largely by narcissistic motives, he is hopeful that the increased attention to narcissistic elements in psychoanalytic trainees will serve to foster much-needed attention to group dynamics within the psychoanalytic movement.

THE CONCEPT OF LEADERSHIP IN GROUP PSYCHOTHERAPY

As I stated in Chapter 2, the relevance of group dynamics for group psychotherapy, even when presented with a Freudian psychoanalytic tinge, was the subject of much heated controversy in the early years of American group psychotherapy. Fortunately, since leadership functions—if only those directed at basic structuring and maintaining of the group—are inherent in the work of all group therapists, the vehement criticisms of anti-group dynamics authors, such as Wolf and Schwartz (1962), were directed primarily at the varied conceptualizations of group-level phenomena and group-level interventions. In other words, even when a group therapist is theoretically persuaded that he or she is treating individual patients merely *in* and not *through* a group, the repeated copresence of a number of people in a room is bound to evoke at least some elements of group process, and with it, group leadership. This is, of course, in the broader framework in which I had depicted leadership at the outset, as a psychosocial process entailing a voluntary influence by one individual upon others in the context of a group situation.

Space will not permit me to examine the specific ways in which the concept of leadership is handled in the myriad theoretical and practice models in the group therapy realm. Instead I will limit myself here to some general observations on this theme.

Many authors tend to use the terms "group leader" and "group therapist" interchangeably. This is regrettable since such a practice tends to further an already marked confusion of terminology in the field of "people-helping" groups which I discussed in Chapter 1. I would like to propose therefore that the two concepts be viewed as belonging to two different, yet understandably related, fields of inquiry. "Leader" and "leadership" are terms which are embedded in the theoretical field of group psychology, a field which is concerned, roughly speaking, with the issues of "what makes groups tick." The term "group therapist," like "hypnotherapist" or "psychoanalyst," belongs to the broader, applied clinical field of psychotherapy, with its primary concern with healing or "repair" of psychopathology by specially trained practitioners in varied settings via a variety of techniques. To put it differently: While the knowledge of group dynamics, including leadership, from the perspectives of social psychology and psychoanalytic group psychology, is nowadays hopefully a part of every group therapist's armamentarium, the group therapist must be knowledgeable about many other subjects, including personality theory, psychopathology, and curative factors. In short, there is much more to group psychotherapy as a change process than to leadership in its technical connotation.

There is the additional fact, persuasively demonstrated by Redl (1942) and more recently by Bion (1959), that the group therapist is not always perceived by the patient as the therapy group's leader, but nevertheless hopefully continues in the role of group therapist. Foulkes and Anthony (1964) and Glatzer (1975) have, in separate ways, also expressed misgivings about the use of the term "leader" in relation to the group therapist's role because it implies an induction of the patients into follower roles. Others have noted that the group therapist's detached stance (however occasional), necessary for cognitive processes of observation and interpretation, requires planful withdrawal from the group's emotionality and from a leadership role. Thus, to be empathetically involved with the group processes and yet sufficiently separated from them to observe objectively, is the almost impossible task of the group therapist. (See also Chapter 3 of this volume.)

The following is a (not necessarily all-inclusive) list of group therapist functions:

1. Structuring the group's composition, time, meeting place, and remuneration procedures.
2. Structuring the conduct of the sessions, with reference to

confidentiality, agenda, physical contact, therapeutic methods (use of free-associative productions), social interaction outside the group, etc.

3. Empathic acceptance and caring for each patient, coupled with a belief in the latter's potentiality for change.
4. Encouraging the open expression of feelings and concerns.
5. Fostering a climate of tolerance and acceptance of variance in feelings and behaviors, coupled with a focus on self and interpersonal scrutiny and awareness in which all group members are encouraged to participate.
6. Controlling within acceptable limits the drive expression, tension, and anxiety level in individual patients.
7. Controlling group manifestations in the interest of both individual patients and the maintenance of optimum group morale.
8. Utilizing verbal interventions, ranging from simple observations through confrontations to psychoanalytic interpretations, aimed at reality testing and eliciting of meaning and of genetic connections.

Even a superficial perusal of this list should help us realize that, despite the understandable overlap, about one half of the enumerated functions belong primarily to the realm of therapy (not group dynamics) and are also operative in the dyadic treatment situation. Examples are: the therapist's basic attitude of empathic acceptance and caring; the encouragement of emotional expression coupled with control of the emergence of undue anxiety in individuals; and above all, the task of various kinds of interpretations, especially of transference and of resistance, in the case of Freudian practitioners.

The call for the desirability of distinguishing between the group therapist's clinical-therapeutic and group dynamic-leadership functions must not be construed as a devaluation of the latter. In fact, such pivotal elements as fostering a group climate of optimism and cohesiveness, safety and need satisfaction, have also been shown to be a part of effective leadership in groups other than therapy groups. Writers such as Whitaker and Lieberman (1964) or Yalom (1970) have rightly emphasized the enormous curative value inherent in the group therapist's group leadership functions related to the setting of empathic group norms, which include elements of peer therapy. Among the major flaws in the group theories of our British colleagues such as Bion (1959) and Ezriel (1950) is their failure to recognize the growth-promoting elements inherent in group psychological regression as well as in all group belonging.

There is reason to believe that group psychotherapy's unique value in successfully reaching patients with severe character pathology, including problems of narcissism, resides in the ease with which the group setting can provide a climate of safety and support for the reenactment of the earliest kinds of parent-child or family-child encounters. In this connection, I am inclined to agree with Malan, Balfour, Hood, and Shooter (1976) that their outcome study of London's Tavistock Clinic group therapy patients might have elicited more positive responses had the group therapists, in their *leadership* roles, consciously fostered such a group climate of support, in addition to the heavy reliance on their *clinical* roles, entailing rigorous, largely group-centered interpretations of transference manifestations.

One possible way to help students of group therapy get a clearer picture of the differences and similarities among the major clinical models in our field might be to use the above list of group therapist functions and apply it to the written contributions of the major authorities. This would involve expanding on Kauff's (1979) recent comparison of the theories and techniques of Bion, Wolf, and Schwartz, as well as Durkin and Glatzer (1973). Following such an approach could, for example, help to juxtapose the marked differences between Yalom's (1970) view of the group therapist's primary here-and-now interpersonal focus in his verbal interventions and interpretations when compared with Ezriel's (1950) position regarding his intricate three-tiered individual and group level here-and-now interpretations, and the ideas of Durkin and Glatzer (1973) as to how the here-and-now group setting facilitates a rigorous attention to individual patients' distortions and resistances.

Presenting the comparative data in such a fashion is likely to be infinitely more useful than the essay kind of presentations which have characterized our literature to date.

Since group psychotherapy's universe of discourse as an applied treatment modality, despite its confusing variety of models of practice, is nevertheless narrower than that of social psychology or even of psychoanalytic group psychology, the overall picture with respect to the understanding of the process of leadership within this realm is relatively more hopeful. To begin with, due in large part to a recent infusion of research interest and talent within our field, some theoreticians and practitioners have begun to describe and record with greater clarity the *what* and the *how* of the complex transactions in their groups. Furthermore, the heretofore fruitless global theorizing has given way, to some extent, to a welcome focus on manageable aspects of specific kinds of groups, and even on momentary group manifestations. (See also Chapter 12 of this volume.)

With respect to leadership studies per se, the justified claim of researchers, among them Lieberman, Yalom, and Miles (1973), that what group practitioners *believe they do is likely to be at variance with what they actually do,* has opened the doors of some group therapy rooms to direct observation and recording of group therapist behavior. In this connection, the *International Journal of Group Psychotherapy* recently presented an Open Forum on Group Psychotherapy Process Research. As a part of this forum, Gruen (1977) studied group therapists in action, and found that positive group movement, cohesiveness, and peer input were enhanced by the therapist's accurate anticipation of individual and group behavior, control of undue group anxiety, and meaningful interpretations. Dies (1977) provided an exhaustive review of the controversial topic of group therapist self–involvement and self–disclosure, ranging from the markedly detached stance of some British group analysts through the intermediate position advocated by Yalom (1970), to the extreme beliefs of existential–experiential group therapy practitioners. He concluded by suggesting that group therapist openness be viewed "as one of many possible interventions available to the group leader, and like most other interventions its effectiveness will undoubtedly be enhanced to the extent that it is systematically integrated into a more comprehensive model of group leadership" (p. 197).

Such valuable research notwithstanding, in all psychotherapy and, with it, group psychotherapy, the therapist's work remains as much an art as a science. As was suggested by Luborsky, Singer, and Luborsky (1975), the ingredients of the effective psychotherapist, regardless of theoretical persuasion, appear to be somewhere on the axis between genuine empathy and caring and an organized cognitive theory of psychopathology and treatment that is communicated to the patient. As for the subtle, and for some people, redundant issue of distinguishing between the group therapist's *leadership* and *clinical* functions, I would propose that the former refer to the interventions aimed primarily at group maintenance needs, while the latter be reserved for interventions aimed primarily at meeting the clinical needs of individual patients. It is the latter aim which is, after all, the ultimate task of even group process–centered group therapists — to ameliorate the problems of individual patients.

There is an old saying, attributed to an ancient Chinese philosopher:

A leader is best
When people barely know that he exists,'
Not so good when people obey and acclaim him,
Worst when they despise him.
Fail to honor people,
They fail to honor you;
But of a good leader, who talks little,

When his work is done, his aim fulfilled,
They will all say, "We did this ourselves."
                               — Laotzu, *The Way of Life*

Perhaps the ideal group psychotherapist in the leadership function achieves such a state of affairs for the group entity. With it goes a perception held by each group patient that, like Mahler, Pine, and Bergman's (1975) parent of "separation–individuation" as enabler and activator, the therapist (be it *in* or *through* the group context) has helped in making each patient stronger (via empathic support), wiser (via interpretations), and better able to cope with life's problems. This is not unlike Modell's (1978) belief that individual psychoanalysis of *all* patients (not only of narcissistic personalities) entails a symbolic reexperiencing of fusion and separateness, in addition to the therapeutic action of interpretation.

In sum, there appears to be no all–encompassing concept of leadership within social psychology, psychoanalytic theory, and group psychotherapy, even though the phenomenon of leadership lies at the very core of human existence and touches our daily lives. We have, at best, numerous partial portrayals, conceptualizations, and research findings, including this overview, all aimed at ascertaining the dimensions of leadership.

Chapter 6

ON SCAPEGOATING IN GROUP PSYCHOTHERAPY

I have chosen the phenomenon of scapegoating, a group phenomenon as old as human history, as the subject for this discussion. My reasons are twofold: (1) Although scapegoating is readily used as a label or as an invective by laymen and professionals alike, it has not been subjected to the kind of careful scrutiny in the group process literature that would lead to its adequate understanding. (2) Scapegoating presents a vexing technical challenge to all group practitioners. At the very least, it involves the simultaneous infliction of pain on a victim, and a threat to group morale. As is well known, the effects are frequently even more profound and tragic, especially when scapegoating surfaces in the society at large.

My focus will of necessity remain on the small, "people–helping" groups, but I find myself impelled (perhaps because it is reminiscent of some poignant childhood experiences) to offer a single sad example from the recent international scene. In the early 1970's the Jewish population of Poland, which had numbered more than three million prior to the Holocaust, had shrunk to a mere 25,000. Faced with marked political unrest, the then leaders of Poland managed to stay in power by rekindling the well–tried flames of anti–Semitism and blaming the few Jews for the nation's problems. Most of the Jews thereupon elected to emigrate, with

Reprinted from *International Journal of Group Psychotherapy,* 32:131–143, 1982, by permission.

only 6,000 remaining in Poland. Nevertheless, even that small remnant was relegated as a scapegoat during the 1980 workers' rebellion. When Poland's communist leaders returned from Russia determined to stem the democratic threat to their leadership, posters began to appear calling on the populace to rise up against the "Jewish-Trotskyist-Zionists." It remains to be seen whether that ploy, now directed at a mere ghost community of only 6,000 Jews, will work again.

HISTORICAL BACKGROUND

The term "scapegoat" originates from the Hebrew "goat for Azazel." According to the Old Testament (Leviticus, 16), in the ritual for the Day of Atonement, one of two goats was chosen by lot and symbolically laden by the High Priest with the sins of the Jewish people. Thus burdened, the goat was sent into the wilderness alive to placate Azazel, a demonic being. In later days, the goat was pushed over a cliff near Jerusalem, to certain death. The other goat, reserved "for the Lord," was sacrificed as a burnt-offering in the Temple. One might speculatively ask here whether this original biblical notion of two goats, one sin-laden for the wilderness demon, and the other marked "For the Lord" repre-sented the perceptual polarization inherent in at least one aspect of scapegoating as we know it — the projected and banished "badness" of the scapegoat versus the Lord-given "goodness" of the scape-goater. (The coexistence of a "good" goat in this original biblical rite has interestingly not been mentioned in connection with scape-goating.)

In popular usage, the term "scapegoat" has nowadays come to stand for any person or group who innocently bears the blame for others. It is part of a magical belief that evil, guilt, and pain can be gotten rid of by its transfer onto animals, other people, and even inanimate objects. These carriers, as amply illustrated by Frazer's

(1922) study of numerous primitive rites, are then destroyed or exiled, not unlike the biblical scapegoat. In ancient Greece, human scapegoats were employed to mitigate plagues and other disasters. In the annual festival of Thargelia a young couple was first feasted and subsequently beaten and exiled, with the idea that the rite would protect Athens from misfortune for a year. Early Roman law permitted an innocent person to assume the punishment pronounced on a guilty party. Furthermore, as in biblical days, Roman priests would sacrifice animals, especially goats and dogs, as embodiments of communal evils.

THE SOCIAL PSYCHOLOGY LITERATURE

In social psychological studies of prejudice (Allport, 1954), scapegoating was generally viewed as displaced aggression, with minority groups being unjustly blamed and attacked for societal problems. The example of Polish anti–Semitism is a case in point. According to the findings of Adorno, Frenkel-Brunswik, Levinson, and Sanford (1950), authoritarian, ethnocentric personalities are especially prone to prejudiced attitudes and to scapegoating behavior toward people who are different and of minority status. Some authors, furthermore, theorized that the perceived qualities in the victimized group, such as the assumed greediness of Jews or the hypersexuality of Blacks, are unconsciously projected and then attacked.

I have noted in another context (Scheidlinger, 1952) how frequently authoritarian leaders tend to use scapegoats to divert the group's attention from their own shortcomings and, in a broader sense, from members' hostility against the father–figure.

In their classical study of leadership styles, Lewin, Lippitt, and White (1939) found that there was much scapegoating in the experimental, autocratically led groups. Interestingly, they explained this in terms of the fact that the attackers were thus enabled to obtain status in a group climate in which other channels for its development was blocked. (I would have explained this in terms of the more likely circumstance of displacement of hostility meant for the frustrating adult against a more readily available victim.)

Modern social psychology texts, such as Shaw's (1971), tend to devote minimal space to the subject of scapegoating. Shaw's handling of the theme is typical, that is, mere brief references to the above-noted studies of prejudice and to the Lewin et al. (1939) experiment.

THE GROUP PSYCHOTHERAPY LITERATURE

In contrast to the writings on family therapy, with its emphasis on the family scapegoat, our own group psychotherapy literature has paid scant attention to the theme of scapegoating. In fact, I could find only two articles devoted exclusively to the subject, with two major texts (Slavson, 1964; Yalom, 1975) not even mentioning it in the index.

In their article on this topic, Kraupl-Taylor and Rey (1953) depicted an incident of scapegoating in a neurotic women's therapy group. A scapegoat was portrayed by these writers as ". . . a person who is made to suffer as the carrier of displaced guilt," with the scapegoaters being viewed as people with "extra-punitive propensities" and a tendency towards "self-deceptive projection of guilt" (p. 253). In the clinical example, a masochistic patient was induced by the others to engage in an illicit sexual affair. She thus became the symbolic carrier of the group's unconscious envy and guilt. Her punishment via guilt absolved the group members from the sins they had secretly desired. The article by Toker (1972), devoted exclusively to scapegoating in group psychotherapy, appeared almost 20 years later. It dealt with aggression rather than sexuality. Toker suggested that scapegoating is an essential group phenomenon as it ". . . provides an arena into which aggression can be channelled and focused without presenting a threat to the psychic integrity of the individual or a threat to the stability and unity of the group itself" (p. 320). Two clinical illustrations drawn from an inpatient adolescent unit referred to the use of the group therapist as a scapegoat for displaced aggression meant for their peers, and to the scapegoating of a group member who was both weak and provocative, hence a ready target.

In the first edition of their book *Group Psychotherapy: The Psycho-analytic Approach,* Foulkes and Anthony (1957) cited the paper by Kraupl-Taylor and Rey (1953) with its emphasis on scapegoating as precipitated ". . . when the urgent need for the group to punish meets an urgent need in a particular member to be punished" (p. 205). In the second edition of their book, Foulkes and Anthony (1965) referred to scapegoating as a process in which angry feelings destined for the group therapist were displaced onto a group member who had been earlier perceived as the therapist's favorite. Foulkes (1980) developed that theme further in another context: "I have repeatedly observed members functioning as scapegoats in place of the conductor. The group, angry with him but not daring to attack him directly . . . will relieve and displace its emotion and fury onto one of themselves, usually a weak or absent member" (p. 154).

Whitaker and Lieberman (1964) portrayed scapegoating similarly as a displacement of hostility onto the group member who was least likely to retaliate. However, they also noted another kind of scapegoating in which the scapegoat served as the recipient of unacceptable impulses that are projected onto him and then symbolically attacked.

While the above references pertain more broadly to scapegoating as a group process manifestation, two other authors laid more limited stress on the group roles inherent in scapegoating. Thus, Kellerman (1979), in his delineation of eight prototype emotional patterns with corresponding group roles, posited an "Emotion of Anger" with a related diagnostic disposition of "aggressivity." In his words, ". . . a member assuming this stance in a group may be described as a scapegoater. Such a person will express an abundance of anger and will confront those who are more likely to absorb the anger. The innocent and the scapegoater roles correspond to the passive and aggressive diagnostic dispositional types . . ." (p.

48). Furthermore, "... the scapegoater shows displacement behavior, is quite angry, and is drawn to people who will absorb hostility" (p. 107). In a more recent contribution, Beck and Peters (1981) argued that every well-functioning group contains four readily differentiated and permanent leadership roles. One of them, the scapegoat role, is usually assumed by a group member rather than the therapist and involves an ongoing function of crystallizing group level issues. In the process, the scapegoat is the recipient of either direct attack or of nonverbal hostility from the other group members.

I hope that this brief review of the group psychotherapy literature has demonstrated that scapegoating, an omnipresent and significant group phenomenon, has been either totally ignored or depicted in such a loose and varied fashion as to preclude an adequate understanding of what is involved.

THE PROCESS OF SCAPEGOATING

To begin with, I would like to propose that although the individual group roles of scapegoat and scapegoater are always brought into play, we never lose sight of the broader dimensions of scapegoating as a complex, interactive group level process. In other words, we are dealing with a phenomenon which entails simultaneous behavioral components from the individual intrapsychic, the interpersonal, and the group–as–a–whole frames of reference. The scapegoat in a small group is likely to range from a wholly innocent person to a more or less willing and involved recipient of the direct or indirect emotionality from a scapegoater or scapegoaters. Although occasionally acting largely in their own behalf, scapegoaters are most often, through conscious and unconscious collusion, the carriers of the desires of other group members as well, if not of the whole group. Scapegoating can be a consciously engineered or a covertly motivated process, and it is readily observed and even more readily felt by the victim. The scapegoat role can be assumed by a group member, the group leader, and infrequently, the group entity. It is worth emphasizing here that unlike Jaques (1955), who asserted that there are no truly innocent victims, since there is always ". . . an unconscious cooperation (or collusion) at the fantasy level between persecutor and persecuted" (p. 286), I believe that, to the contrary, innocent and unwilling persons and groups can, indeed, be subjected to scapegoating.

In psychodynamic terms, scapegoating constitutes a group defensive manifestation, a shared fantasy or act, designed to deal with unacceptable emotions such as hostility, sexuality, and guilt. The mechanisms for the transfer of those emotions have been denoted as various kinds of displacement or projection. Included within the concept of projection is the controversial Kleinian projective identification, with its assumed primitive intent of "splitting," that is, separating "good" experiences and objects from "bad" ones.

Scapegoating can also ensue as a means of dealing with a group's anger by injured self–esteem and narcissism, which Kohut (1976) termed the "group–self." The scapegoating of innocent Iranians in America in response to the perceived humiliating holding of our hostages in Teheran serves as a recent example.

It occurred to me that an initial way to facilitate the study and understanding of scapegoating would be to narrow its unnecessarily broad definition. I see no use, in this connection, in subsuming the commonplace displacement of hostility to group leaders, or for that matter to other people, under the rubric of scapegoating. In our ever–present hostility toward persons in authority roles, we are evidently dealing with a transference–like displacement of feelings from our past, if not also a relatively simple temporal discharge of overflow emotions onto a substitute.

The following quotation illustrates what I would consider a questionable use of the term "scapegoat": "The leader as a scapegoat. . . by accepting verbal attacks. . . promotes a situation where the goal orientation becomes an object substitute upon which destructive forces can be vented" (Arsenian, Semrad, and Shapiro, 1962, p. 432). Why not call that common group phenomenon what it is? — a displacement of emotions toward a leader or other persons. Doing so would permit us to delimit the complex and unconsciously generated process of scapegoating as a group defensive maneuver in which the mechanisms of projection or projective identification are used. In a sense, that would constitute a return to scapegoating's biblical roots in which one dealt with a symbolic projection of the Jewish people's sin and guilt onto a victim, a goat, who was then subject to expulsion.

Following this train of thought, I would like to propose further that the phenomenon of scapegoating be viewed as occurring in two different, yet related ways: (1) A group defensive process where shared, unacceptable impulses or ideas are projected onto a victim with the intent of thus getting rid of them. The recipient of the projection here might be innocent though vulnerable, or perhaps a willing partner in the short–lived interaction. (2) A more primitive process akin to projective identification, in which there is a longer and ongoing unconscious interaction between the scapegoater and the scapegoat. This formulation is in line with a part of Ogden's (1979) formulation of projective identification in which ". . . the projector phantasies ridding himself of an aspect of himself and putting that aspect into another person in a controlling way. Secondly, via the interpersonal interaction, the projector exerts pressure on the recipient of the projection to experience feelings that are congruent with the projection" (p. 371).

In line with my earlier discussion of regression in group psychotherapy (Scheidlinger, 1968b), scapegoating via projection is likely to occur with considerable frequency during the "normal" group formative phase of all unstructured small groups. Such primitive defensive manifestations, including "splitting" and introjection, have been described by Bion (1959) and Saravay (1978), among others, as characteristic of the anxiety–laden group transactions. The so–called "revolt" against the leader observed in training groups was explained by Gibbard, Hartman, and Mann (1974) and by Ruiz (1972) in terms of scapegoating of the "bad" leader in the hope that his expulsion would lead to an ideal and "good" maternal group entity. During later phases of group development, both kinds of scapegoating—by *projection* and by *projective identification*—can be at work. I have a hunch, however, subject to further verification, that scapegoating by projective identification is more expressive of individual member pathology and, accordingly, more prevalent in groups comprising patients with so-called borderline personality organization. The less intricate scapegoating by projection, on the other hand, with its theme of expulsion, appears to me to be more readily related to such common group-level disturbances as the introduction of new members, separation issues, and generally to any perceived threats to the group's well-being and self-esteem.

The clinical handling of scapegoating, even with its meaning understood, is no easy matter. There is, first and foremost, the group maintenance element, which refers to the therapist's function of maintaining at least tolerable and, in the long run, optimum individual patient and group anxiety levels. In other words, the most elegant process interpretations may be of no use during highly charged instances of scapegoating. They may have to be preceded by more direct measures of control and support in order to restore a degree of equilibrium. That may have to involve psychological "first aid" to the scapegoat as well as to the scapegoater. Only then, and probably by repeated "working through," can one hope for the interpretive interventions pertaining to the multiple motivational elements at work in scapegoating to be heard and absorbed.

What of the main therapist countertransference themes inherent in scapegoating? There is, to begin with, the element of injustice inflicted on a weak victim by a cruel aggressor, who is frequently aided and abetted by a gang of "meanies." With it can go resentment at the troublemakers who disturb the group's tranquility. Since many scapegoating episodes entail sibling rivalry, unresolved issues from that realm can also be reactivated. There is, in addition, the whole array of feelings spawned by virtue of the therapist's frequently being maneuvered into the role of scapegoat through projective identification, which has been discussed by

Kernberg (1976) and others in the literature on the treatment of patients with borderline pathology. In this connection, I think that Roth's (1980) vivid portrayal of the powerful collective projections of identity–impaired patients onto the group therapist offers clear examples of scapegoating by projective identification with associated countertransference reactions.

CASE ILLUSTRATIONS

The following examples of the two kinds of scapegoating outlined earlier were drawn from children's therapy groups because of my belief that children's behavior is infinitely more transparent than that of adults. To paraphrase Eric Berne, the "games children play" are in actuality very much more for real!

> Carla was a short, 10½-year-old girl who was referred for treatment because of severe temper tantrums and marked sibling rivalry at home. At school, she was unduly compliant, with poor social skills, which led her to be both isolated and the object of teasing.
> During the early sessions of her combined activity–discussion therapy group, Carla stayed by herself, appeared to be easily hurt and was acutely watchful of the noisy interaction among the more impulsive girls. When rubber darts began to whiz across the room — a usual part of the initial testing of limits — she became especially fearful, hiding her face in some crafts work. When a dart accidently landed near her, she protested with a startled expression, "Hey, what did I do this time?" As if on signal, her response evoked more deliberate acts of throwing things in her direction amid a climate of laughter and derision. There were suggestions that she leave the room, for she was a "troublemaker" and a "cry baby" (a "cry baby" because the therapist had chosen to stay in Carla's vicinity). For the next two sessions, similar incidents of collusive acts of scapegoating of Carla continued. There was no physical hurt involved, and all comments from the therapist about this patterned behavior were met with a shrugging of the shoulders and curt denials. When a new member arrived, the group's attention was diverted from Carla. Carla, cautiously at first, in fact joined the

other girls in subjecting the newcomer to somewhat trying initiation rites. The scapegoating of Carla did not reappear.

This illustration of a short–lived scapegoating episode, characterized by projection and apparently related to the group's initial regressive phase, stands in marked contrast to the next example of a more complex scapegoating process in another group, that persisted intermittently for a period of about 30 sessions.

Donald, aged 9, was referred for group therapy because of difficulties in his peer relations, markedly low self–esteem, and poor frustration tolerance. Those problems had become exacerbated after his father's recent departure from the home. Psychological test findings suggested that he was a vulnerable, confused boy who viewed adults as unsupportive and unresponsive to his concerns, needs, and fears. He was also very frightened by the intensity of his anger toward his younger brother.

Donald's demeanor in the group, conducted by a team of male and female co–therapists, stood out as significantly different from that of the other boys. Except for the occasions when he managed to get an adult to play or work with him, Donald was restless, climbing on chairs and searching through cabinets. There was minimal frustration tolerance and much whining for attention with his unusually high–pitched voice. He was readily drawn to playing with water or to messing with paints. Critical comments from the others regarding his "babyish" behavior were ignored. He proceeded to call his critics derogatory names, and, when they tried to retaliate, Donald tearfully beseeched the male co–therapist for help. There were repeated occasions in which Donald, even under the mildest threats of attack, literally climbed on the therapist's lap and half–mockingly cried: "Mama, mama help me!" When confronted with his obvious provocations, Donald's typical stance was one of tearful denial and accusation of his attackers. There were also rare whispered admissions to the therapist, especially after failures due to his physical ineptness, that he was "the stupid one here." Before that, one of Donald's more vociferous scapegoaters had labeled him "retarded." That label became the password for the scapegoating episodes that characterized at least a part of most of the meetings. Donald did not miss a single session throughout the year and never complained to his mother about what transpired in the group.

During the group's middle phase, instead of landing in the therapist's lap, Donald tended to run out into the hall after the usual ganging-up against him. It should be noted here that the ganging-up was now mostly verbal, as the therapists routinely intervened when there was physical attack. As might be expected, Donald did not respond to the therapists' repeated confrontations and interpretations regarding his role in the repetitive, interactive cycle. The other boys, the scapegoaters, were more prone than he to accept the suggestions that Donald was being made to reenact their own unwelcome fears and wishes, such as being a baby again, or feeling like murdering a pesky sibling. When Donald on one occasion again went through his routine litany that "everyone here wants to hit me," one of the boys seriously confronted him by saying, "You are really asking for this."

Such repeated interventions, aimed at eliciting the meaning behind the scapegoating episodes, appeared to cause a gradual lessening in their frequency and intensity. With the dimunition of these episodes came an increase in willingness on the part of the boys to include Donald in structured games, many of which were initiated by the therapist. Donald's conduct became, in turn, more age-appropriate as he was noted on a number of occasions to converse with the others about television programs and comic book characters. A true turning point was reached when Donald succeeded in finishing his first project, an airplane model.

The scapegoating pattern of Donald by his group, which lasted intermittently for a period of more than seven months, appeared to contain the earlier-delineated elements of a projective identification. In this largely covert interaction, the scapegoaters not only projected unwanted aspects of themselves onto the ready and willing target, but also symbolically and really continued to banish him from their midst. In addition, not unlike the scripts in the pre-fated Greek plays, those same scapegoaters seemed to unconsciously direct Donald's behavior and feelings. By doing so, they could vicariously reexperience them in the open and work them through, with the aid of the therapists' interventions. As for Donald, his growth toward age-appropriate conduct was promoted by the direct gratification entailed in the interactions with the empathetic parental figures of the therapists, coupled with the interpretations of his self-defeating behavioral patterns.

In sum, beginning with its original mention in the Old Testament, the phenomenon of scapegoating has been subjected to a historical review. The tendency of human groups to project onto other such emotions as fear, aggression, and guilt—emotions they must negate in themselves—is as old as history.

The group psychotherapy literature fails to give the omnipresent and vexing subject of scapegoating the attention it deserves. The few existing references appear to be overly general and inconclusive.

Scapegoating can be viewed as a group process manifestation, occurring in two different yet related forms: (1) a short lived one, characterized primarily by the mechanism of projection, and (2) a more complex and persistent one, preempted by the mechanism of projective identification.

It is hoped that this attempt to integrate the existing findings about scapegoating and to propose a theoretical and practical framework will enhance our understanding of this phenomenon and help to clarify some of the issues arising from the multiple ways in which it has heretofore been depicted.

Part III

GROUP TREATMENT OF CHILDREN AND ADOLESCENTS

Introduction

Parts III and IV of this book deal with the clinical practice of group psychotherapy for children and adolescents, as well as for adults, respectively.

Chapter 7 offers a historical and conceptual background on the origin of activity group therapy for latency–age children. The unique developmental issues of these children are depicted within a psychoanalytic framework together with the impetus which surfaced in the 1930's to effect the initiation of this new group intervention modality. Traditional activity group therapy is described and contrasted with some modified group treatment methods, which were designed for different kinds of childhood maladies.

Chapter 8 contains a detailed presentation of one such modified treatment model, which was developed through trial and error to reach children with severe ego pathology who had failed to respond to the traditional methods. These children had been variously diagnosed as "atypical," borderline, or schizophrenic. Originally devised in the 1950's, this experiential approach appears to have stood the test of time, if one judges by the current literature on the group treatment of severely deprived children. The lengthy clinical illustrations in this chapter are designed to enhance the reader's comprehension of the subtle theoretical and technical issues inherent in work with such markedly impaired children.

Chapter 9 comprises a comprehensive overview of the major group treatment models in the broader realm of child and adolescent group psychotherapy. In line with the classification proposed in Chapter 1, the "therapeutic" (or "para–therapeutic") modalities are presented apart from the truly clinical ones. The synopses of the varied models coupled with the detailed clinical vignettes, illustrate the nuances of the group therapeutic process. Among the modalitites covered in this chapter, including appropriate references, are groups for preschoolers and for older children, including diagnostic groups. As for adolescent group psychotherapy, there is a discussion of the unique issues facing the group therapist of socially disadvantaged teenagers when compared to those from middle–class backgrounds. Group treatment approaches for delinquent and drug–abusing adolescents are covered as well. The chapter concludes with the puzzling question of why child and adolescent group therapy has been outstripped by the group treatment of adults. As suggested also in this volume's concluding Chapter 12, dictates of the marketplace coupled with the sponsorship of current training programs in child psychotherapy are the likely causes for this regrettable circumstance.

Chapter 7

THE CONCEPT OF LATENCY: IMPLICATIONS FOR GROUP TREATMENT

The concept of the "ideal of latency" coined by Freud in 1905 grew out of his assumption that between the ages of six and thirteen, or puberty, there is a relative dormancy of sexual pressures and conflicts in personality development. He later elaborated on the relationship between the resolution of the so-called "Oedipus complex" and the onset of latency, emphasizing strong repression, the replacement of object cathexis on the parent by identification, and the beginnings of the formation of the superego. As noted by Margaret Fries (1958), this view of latency was reflected in the psychoanalytic literature until the early 1940's. In fact, the definition in a dictionary published in 1958, still referred to latency as "a period from about age 4 or 5 to about age 12 during which interest in sex is sublimated" (English and English, 1958). Today, anyone familiar with children between those ages is likely to question whether their interest in sex is actually sublimated and, above all, whether the latency period, however conceptualized, stretches beyond the age of ten. The well-known preadolescent conflicts and regressive patterns which include expressions of aggression characteristic of even so-called "normal" children cannot possibly be subsumed under the notion of latency.

PSYCHOSEXUAL DRIVES

What are the more recent psychoanalytic ideas about the fate of the psychosexual drives during the latency period? Berta Bornstein

Reprinted, in part, from *Social Casework*, 22:363–367, 1966, by permission of the Family Service Association of America, publishers.

(1951) suggested that latency is constituted by two distinct phases: (1) the period between the ages five and a half and eight, which is characterized by a continuation of the infantile neurosis, and (2) the period between the ages eight and ten, during which there is a relative weakening of genital impulses and superego demands. During the first period, according to Bornstein, the child's ego is threatened by both his impulses and his newly developed superego. (It is not surprising that some people have referred to the first stage of latency as "the little adolescence.") Bornstein argues that two sets of defenses are employed by the child in trying to cope with the genital impulses: initially, regression to pregenitality and, in turn, reaction formation. A heightened ambivalence characterized by alternating obedience, rebellion, and self-reproach are part of the picture. Additional defenses utilized by children during the first period of latency are identification with the aggressor and projection. The second period, which agrees more closely with the notion of latency as a time of emotional calm and relative equilibrium, is characterized by freer and more consolidated ego functioning. A marked orientation toward reality and and toward object relationships permits the development of healthy defenses, of adaptations, and of ego mastery.

In a subsequent contribution, Sarnoff (1976) questioned the assumed decline in drive energy in all latency-age children, suggesting instead that fantasies and group activities become the channels for the discharge of continuing sexual and aggressive impulses. He noted, in particular, that in preadolescents these group activities, which include transference-like symbolizations and the sharing of group myths, tend to replace fantasy as a means of drive expression.

Of particular importance to those working with latency-age children is the observation of psychoanalysts that together with the forces conducive to healthy character formation goes a persistent, though repressed, struggle against a temptation to masturbate. Anna Freud argues that the many pregenital fantasies of the child come to be compressed into a single fantasy with the onset of latency. In her words, the fantasy is "from then onwards, the sole carrier of the child's sexuality and finds its bodily outlet in phallic masturbation" (1949, p. 202). The child's struggle against masturbation may focus on the content of the fantasy, on the act itself, on his hands, or on the genital organ. Despite the elaborate defenses, the child's ego occasionally succumbs to the pressures to masturbate. This is likely to lead to a cycle of guilt, self-punishment, and defensive maneuvers. According to Sarnoff (1976), overt masturbation is less prevalent among latency-age girls than boys. It tends to be replaced by orally regressive activities, reaction formations, and symbolic fantasies. Bornstein (1953) has described how children frequently resort to such regressive substitutes for masturbation as nail-biting, picking on things, and ear-pulling. Similarly, compulsive nagging or provocativeness may become the disguised expressions of sadomasochistic fantasies that have become isolated from the masturbatory act.

The parallel struggle against the emergence of aggressive impulses in latency-age children is of equal importance. The well-known preoccupation of those children with gory subject matter, be it on television or in the comics, represents a means of vicarious, socially acceptable gratification. The elaborate rules in games, the many hobbies, and the rituals or mannerisms with a strong obsessive-compulsive flavor, are examples of the latency-age child's more disguised ways of dealing with the underlying aggressiveness. In this connection English and Pearson (1945) have referred to the frequency during latency of tics and rituals, such as counting and touching fence posts, that are associated with notions of bad or good luck. The game of avoiding stepping on cracks with the related rhyme, "Step on a crack, break your mother's back," is perhaps the clearest illustration of an obsessive-compulsive activity utilized to deal with an aggressive wish.

Ego Development

What about ego development in the latency-age child? The frequent difficulties prior to the age of eight in separating from the parents and the family give way to strong urges to be independent, to socialize, and, above all, to learn. As Erik Erikson stated so well: "At no time is the individual more ready to learn quickly and avidly, to become big in the sense of sharing obligation, discipline, and performance rather than power. . . ; and he is able and willing to profit fully by the association with teachers and ideal prototypes" (1959, p. 81). In relation to children's ego and superego development at this age, the importance of teachers, group leaders, and other meaningful adults, apart from the parents, cannot be overemphasized. Because the child spends most of his waking hours at school, it is important to define the roles and functions of the teacher, especially as a leader of the classroom group. Some years ago I listed the following teacher roles: (1) realistic object of love or hate, (2) object of identification, (3) source of support as enabler and helper in maintaining ego control, (4) carrier of society's mores, (5) source of knowledge and skills, (6) evaluator of performance, (7) mediator in conflicts, (8) symbol of group values, and (9) friendly counselor (Scheidlinger, 1955).

In addition to the school group, indigenous peer groups play a significant role in the latency–age child's social development. Group relationships offer not only a sense of belonging and of emotional support, but also an opportunity for the sublimation and redirection of aggressive and libidinal impulses, especially via fantasy. The provision of this opportunity is particularly important in view of the urgent need of latency–age children to deal with the sexual and aggressive drives carried over from their oedipal conflicts; they also have the related need to emancipate themselves from earlier dependency on the parental figures. In addition, a most critical task for the child is the evolution of an ego and sexual–role identity in his ever–broadening arena of living, which has come to include the school and other community institutions. It must be noted that spontaneous peer groupings contain, at the same time, elements of considerable conflict and potential hurt: The ready use of cliques to control and bully others, scapegoating patterns often bordering on cruelty, and delinquent escapades, come to mind in this connection.

There is little doubt that children's behavior in latency is strongly influenced by environmental and cultural factors. To begin with, it is most unlikely that, in the face of the continual erotic stimulation emanating from the mass communication media, children's sexual interests and responses can nowadays remain latent in any sense of the word. This stimulation is compounded in socially and economically disadvantaged families in which crowded living conditions and early sexual experimentation are commonplace. Furthermore, parental pressures directed at regimenting the little free playtime available to children — be it for cultural enrichment, chores in the home, or earning money — are also likely to undermine the equilibrium of the latency-age child. Nevertheless — though the literature all too frequently fails to underscore the fact — in most latency-age children, the maturational and adaptive forces outweigh those tending to produce intrapsychic conflict, thus leading to the strengthening and integration of the ego.

Fries and Lewi (1938) discussed the importance of maturational elements from birth on, whereas Hartmann (1958) has contributed the significant concept of autonomous and conflict-free ego functions — all of which are relevant to the concept of latency. Erikson's idea of mutuality in the basic relationship between the developing individual and his social environment offers a theoretical link between intrapersonal and group processes (Erikson, 1959).

PATHOLOGY AND TREATMENT

Gordon Hamilton's (1947) observation that disturbed children really do not have a latency is consistent with the concept of latency that has been presented. Hamilton adds that the sources of disturbance in these children usually reside in unresolved conflicts or patterns from the years preceding the latency period. Sarnoff (1976) also noted that all acute stress in such latency-age children is likely to lead to anal–sadistic regressions such as smearing, teasing, and provoking.

It follows from the foregoing formulation of the conflicts typical of latency that problems are most likely to manifest themselves in overly rigid defenses and related inhibitions at the one extreme, or ineffective defenses leading to undue impulsivity at the other. Although anxiety states and phobias are frequent during the early phase of latency, obsessive–compulsive pathology is more likely to appear after the age of eight. Neurotic manifestations of this kind are rooted essentially in the oedipal period. In contrast, the reactive behavior disorders and conditions involving severe ego damage are more likely to stem from conflicts in the earliest years, not infrequently compounded by constitutional factors. It is noteworthy that presenting complaints pertaining to latency–age children tend to focus on disturbances in learning or the realm of social adaptation. Since, as has already been noted, learning and social adaptation are two essential spheres in these children's personality development, such complaints warrant careful study and, if indicated, early intervention. Erikson (1959) has warned against the lasting harm to the developing identity if the child's sense of industry is supplanted by feelings of inadequacy and inferiority.

An observation of Bornstein's (1951) has especially important implications for the education and treatment of the latency–age child. She argues that, in view of the latter's strong need to maintain the newly gained ego organization, free–associative productions and attempts at promoting introspection constitute a massive threat. This is especially true during the second phase of latency, when some measure of equilibrium is likely to have been established.

It is no accident that, except for instances of neurotic suffering, latency–age children tend to resist treatment measures based solely on verbal communication. They even resist any encounter with adults in which the expression of subjective feelings is elicited directly. In contrast, when it comes to manual activities or sports, they respond eagerly. Latency-age children represent the bulk of the clientele of group service agencies, such as neighborhood houses, and of leisure–time recreational programs; they are also readily involved in such youth–serving programs as those provided by the "Y's" and the Boy Scouts and Girl Scouts.

The predilection of latency–age children for group experiences was first exploited for therapeutic purposes in the early thirties with the development of activity group therapy (Slavson, 1943) and "diagnostic groups" (Redl, 1944). Activity group therapy, as its name implies, stresses the expression of fantasies and drives through play and action. A permissive group climate promotes a benign regression in which earlier conflicts can be relived in the context of a stable and accepting environment. The basic therapeutic forces arise from the interaction of the children with each other and with the therapist. The proper placement of children in such a way as to achieve a "group balance" is therefore essential for favorable therapeutic results; a group of about eight boys or girls of similar age and complementary behavior patterns is generally considered desirable. Materials and tools, selected games, and food are provided, and are utilized by the therapist to serve therapeutic ends.

In addition to such groups, in which the therapist's role is one of neutrality, and in which no interpretation is offered, some approaches combine the elements of activity and play with discussion and interpretations by the therapist. These range from the diagnostic groups mentioned earlier to "activity interview groups" (Slavson, 1952) for children six to ten years of age. More recently, Foulkes and Anthony (1964) have described a group approach for latency–age children in which each group session is divided into a discussion phase and an activity phase. During the discussion phase the children are encouraged to talk about their concerns, such as sexuality, and about various fantasied and real fears. Following the discussion period, the children are free to choose an activity for the day.

The next chapter portrays a group treatment approach developed especially for severely disturbed latency–age children, in which verbal interventions are also employed.

Despite the numerous successful demonstrations of various kinds of group approaches in selected child guidance clinics (Coolidge and Grunebaum, 1964) and family service agencies (Scheidlinger and Freeman, 1956), outpatient group treatment for latency-age children has, in general, failed to flourish. It has not kept pace with the striking growth of therapy groups for adults, despite frequent acknowledgments that for many latency-age children group treatment is probably the most desirable and efficacious method of treatment available (Lockwood, 1981). The failure of group therapy for latency-age children to keep pace with the rapid development of group treatment for adolescents and adults is probably related to the prevailing modes of training in child psychiatry and child psychology, including the resulting preference of therapists for verbal and dyadic approaches. The need for special physical facilities for group therapy for children may be another factor.

With the tremendous demand for new treatment modalities appropriate for the special needs of socially and emotionally deprived youth in our urban centers (Riessman, Cohen, and Pearl, 1964), group therapy and related attempts to influence children through groups are eventually bound to play a new and major role.

Chapter 8

EXPERIENTIAL GROUP TREATMENT OF SEVERELY DEPRIVED LATENCY–AGE CHILDREN[1]

There has been an increasing recent interest in the problem of children with severe ego pathology. They have been variously termed "severe non–neurotic ego disturbance," "borderline," "atypical," "pre–psychotic," "autistic," or "schizophrenic" (Ekstein, Bryant, and Friedman, 1958). The treatment efforts described in the literature most frequently involve the provision of a therapeutic environment in an institution. There has also been some experimentation in extramural settings, modifying the usual techniques of individual psychotherapy to suit the special needs of these children. In line with the frequently held view of a guarded prognosis unless treatment is initiated prior to age six (Buxbaum, 1954), much of this work has been carried on at the preschool age level.

This chapter deals with an experimental use of activity group therapy for such *latency–aged children* (aged 8–13), who have experienced marked deprivation in their lives and consequently developed serious disturbances in ego functioning. Carried out within the framework of a nonsectarian family service agency, the observations and techniques to be discussed were gradually evolved in

Reprinted from *American Journal of Orthopsychiatry*, 30:356–368, 1960, by permission of the American Orthopsychiatric Association, Inc.

[1] The term "latency–age" is employed loosely here, and includes preadolescents, in line with the discussion in the previous chapter.

the course of six years of work with these clients. (A few of the groups contained a majority of such cases; in most of them, they were in a minority. In all, they constituted about one third of the total number of 60 children in group treatment at the agency.)

PRESENTING PROBLEMS

These boys and girls invariably came from families of severe social and economic disadvantage, ethnically, almost 90 percent were Black, the small remainder whites and Puerto Ricans. Marked emotional deprivation, especially in the earliest years, absence of parental figures (usually the father), and transient relationships by the mother with several men were repetitive features. Such problems as lack of mothering, frequent parental neglect with inconsistent handling, and harsh physical punishment stood out. Not infrequently the child was exposed to direct sexual seductiveness and delinquent patterns.

Case Illustrations

Carl, 9½, was extremely moody, sullen and withdrawn. His moods seemed unrelated to external factors. He had no close relationships with anyone and gave the surface impression of passivity. Suspiciousness and shyness with adults were noted. There was a twitching of the face, and both fear and fascination at the theme of death. At school, Carl stood out as different and aloof. He worked far below his capacity, and was markedly retarded in reading. Though of Black background, Carl insisted that he was of Indian blood.

His psychotic mother had been in and out of mental hospitals for years. During those periods, the children (including an older brother and a younger sister) were neglected, often without any adult supervision for a number of days. Later on, a great-aunt, a sickly woman over 70 years old, would assume care of the children until her niece's return from the hospital. The parents had been divorced when Carl was a baby.

Bernice, 9, was brought to the agency because of disobedience, poor social relationships, fighting with siblings, playing with matches, bed-wetting and occasional thumb-sucking. She was described as an impulsive, slightly delinquent youngster who exhibited little capacity for control. At school she was defiant with adults. She stole money and small objects, mostly to "buy" favor with other children.

Bernice was born out-of-wedlock, as were her two younger siblings. Each of them had a different father, which served to enhance their confusion regarding their identity. The family unit, consisting of the mother and the three children, lived in a one-room apartment. Bernice and her sister had to share a bed with their mother.

Bernice became enuretic at the age of seven after the mother had forced her to stop sucking her thumb. Once the restrictions were removed (bitter fluids on the thumb—described to the child as poison), Bernice began sucking her thumb again, and the bed-wetting ceased. Shortly before the group treatment commenced, Bernice broke herself of the thumb-sucking habit by putting a piece of tape on her thumb. While successful in stopping the symptom, Bernice became more withdrawn and depressed, sulking or crying frequently, for no apparent reason.

Vivian, 10, was described by both her mother and her teacher as a "nervous" child. She reacted to stress situations by becoming frightened and going to bed. Threats of whipping by the mother left Vivian shaking and trembling. She was also very fearful of insects. The mother further described her as a restless sleeper who cried out at night and sleepwalked on occasion. There was rivalry and aggressiveness with an older brother. Vivian was depicted by the agency's homemaker as quiet and withdrawn. She did not play like the other children and would often go off to a corner, sit in a chair, and rub her lip.

Those at school spoke of Vivian as fidgeting and as talking out of turn. At camp, she displayed occasional temper outbursts and rapid mood shifts. Vivian had become more "nervous" after the death of a brother several years before. Vivian and her sister had to help in caring for the youngest child.

The mother was described as a dull woman, noncommunicative and markedly depressed. She was hospitalized for cardiac disease, and during this time a homemaker helped in caring for the children. Upon the mother's return, she became pregnant again, even though she had not wanted a fifth child—the four children were already too much for her. The father, a passive and ineffectual person, was extremely dependent on his own domineering mother.

Vivian's severe pathology emerged with particular clarity during the first few group sessions. She looked at times as though she were in a trance. She made faces, smiled, talked to herself and even addressed inanimate objects. She was completely unable to relate to the other girls, staying close to the adult.

The illustrations readily suggest a similarity of these children with the severe ego-disturbed cases described by Alpert (1957), Mahler (1952), and especially those depicted by Weil (1953). The latter had discussed in considerable detail the failure in adequate ego development characterized by poor social-emotional adaptations, problems of control, and various anxiety manifestations, ranging from fears to obsessive-compulsive mechanisms.

Perhaps because of the greater actual (in addition to emotional) deprivation and want in our samples, we were particularly struck with the degree of oral fixations in these children, with a primitive, oral greediness coupled with an impatient, hostile expectation that their needs would not be met. Hand-in-hand with poor reality testing and difficulty in distinguishing between inner and outer sources of tension, went serious distortions in the perceptions of other people, especially adults. Related to this was an underlying tone of depression with an extremely low self-concept and the problem of confused identity.

While none of these clients fitted into the concept of latency as summarized by Fries (1958), it is also noteworthy that we never worked with any in whom the ego pathology was all-embracing. Thus, arrested or regressed ego functions invariably occurred with others which were reasonably well developed and served as anchorage points for the therapeutic intervention.

GROUP THERAPY TECHNIQUES

The group treatment techniques that we evolved for these children constituted, in effect, a modification of the activity group therapy developed by Slavson (1943) in the late thirties. Briefly, the latter method, as already noted in the previous chapter, was devised for less severely disturbed children. It stresses the *acting out* of conflicts and deviant behavior patterns within the framework of a permissive environment. The basic therapeutic elements accrue from the interaction of the children with each other and from their relationship to the therapist.

The potentialities inherent in activity group therapy for helping children with severe ego pathology suggested themselves to us through coincidence. It occurred in connection with our use of groups for observation of clients on whom there was inadequate diagnostic data. In the course of these observations the striking pathology of the children readily emerged to view. In addition, the group experience seemed to assume a positive meaning to them from the very beginning. Considering that most of these clients were totally inaccessible to individual contact without motivation for help or change, this was an especially important finding. We began to experiment with more and more such children, modifying our techniques along the way in line with their special needs.

The changes we experimentally introduced differ in a number of ways from the techniques usually associated with activity group therapy. First of all, from the very beginning the therapist had to abandon the role of neutrality and extreme permissiveness which had worked so well with less damaged personalities. These children's ego faculties were simply not sufficiently developed to perceive the adult as a warm and helpful figure when he kept his verbal responses to a minimum, and particularly when he planfully failed to interfere in the face of what appeared to them as psychologically threatening group developments. As Slavson (1955) had stated regarding the general kinds of activity groups, they require children with at least "a minimal development of ego strength and superego organization so that impulses can be brought under control through reactions of other children and the demands of the group" (p.17). Thus, for the children under discussion, the therapist had to become more open and direct in his emotional reactions and verbalizations.

As to restraints, the therapist had to be readier to use them (preferably indirectly) in the face of verbal or physical impulsive acting out. It should be noted, however, that direct physical attacks rarely occurred in our groups. First of all, there was the careful selection and "balancing" of the membership. Then, there was the amazing tolerance of these children for individuals who are "different" and particularly vulnerable. Nonetheless when controls had to be instituted they were rarely perceived as hostile acts; quite to the contrary, we have had indications that, as with nursery–age children, adults' help to the ego against the threat of uncontrollable impulsivity is received with relief and relaxation. Prior to this shift in the therapist's role, these children, when asked about the groups, would describe the leader as "not caring" or as "being afraid of the kids."

Another related modification referred to the planful structuring of the group climate toward constancy, nurturing, and feeding, even further than is usually the case. Besides the availability of plentiful supplies, especially in the early stages of the group, the traditional snack became a full–fledged meal, carefully prepared by the therapist. While deliberately providing a few "extras" (plus the food of absentees) for the group to deal with as it pleased, the therapist did not permit the customary free group interaction with respect to basic portions. These were assured to each child, no matter how persistent the attempts of the more aggressive group members to grab food away.

We also decided that, because of these children's deficiencies in reality testing, the well–known nonverbal techniques of situational interferences were inadequate. The children required, in addition, frequent verbal interventions on the part of the therapist. These could be directed toward confronting behavioral responses, i.e., "You are now quite upset," or "You are taking the wood which belongs to Fred"; or more frequently, were in the nature of clarifying external reality. For instance, some of the members of a boys' group giggled and playfully threatened to beat Robert up after the meeting. The therapist clarified the reality for the child by saying, "They are only teasing." Or, the adult might say, "I will not let anyone in this club beat you." In a girls' group a child once said to the therapist, "Get the girls out of the bathroom or they will fall in the toilet and get swallowed up." The therapist replied, "That cannot happen."

THE TREATMENT PROCESS

With the above kinds of modifications we found activity group therapy eminently suitable for helping such clients with severe disturbances in ego development. In *all* children, acting is the natural form of communication. Also, with their more pliant personality structure, they respond more readily than adults to new perceptions inherent in a current experience. Expressing problems through action rather than words is especially true of personalities with early fixation levels, for, as is well known, the earliest form of communication in life is nonverbal. Consequently, *the actual experiencing of gratifications* and the *reliving of earliest traumata* inherent in this approach are most valuable. Insofar as the group treatment constitutes, in effect, a *guided gratification, regression, and upbringing,* current conflicts as well as earlier unresolved interpersonal experiences can be relived, but with different actors, and what is even more important—a different ending. As one girl put it (when her mother noticed that she was not overeating as much at home), "They stuff you so much all the time in the club that I don't care to eat as much now." The therapist's feeding her once a week during the sessions had begun to carry her for the whole week!

Case Illustrations

In both the illustrative cases which follow, the reactivation of oral conflicts in relation to the group therapist as a maternal figure is underscored. This is no coincidence, for as we have noted at another point regarding these groups, ". . . it is around the theme of food—the buying of it, the bringing of it to the meeting room, the cooking and serving—that the most dramatic and meaningful interactions occur. The conflicts reenacted here involve not only the reliving of the earliest problems in mother–child relationships, but they are at the same time anchored in the current reality of the children's home experiences" (Scheidlinger, Douville, Harrahill, King, and Minor, 1959). In this context, sibling rivalry actually became a struggle for mother's food — for her milk in a symbolic sense.

> Bernice, the earlier-mentioned impulsive child, who sucked her thumb, fought with her sister, wet her bed, and played with fire, was enraged at other girls for bringing visitors to the group meetings. Her anger about this kind of sharing of the food was so intense that, in retaliation, she brought her hated younger sister to some sessions provisionally, just in case another girl had again invited her friend to attend. Quoting from a session:
> Like a racing locomotive suddenly brought to a halt, Bernice stopped short at the ping–pong table. Her sister Doris followed behind. Bernice did not bother to say "hello" or to take off her coat. After greeting Bernice I asked her if she wanted to have her sister visit for today. Bernice said it depended on whether or not Sally's friend was going to stay. When Sally announced that she had brought Dora at the designation of the girls, Bernice bellowed at Doris to take off her coat.

The fact that by bringing her sister she had further diluted the food available for sharing did not count. One of the prime factors was that she had to get even. Perhaps also on a deeper level, her sister constituted an extension of herself, thus neutralizing the food given to the outsider, to Sally's friend. A similar self-defeating mechanism on the part of the same girl, which ended in her destroying the food, is seen in the following quoted incident:

> Once again Bernice claimed the food of the absent club member. She and Sally raced for the empty seat, with Bernice pushing Sally out of the way. Sally asked Bernice if her mother did not teach her manners. Bernice warned Sally not to talk about her mother in that way, but Sally provocatively repeated her question. Bernice slapped Sally, and Sally hit Bernice back. Bernice landed a hard smack on Sally's arm and the latter began to cry. After Barbara's intervention "to break it up," Sally cried a little while longer. Bernice seemed

somewhat apologetic and told Sally she had warned her not to say anything about her mother. She offered Sally the contested seat, but Sally refused it. After some further angry interchange, Bernice poured soda all over the sandwiches. She sat at the table pouting. Sally asked why she did that, spoiling the food for everybody, but Bernice did not reply.

As we have noted earlier, such reliving of conflicts in the sphere of orality alone, encompasses much of the treatment process with these severely deprived children. This should not be construed, however, as meaning that in this kind of guided regression other psychosexual levels and their related fixations, particularly pre-oedipal ones, do not get stimulated as well. This could occur in relation to food or any other aspect of the group interaction, i.e., bathroom play, use of materials or tools. To quote from another session:

> As I continued to go around the table to serve the franks, Doreen said, "It looks like we are stealing something from the boys." Mary impatiently asked Doreen what she was talking about. After a second, Sandra looked at Doreen and said, "I get you." Then all the girls laughed. As she bit into her frankfurter Doreen said, "Mm. Mm." Sandra said, "Very funny." Nonie added sarcastically, "Haha." Mary was the only girl who failed to perceive the phallic reference.

Therapeutic Success and Failure

The children in our groups frequently showed open awareness of the changes which occurred in them and in others. The following is an illustration: Jean took hold of Winnie's hand and began whirling her around. "Last year," she said to her, "you used to be afraid of me. I told you that I would beat you up and you believed me. What about that now?" Winnie laughed at her in an easy way and said, "I don't; you'd better not try it now."

While the group treatment depicted so far has been markedly successful in modifying, to a degree at least, the functioning of a large majority of these severely disturbed clients, we have, of course, also had failures. These seemed to fall into two major categories: (1) The overly provocative children, who despite the therapist's repeated interventions continued to so goad the other group members that counterattack and scapegoating could not be prevented. Eventually these children had to be removed from the group (see Chapter 6 for a discussion of scapegoating). (2) The children who improved in their group behavior, but failed to carry this over to the outside. This seemed related most often to a highly charged mutual provocativeness or sadomasochistic pattern operating at home, which defied modification through the casework efforts with the family.[2]

Jane exemplifies a child with extremely provocative behavior in the group. She was referred by the school because of a violent temper and constant arguments with her peers. With adults, Jane was anxious for attention and affection. The mother openly preferred Jane's older sister and complained that Jane was willful, lied and stole money. She was generally dissatisfied with what anyone tried to do for her. From the very beginning, Jane behaved aggressively toward all the girls in the group. Her major efforts seemed focused on hoarding supplies and food to take home with her, and on provocative teasing of the other children. The girls tried to put up with her, tolerating much of her provocativeness. Instead of calming her down, this only made things worse as she continued her sarcastic barrage directed at almost everyone. The girls soon verbalized the truth: whenever Jane came she caused trouble. The therapist's efforts to get close to Jane and to support her were of no avail, as she could not perceive the therapist as trying to help her. Her projection mechanisms and denial were so pervasive that in the face of all reality confrontations, she kept on insisting: "I never do anything to the girls. They pick on me, so I must hit back."

Bernice, whom we mentioned earlier in this chapter, belongs to the other category, namely the children who fail to transfer the behavioral changes achieved in the group to the outside world. This

[2] In line with common practice in the family service field, a caseworker always assumes responsibility for the treatment planning for the family and each of its members. While the children discussed here were treated in the group, individual contact with the parents was maintained. However, because of the marked pathology in these cases, such contacts were frequently sporadic and of limited effectiveness.

severely impulsive, hostile girl with complex symptomatology began to show signs of responding to the treatment after a year and a half. Aside from conscious efforts to control her intense oral-sadistic tendencies, she began to accept limitations, to cooperate with the therapist and to abide by group decisions. Her consistently warmer feelings toward the therapist were striking. On Valentine's Day she was the one who suggested that the girls make a heart for the therapist. In addition, she herself made a change purse for her, delaying her coming to the table to eat, for a considerable period of time. Quite an achievement for this voracious youngster! When the gifts were presented, Bernice called out twice: "Mrs. K, we love you," to which the therapist replied gently, "Yes, Bernice."

Despite these changes in the group, Bernice continued to get herself into difficulties in the community. It was felt that this was due to the pervasive pathology in the mother–daughter relationship. The mother admitted that since the birth of her latest out-of-wedlock child, the "lickings" she administered to Bernice gave her satisfaction, "relieving everything I feel inside." Besides these whippings, there were frequent trips to the local police precinct, coupled with threats to send Bernice away. This unchanging mutual provocativeness at home is likely to necessitate the placement of Bernice away from home.

In the latter event, the group experience, which demonstrated this girl's capacity to change and grow in a supportive environment, will have served as a significant steppingstone.

The Group Treatment of Carl and of Ellen

The problem of reliving earlier traumatic experiences, especially in the sphere of orality, could be exemplified through Carl's group treatment. This is the earlier–mentioned 9½–year–old boy with extreme mood swings, a marked distrust of adults, fear of death, no social relationships, and severe retardation in reading. His lack of "mothering" was due to the psychotic mother's frequent hospitalizations with resultant neglect of the children.

During the first period, Carl began by relating to the group with extreme caution. He was very suspicious toward the therapist. In spite of the fact that he spent most of his time away from the others at the "isolate's" table, he was the first boy to announce during the meal-time that the group should meet more often than once a week and for longer periods. Of particular significance was his voracious manner of eating, his grabbing for food and stuffing it into his mouth, using the fingers of both hands. This behavior was so much more exaggerated than that of any of the other boys, also deprived, that they quickly dubbed him "Greedy." This would always cause Carl to glower at them, but in no way deterred his grabbing for all extras. The boys rather quickly accepted his tremendous needs and would usually, by tacit agreement, allow him the extra food without competition.

While there was gradual improvement in the boy's relationship to the others by the second year, there was little change in his atti-tude toward food, or the therapist. By the third year, Carl became friendlier with the therapist, coupled with an increasing dependence on him for help with tools and materials. Concurrently, there was a dramatic change in Carl's consumption of food. At times he would pass up seconds, or would be slow enough in reaching for them, so that the other boys began competing more actively and directly. Carl didn't seem to be upset if they got ahead of him. His table man-ners had by now become quite acceptable. The mood swings were hardly in evidence. The summer camp noted for the first time a marked gain in impulse control. In contrast to the previous year there, Carl would become realistically angry without "flying to pieces" or appearing to have to "sit on himself" to keep from blow-ing up.

During the fourth group year, the therapist noted a definite relationship between Carl's attitude toward him and his food con-sumption. When he was particularly hostile to the therapist, he did not even take his basic portion. During the same year Carl brought some candy for the therapist, after the latter had kept a chocolate rabbit for him from the Easter party that the boy could not attend.

The case of Eileen, who was not described previously, could serve to illustrate the group treatment with an even more seriously disturbed youngster.

Eileen was referred to the agency at the age of 8½. She was with-drawn, fearful, and had difficulties in relating to children and adults. Her hands trembled at times and she cried easily. She had expressed concern over "sin," which seemed related to sexual fan-tasies and to growing up, generally. She had a great many fears of noises, insects, and animals. At school she was on the fringe of the group, working far below capacity. A camp report from a prior year stressed her bizarre behavior. She would roll her eyes, ask seemingly unrelated questions and had poor reality orientation. There were also difficulties in physical coordination, some involuntary movements, and considerable overweight. Eileen, on occasion, would speak of herself as "crazy."

Eileen's mother, a primitive, self-centered woman with delinquent tendencies, had had a very unhappy childhood. She had lost her mother at an early age. Following an out-of-wedlock pregnancy in her early teens, she was treated by her relatives as an outcast. Eileen was the later product of a short-lived marriage, characterized by much conflict from the very beginning. Eileen was especially upset when her father deserted the family during her early childhood.

The group therapist described Eileen as pretty, somewhat overweight, with smooth brown skin and rounded regular features. She was quiet and unobtrusive, with a facade of social ease. When ignored by the other girls, as she often was, she resorted to a mannerism in which she smiled, raised and lowered her eyes slowly, sighed, then smiled again, and turned away. Underneath, there was a mild depressive quality. When thus left out, Eileen spent much time working with materials. In this she needed considerable help from the therapist. To the first girl using a tool, Eileen said, "Do you want to be a boy—I mean carpenter?" thus suggesting primitive thinking and confusion regarding her identity. In the seventh session she was greeted as "Fatso," and criticized for not talking. Her response was to smile again in the manner indicated above. Eileen announced that she was dieting because of her overweight. She never competed for extra food, quoting her mother as saying: "You eat like a bird, his beak, that is." In contrast, during a group trip to a restaurant, Eileen ate with fascinated gluttony. Eileen related to the therapist with a dependent, superficial charm. The therapist also observed peculiar twitching or rotating motions of her hips, when Eileen was engrossed in her work. She stopped this when another child brought it to her attention. Eileen continued to talk about her diet, but put so much mayonnaise or ketchup on her sandwiches, that they literally dripped. Although usually alone or withdrawn, Eileen joined promptly in games when she was invited to do so. She was compliant and passive in relation to all requests made of her. She frequently did not seem to understand group decisions, being markedly preoccupied with herself. Her work with clay seemed unique and represented considerable fantasy, with sexual symbolism. The same held true for her colorful, abstract paintings. Eileen preserved in the group's cabinet the sculptured head of a man, with the notion of sending it as a gift to a well-known older male comedian. She was unaware that the girls viewed her repeated preoccupation with this piece as bizarre.

For a few months there was a difficult period during which the girls derided Eileen as "crazy." Through the intensive activity of the therapist, involving both direct support of Eileen and indirect restraint of the others, there occurred a significant shift in the group attitudes. Most of the members, in identification with the therapist, began instead to be supportive of the girl, including her in their games. They insisted, however, on her stopping her "crazy" acts, i.e., singing or talking to herself, or hip movements; and she complied readily. Not only did the girls accept the special closeness Eileen required of the therapist, but they often even drew her attention to Eileen's needs. At the end of 36 sessions, Eileen had shifted from a position of scapegoat to that of being a source of group concern and support.

Eileen responded with mild, tenuous expressions of affection to the therapist's activity in her behalf. Her awareness of support was evidenced by her revealing some of her concerns about the outside world such as school or camp. Each time the therapist brought these concerns to the attention of the family caseworker, there seemed to be another spurt of improvement in Eileen. She related better to the girls, and her reality perceptions seemed improved. Eileen would on occasion bring bizarre-sounding fantasy material to the therapist. While not discouraging her, this was always handled through enabling her to focus on the reality aspect.

The mother reported marked improvement in Eileen's functioning. The girl was now cooperative and helpful around the house. She began going out to play with the children in the neighborhood. With support from her caseworker, the mother could permit Eileen to begin to be on her own.

At camp, Eileen enjoyed herself more than during the previous year. She was less fearful and could participate in group activities much of the time. Occasionally, she still seemed confused, unable to grasp the reality expectations, being content to remain by herself. Her relationship to the therapist was one of a clinging, warm dependency.

During the second year of group therapy the girl's attendance continued to be excellent. She was noted to be taller and slimmer, with marked gains in her physical coordination. The bizarre behavior patterns had disappeared. The therapist felt that there had been a definite gain in her self-concept and in the mastery of environmental demands. While alone during part of each session, she was infinitely more involved with the others. She joined in when the girls initiated games. She withdrew, however, when they discussed boys and sex. While still in need of support, and functioning less adequately than all the others, she hardly stood out as different to observers. (Our group sessions can be observed through one–way screens.) Eileen now rarely expressed fantasies to the therapist or the group and was seldom noted to be idle or self-absorbed. Her efforts to be like the others and master conventional projects, occurred apparently at the cost of the more creative fantasy–laden projects of the previous year. While still needing the support of the therapist, Eileen paid little attention to her when really involved in activity with the group. Not only had she become a fully accepted member, but on rare occasions she even stood up to other girls.

After the family moved to larger and more attractive living quarters, there was an interesting change in Eileen's use of the special group cabinet. Heretofore (until the 53rd session), it had been a repository for her many "treasures," including the earlier-noted head. She valued it so highly and constantly as to give the impression that an important part of her emotional life had centered there. It was as though with a room of her own in the new apartment she no longer needed this cherished, private place. Perhaps, in addition, it connoted her broader freedom to move out of the protective setting of the group.

Following the second period of group treatment, the caseworker reported further improvement in Eileen's symptomatology and functioning. This was particularly significant inasmuch as there had been some upsetting developments in the family. Not only did the mother marry again, but she also became pregnant prior to this marriage. She sent her youngest child, Eileen's stepsister, out of the state to the child's father. This move, as well as her decision to offer the expected baby for adoption, upset Eileen considerably. On the constructive side, there was more consistency in Eileen's father's contacts, and he began visiting her once a week.

While the relationship with the mother was much better "Eileen's no trouble"—the latter's primitive and punitive measures continued on occasion. She described, for instance, how about once a month she would make Eileen kneel on the floor and would beat her with a strap.

Eileen's schoolwork improved to the extent that, upon her move to the new apartment, she was promoted from an "opportunity class" to a regular one. Her reading advanced noticeably, and the mother was pleased that Eileen was now eager to read the newspaper.

Despite these gratifying changes for the better in Eileen, the psychiatric consultant recommended that the long-range plan be to place all the children away from home. This was because of the mother's severe personality pathology and her complete inability to tolerate assertiveness and independence in any of her children. In line with this recommendation, Eileen was assigned to a separate caseworker for supportive contact three months prior to the termination of the group treatment.

It is noteworthy that an important subsequent step in our experimental work involved careful follow-up evaluations of our cases, especially during and after adolescence. The few instances in which we were able to undertake this in an organized fashion seemed promising. They suggested that the clients had generally managed to at least maintain the gains in ego functioning achieved through the group treatment (King, 1959). On the other hand, we suspect that Weil's contention of a remaining underlying "deficient personality structure" (1953, p. 277) in these kinds of individuals is probably true.

In trying to assess in general the therapeutic possibilities in this group approach, the following observations emerge:

1. The children are offered a benign familylike setting where, in contrast to their homes, there is a maximum of constancy and gratification, and a minimum of frustration. All this is enhanced by the special modifications we introduced in the therapist's role of greater directness, protective restraint, and verbal clarification.

2. The group as an entity represents a physical and psychological reality with which even a deficient ego can cope. It permits new perceptions, possibly ranging from the deepest unconscious levels

(i.e., primitive identification with the mother–group) to the initially unsettling conscious realization of this uniquely different kind of "club." (See also Chapter 5 of this volume.)

3. Within the climate of controlled gratification and regression, early conflicts are reenacted with a consistent, strong and accepting parental figure. The emphasis is on the anticipation and on the unconditional meeting of needs.

4. Various degrees and types of relationships are possible — none are demanded. These range from isolation through the most tenuous primitive identifications involving the borrowing of another object's ego strengths — to real object ties.

5. The dosage of gratifications (love offerings) is determined by the child on the basis of his readiness to accept them, thus permitting gradual removal of defenses. At the same time, demands made upon him are minimal.

6. The support of the other group members, the reality–geared group environment, and the nondirective role of the therapist tend to minimize and counteract the fears of overwhelming impulsivity and of domination or destruction by adults, so frequently inherent in these kinds of problems.

7. While no attempt is made to enter these children's inner autistic world with their primitive fantasies, the boundaries between reality and fantasy are repeatedly emphasized.

8. With the free flow of emotional gratifications, arrested ego development can be resumed, step by step. The child learns to postpone immediate satisfactions; to recognize and respond to the requirements of reality; to find pleasure in playing games, or working with tools and materials.

9. Inevitable changes in individual self–concepts are closely intertwined with healthier perceptions of the adult, of other children and the group as an entity, thus counteracting identity confusions.

In summary, I have depicted the usefulness of a guided gratification, regression, and upbringing through a modified form of activity group therapy for severely deprived latency–aged children.

Conflicts are expressed and reexperienced in this kind of setting through action, rather than words. The direct gratification of unmet oral and other pregenital needs through food, arts and crafts materials and the like, offered by an adult counselor, was found to be markedly effective in fostering improved ego functioning. The consistent, accepting parental figure, coupled with the benign image of a group entity, promoted changes in the clients' perceptions and expectations of the environment and of the people in it. The cumulative effects of these group experiences were an improved self-concept, better ego control over impulses, and enhanced reality testing.

I hope that further experimentation with such groups may well show the way toward reaching children during the latency period, who, if not treated, tend to succumb to active psychoses or to develop highly destructive antisocial patterns in adolescence.

Chapter 9

GROUP PSYCHOTHERAPY
WITH CHILDREN
AND ADOLESCENTS

In line with the discussion in Chapter 1, the term "group psycho-therapy" will be employed here in its narrowest sense, connoting a clinical method utilized by a specially trained professional. Simi-larly, all extensions of group psychotherapy, including the many more broadly conceived group intervention measures, will be termed "therapeutic" group approaches (or "para–therapeutic")— allied to, and yet different from, group psychotherapy.

Schamess (1976) reviewed the current group treatment modal-ities for children and classified these into the following four broad diagnostic categories: (1) groups for children with preoedipal developmental and personality problems, (2) groups for "atypical," ego–damaged children, (3) groups for "impulse–ridden," acting-out children, and (4) groups for neurotic children.

Schamess' first category (preoedipal) encompasses Slavson's (1943) classical activity group therapy as well as Axline's (1947) and Ginnott's (1961) play therapy. Schamess believes that each of these three approaches is uniquely suitable for immature children with ego deficiencies stemming from fixations in the anal and phal-lic periods, including problems in gender identity and in separa-

---

Reprinted, in part, from a chapter co–authored with Estelle Rauch, in *Handbook of Child Psychoanalysis,* ed. B. B. Wolman. New York: Van Nostrand Reinhold, 1972, by permission of the publisher.

ation from the mother. Such activity play groups are counterindicated, however, for psychoneurotic children as well as for those with problems of autism, high impulsivity, or sadism. An example of the second group treatment category (atypical children) is the modified activity model for ego–disturbed or borderline children, which was described in the previous chapter. To remind the reader, after an initial stage of "guided gratification," these modified activity groups subsequently went through a period of controlled therapeutic "regression" where pathological perceptions and behavior were relived. In the final stage, of "guided upbringing," reality–geared behavior was fostered. Schamess' third category (impulse–ridden) covers Foulkes and Anthony's (1957) "Small Room Technique," Epstein and Altman's (1972) "Common Sense Club," and the "Intermediary Group Treatment" depicted by Ganter, Yeakel, and Polansky (1967). These modalities were designed especially for homogeneous groups of impulsive children with antisocial behavior, who in Redl and Wineman's (1952) words, ". . . demand gratification at any cost . . . without concern for either reality or superego prohibitions" (p. 17). Given the depth of pathology, therapeutic success here was by no means assured. However, some substantial results were achieved through providing a structured group environment where aggression could be expressed without retaliation, and identification with the authority fostered. Teaching of specific skills served to build a sense of mastery and to enhance self-esteem.

Schamess' last category (neurotic) deals with groups for psychoneurotic children. Depicted by Slavson (1950) and Schiffer (1977) as "activity–interview group therapy," it is similar to the approach of Foulkes and Anthony (1965) described later in this chapter. These modalities embody conflicting data regarding their suitability as *exclusive* treatment measures for psychoneurotic children. The paucity of supporting clinical evidence raises the question whether the kind of reconstructive "working through" of unconscious conflicts and of transference reactions called for in crystallized psychoneuroses can really be accomplished through group therapy alone. However, when employed together with dyadic sessions, the effectiveness of group therapy with psychoneurotic children has been more convincingly documented (Hamilton, 1947).

GROUPS FOR CHILDREN

Traditional Activity Group Therapy: Case Illustration

The following is an excerpt from a recording of a traditional preadolescent boys' activity group session, taken after the group had been well under way. It illustrates the process in general, and highlights the reaction of this type of group to the arrival of a prospective new member. (The reader can compare the markedly nondirective stance of the present group therapist, with that employed in the experiential groups described in the previous chapter.)

In general, up until about this point (15th session of the second season), the boys had been working much more quietly than in the previous sessions. There was little verbal interchange when compared to the prior year, and what there was, occurred in whispered tones. The only noise came from hammering and sawing, and the latter in moderate tempo. Charles continued painting; Melvin was sawing on wood when not talking to Thomas; Errol worked by himself, hammering together what seemed to be a box–like structure; Joseph had taken a piece of plywood and was drawing the side view of a man's head and doing pretty well at it; Melvin had gone back to the second work bench and this time was trailed by Thomas.

At about 4:15 P.M. there was a knock on the door and Wayne (a planned visitor, who was being considered for this group) entered, escorted by his mother (Mrs. L.). I met them in the middle of the room as Mrs. L. handed me a letter of introduction from her caseworker. She was a slender woman, pleasant–looking and soft–spoken. She got confirmation that the meeting would end at 5:30 P.M., informed Wayne that she would be back for him at that time, and left. I introduced myself to Wayne, who was already beginning to peel off his clothes. Wayne was a small youngster of slender build, about the same size as Charles and Melvin. He wore a bright yellow, long-sleeved T-shirt and dungarees. He was hanging up his coat as I invited him to meet the other members, and I proceeded to introduce him to Charles, who looked expectantly, standing aside from his work, and more or less ducked his head in a nod. The boys did not shake hands, Wayne responding to my introduction with an uncertain smile, Charles reciprocating pretty much in a like manner. I then introduced him to Errol, who also stopped working, turned away, and seemed uncertain whether or not to reach out his hand to shake, though he did not in the end. He also ducked his head in response to the introduction. As I approached Thomas and Melvin, introducing them, they moved their heads in an abrupt nod, accompanied by the watchful expressions of Wayne.

There ensued a hasty whispered discussion between Melvin and Thomas, with Thomas calling to me and asking if Wayne was going to be a group member. Charles, Joseph, and Errol had more or less gone back to their work, but I had the impression that they, too, were listening behind me, as the room was silent. I had the letter of introduction in my hand and, glancing at it, replied that I understood from the group department that Wayne was visiting with us. Thomas and Melvin again engaged excitedly in a whispered discussion (obviously about the newcomer), with Melvin eventually going back to his work, while I proceeded to show Wayne about the room. When I had done this, I returned to some work I had been doing, Wayne trailing me and remaining in close proximity. Wayne's unease in this new situation was apparent as he watched me put some pieces of wood together and asked what I was doing. I told him that I was working on a shoeshine kit. He inquired whether I was making it for one of the fellows, or if it was for myself. Following my reply, Wayne remained close by, watching me for another few minutes. Only occasionally would he sneak a furtive glance at the others.

Joseph had finished drawing on the plywood, placed it on a tool shelf, got into the supply closet and now was working with leather and gimp. Wayne finally drew up his courage and drifted over to watch Joseph, who moved away from the supply cabinet and then wandered over to watch Charles. Thomas was leaning on a large table, watching Charles too. Again, he called Melvin over and they seemed to be in some discussion which I believe had to do with school, as I heard the word mentioned and something about Melvin being in a certain class. Wayne stood off to the side listening to the conversation between Melvin and Thomas, but not joining in.

At about 4:25 P.M. I began preparation for the meal, putting the water on and then returning to the vicinity of the tool cabinet. Errol had painted the roof of his box structure and was now also in the vicinity of the tool cabinet, examining the birdfeeding station I had placed on it. Errol had asked at the last meeting if he could have it, but had left early without taking it with him. At a point where I was close to Errol, I remarked that he could now have the box, if he still wanted it. As I moved away, Errol, who had at first been listening more or less impassively, nodding as I finished speaking, now turned about, striking the palm of one hand with his fist happily, and whirling in another direction once or twice, again examining the feeding station and moving back to his work. (He was apparently thrilled that I had remembered his request.) I put my work away and replaced some tools I had used in the tool cabinet, then returned to the kitchen area to resume preparation of the meal. As I worked there, the tempo of the group's activity seemed to pick up in terms of hammering, talking, and moving about. (Even in this second year, the food preparation continued to evoke restless tension.)

Wayne initiated the idea of a game of ping pong, asking if Wayne or Melvin knew how to play, and the latter two started to play singles. Melvin emerged as the better of the two players and won the game. He then engaged Joseph in play. Thomas, at the large table, moved in closer to Charles, who continued painting away. Errol worked alone at the second bench. A couple of times Charles came over to the kitchen area to clean the paintbrush, glancing at what was cooking. Over at the ping pong table the game had turned into a three–sided exchange with Joseph, Wayne, and Melvin batting the ball amongst each other. The boys were batting it around the room yelling at each other. Thomas moved in crying out, "Who wants to play tag?" There was a concerted dive on the part of all but Errol to get under the table, for the last boy "under" was supposed to be "it." I did not get to observe whether Errol participated in this game or not. There was, however, a good deal of running around with shouting on the part of everyone. (The ready acceptance of Wayne, the visitor, stands in marked contrast to last year's systematic scapegoating of all visitors.)

Just about the time the game of tag got under way, Joseph had taken off his glasses and put them on the tool cabinet. As I began laying out the food at about 4:55, Melvin and Thomas broke away from the game, somebody yelling "time out." They came over to the sink, beginning to wash up. Wayne and Joseph locked themselves accidentally in the bathroom. Charles on the outside, with his back to the door, seemed to be half–heartedly kicking at the door. After a few minutes the boys came out, but Charles did not enter; rather, he trailed them to the table. Thomas and Melvin were the first ones to be seated, with Thomas announcing that he was going to take his old seat. Wayne, the newcomer, the last one to sit down, unknowingly took the seat that I had regularly occupied. I heard Thomas whispering excitedly to Melvin, but I did not quite pick up what he said. I believe it was in reference to my seat that Wayne had taken. (The boys' ready acceptance of this is another sign of their growth.) The seating arrangement was: Wayne on my immediate left, then Charles, Errol, Joseph, Thomas, and Melvin on my immediate right.

The meal consisted of franks, beans, chocolate milk, and cupcakes. There was a bottle of ketchup and a small jar of pickles on the table. Errol, as soon as he was seated, began eating, followed by Melvin and Thomas. The latter two struck up a conversation about camp. Both had been there. Joseph chimed in and there soon was a three-way conversation among Joseph, Thomas, and Melvin, while Errol, Charles, and Wayne listened silently. The conversation centered around Melvin and Thomas at first wanting to know when each had been to camp, and to make sure that they were both talking about the same camp. They talked about their counselor, Tony, at which point Joseph chimed in, and then Melvin announced that there were two counselors named Tony. They talked about the group in which they had been, with Melvin asserting that neither of them could have been in group four, because they were not old enough. They talked about the various activities they participated in and about the physical features of the camp. At one point, as Melvin was describing the lake, the therapist accidentally coughed and there was a sudden silence. After a few moments of this silence, Thomas and Melvin seemed to look around the table, then at each other. They grinned briefly (as if needing to remind themselves that this adult was not to be feared), with Melvin resuming talk about other features of the camp.

The therapist noted that on their way home, the boys engaged in a loud conversation from which Wayne was excluded while trailing behind the others.

Play Group Psychotherapy

For children under the age of seven years, a modified form of activity group therapy, termed "play group psychotherapy," has been in use. The approach is akin to that encountered in psychoanalytically oriented nursery schools. Besides setting definite limits on the amount of impulsive activity, the therapist offers interpretations of behavior patterns in order to promote self-understanding (Ginnott, 1961). Sometimes the children's parents receive simultaneous group treatment.

Barcai and Robinson (1969) reported on the use of discussion group therapy with a group of fifth and sixth-grade children from two slum neighborhood schools, who were referred because of difficult classroom behavior or poor academic performance. The authors concluded that conventional group psychotherapy was considerably more effective than supervised art classes offered to the same kind of children.

As already noted, traditional activity group therapy has been found uniquely suited to the treatment of children with mild character and neurotic disorders (Coolidge and Grunebaum, 1964). A modified version of it, which made it possible to reach more severely disturbed and atypical children, was depicted in the preceding chapter.

There appears to be a growing body of evidence for the successful utilization of varied techniques of behavior modification in treating maladjusted children in groups. As noted by Rose (1972), such approaches, often employed in school settings, tend to be directed at the correction of specific maladaptive behavior. They turned out to be not only least expensive, but also most efficient with children who were not markedly disturbed.

Para-Therapeutic Children's Groups

Among the first workers to apply the techniques of activity group therapy to children's play groups in elementary schools is Schiffer (1969). Begun in 1950, his groups included six to nine-year-olds, and were led by school guidance counselors. As in activity groups, the counselor's stance was essentially permissive and nondirective, promoting limited regressive behavior and transference reactions. However, with these younger children there appears to be more emphasis placed on a balanced composition of members and more frequent leader interventions to prevent uncontrolled emotionality.

Most treatment groups in elementary schools today are regrettably devoid of the systematic approach and pretraining of practitioners which characterized Schiffer's approach. Nevertheless, as was noted by Frank and Zilbach (1968), such undertakings tend to be relatively successful whenever the method reflects an awareness of the reality of the school setting and of the unique psychology of the latency-age child. For example, in one school a "reading club" was devised for eight-year-old boys with behavior problems and reading disabilities. The boys were supplied with food and a variety of reading materials and word games. In the absence of any "push" from the adult, the youngsters gradually chose to engage in reading rather than in play, asking the worker for help with it. At the end of the year, the teachers reported marked improvement in the boys' behavior and several of them had even gained a year in their reading level.

A modified kind of activity group was applied in an educational project to a sample of about 40 underachieving, disadvantaged latency-age children with superior intelligence (Scheidlinger, 1965). The design called for the ready possibility of replicating this group intervention measure in the schools, under the direction of guidance personnel. In addition to the usual tools and craft supplies characteristic of traditional activity therapy groups, special materials, such as science sets, educational games, musical instruments, and maps, were provided. In contrast to the regressive climate encouraged in traditional group psychotherapy, reality considerations were planfully injected from the start, by limiting the amount of food available, by not allowing visitors to attend, and by permitting only completed projects to be taken home.

The worker's role was quite different from that of the activity group therapist. Along with the role of accepting adult, went that of active stimulator, guide, and teacher. Realistic praise and support were offered, together with confrontation of undesirable behavior patterns such as undue dependence. The major focus was on strengthening the children's relatively unconflicted ego functions through individual interventions and group discussions. These were evoked from the very beginning as a means of enhancing the group's cohesiveness and helping it to resolve its conflicts as well as to make plans for the future.

It was impressive how ready these groups were, not only to absorb the small number of severely disturbed children in their midst, but also to actively help bring about improved functioning. This was accomplished largely through direct intervention by the leader in regard to undesirable behavior patterns, coupled with enlistment of the group's understanding and help.

Diagnostic Groups

Short-term diagnostic groups for latency-age children represent yet another adaptation of activity group therapy. As depicted by King (1970), these groups contained five boys and girls aged 7–11½ years, who met for a total of four sessions with a female social worker. In contrast to some other similar programs (Redl, 1944; Churchill, 1965), these diagnostic groups were utilized as an integral part of the intake study and planning process in a family service agency. The unique advantage of these groups resided in their flexible character. They could thus accommodate children of both sexes about whom almost nothing was known, as well as those where specific diagnostic questions were being posed. Control of impulsivity presented no undue problem, once the traditional nondirective stance of the activity group therapist was modified. Immediate adult intervention coupled with a role of benign authority worked best. As might be expected, the worker had to have a wide variety of intervention measures available. The need to exert limits for the benefit of the weakest child was balanced by the desirability of allowing sufficient freedom for the emergence of spontaneous behavior. Availability and use of tools and materials were managed with a view to the short–term diagnostic purpose of the group, as well as flexibility in controlling the amount of impulsive behavior.

As noted by King (1970), certain aspects of the children's developmental levels and functioning emerged more than others in this diagnostic group experience. Thus, each child's current ego functioning was most clearly demonstrated, especially in regard to object constancy and relationships, reality testing and judgment, impulse control, frustration tolerance and characteristic defenses.

There emerged, in addition, much useful data pertaining to levels of psychosocial development, aspects of the self-concept, and sexual identification. Also revealed were such areas of functioning as the degree and quality of energy as expressed in motor activity and outward-directed interests and curiosity, and the child's span of attention and ability to concentrate. Some indications regarding withdrawal and excessive fantasy presented themselves as well.

As might be expected, children's residential treatment settings abound in group treatment modalities. These range from milieu groupings encompassing the whole institution or living-in units, to small socialization or recreational groups (Konopka, 1970). There has been little systematic utilization of activity or discussion group therapy in institutions, largely due to the difficulty of combining the permissive role characteristic of these approaches with the need for authoritative handling of the generally impulse-ridden patient population.

In general, as has also been concluded by MacLennan and Levy (1969), despite the fact that the need for the treatment of children has approached the character of a crisis, the literature on group therapy for children still fails to reflect this fact.

Groups for Adolescents

It is well known to clinicians that there are as many ways to go through adolescence as there are people—but the core issues to be dealt with and the ultimate goals to be achieved appear to be universal. The adolescent must accordingly deal with the still powerful, dependent tie to parents, and at the same time learn to cope with the anxiety about trying to manage on one's own and find security in oneself and in extrafamilial objects. Adolescents must permit themselves some socially acceptable gratifications of their aggressive and sexual drives, and resolve the bisexual identity characteristic of preadolescence in order to arrive at a firm heterosexual orientation. Ultimately, there must also emerge a clear sense of self and along with this, of one's values. They must select a career and follow through on training for that objective. This is a tall order—and all to be dealt with against the background of tremendous physical upheaval and a difficult social reality.

Adolescent development is to a large extent determined by the way the personality has progressed through the earlier stages, but, according to Blos (1962), "Adolescence often affords spontaneous recovery from debilitating childhood exigencies which threatened to impede progressive development" (p. 10). Blos goes on to describe the importance of latency as preparation for adolescence: As was already noted in the preceding chapters, within latency much sexual and aggressive energy is channeled into fantasy and sublimated activities; there is normally considerable broadening of the conflict-free spheres encompassing perception, memory, thinking, etc., and superego functions are fairly well secured. Thus, the increase in drive pressure in early adolescence does not usually undermine most aspects of reality functioning.

Not infrequently depicted as the "crazy" period, early adolescence, brought into existence in part by profound bodily changes, is characterized by a fairly chronic state of emotional lability. Conflict is everywhere; in the home the issue is whether to separate from parents or remain "safely" a child; at school one will be either popular with the opposite sex and make it with one's peer group or be a failure; and we must not forget the necessity of meeting the academic requirements, a task often providing much cause for conflict. The one-sex peer group gradually gives way to intense heterosexual curiosity, then dating, as both girls and boys move away from the primal love objects and alter the overwhelmingly narcissistic orientation normally characteristic of the earlier period. Devaluation of parents occurs and considerable open conflict with them is usual, and perhaps even necessary, to facilitate ultimate separation. The relatively healthy individual will have repressed the sexual wishes toward the opposite-sex parent by late adolescence, and will have identified with the same-sex parent, thus permitting a resolution of the childhood ties. This ultimately will allow for selection of an extrafamilial heterosexual object.

With diminished pressures internally and within the home, the 16–
to 18-year-old can thus more readily focus on intellectual and
career pursuits (Blos, 1979).

It is a known fact that breakdown can occur at any point in
adolescence. Studies have suggested, in this connection, that the
onset of schizophrenia takes place with considerable frequency
within the adolescent period. In terms of the less pathological
symptomatology, we observed that most often girls are brought for
treatment because of intense mother–daughter conflict, unwanted
pregnancy, or depression. Boys are more likely to be referred by
the school due to truancy, academic failure, or unduly aggressive
behavior. In recent years, youths of both sexes are frequently using
drugs. One often encounters teenagers who are friendless, or who
are neither feminine nor masculine, but asexual; or, those who are
in fact already beginning to act like and appear as members of the
opposite sex. Almost invariably these are youths who are suspicious or even hostile to authority figures since they have failed to
deal with the adult world both at home and at school. Many of
them have turned almost frantically to their peer group for support. This reluctance to depend upon adults, coupled with the
natural inclination toward peer group formation, are two major
reasons why group therapy is often considered the treatment of
choice for most adolescents (Torda, 1970).

In fact, there are adolescents who from the outset make it clear
that they are unwilling to work on an individual basis with a therapist, or who agree to come and do so only to remain totally silent
within the one-to-one treatment setting. Common concerns
among these youths are that they will be thought of as "crazy" or
that the therapist can read their minds. On a deeper level, they frequently fear the attachment to the adult. For many of these adolescents, the comfort of a group permits sufficient anonymity and
distance from the parental representatives so that the thoughts and
feelings can be shared more naturally.

Some adolescents cannot readily fit into the usual therapy
groups. Those who exhibit overt psychosis or psychopathy are

accordingly excluded from group therapy except where special groups are set up to treat individuals with this type of psychopathology. Similarly, there is agreement in the field that youngsters who are extremely vulnerable, intensely jealous of peers, and those who are paranoid, with practically no social relationships, are not ready for any kind of a therapy group. For them, the primary object is not the peer group but the adult, and until they work through some of these dependency problems in individual therapy, they cannot manage in a peer group. Slavson (1950) emphasized the importance of careful selection of group members; he suggested that adolescents should be grouped according to their general level of psychosexual development, believing that such homogeneous groups would help the members be more attuned to each other's unconscious motivations, and thus be more able to make astute observations concerning one another. He also stressed the need for group balance, as between "talkers" and "silent" members, the acting–outers and the withdrawn, and in relation to levels of pathology and hostility. It should be noted here that such therapy groups, which call for verbal communication, can absorb people from different socioeconomic backgrounds and with a wide range of intelligence, providing all members have an at least low average intelligence.

The setting for the group is of crucial importance; it must, to begin with, have a regular place available for meetings. The room should be large enough to permit a sense of spaciousness, but not so large as to make people uncomfortable (MacLennan and Felsenfeld, 1968). Most teen group meetings are held around a table, which facilitates discussion. Often, adolescent groups have soda served, and at the beginning they frequently need supplies, such as drawing materials, to help the more anxious members physically drain off excessive anxiety, which might otherwise drive them away. The group therapist makes it clear from the outset, however, that the expected means of communication is verbal.

During the initial part of such a group's life, absenteeism is often so high that many a clinician has wondered whether the group will fall apart. Some authorities recommend a brief individual contact with each adolescent prior to the commencement of group treatment. It is believed that the relationship thus formed will hold the youth in the group during the initial period of high anxiety. Early group sessions are frequently characterized by spurts of chatter, especially by girls, followed by painful silences which are difficult for most teenagers. The group therapist must come across from the outset as a warm and interested person who will not take over, who can tolerate some regression as well as contempt for authority, and who will maintain total confidentiality. Once the level of intense suspicion and anxiety related to the adult is reduced, the natural tendency toward peer group formation will take hold.

The above-noted developments are illustrated by the following all girls' group which was conducted at a family service agency. The girls had been interviewed at least three times each by the group therapist before the decision was made for placement in the group.

Case Illustrations

An All Girls' Group

The group consisted of eight girls, six of whom had been participants from the outset. (Two girls had withdrawn after one session, so that two new members were added at the seventh meeting.) Ann, 16, white, Catholic, pretty and articulate, an only child, was having severe difficulties with her mother and was extremely reluctant to be seen individually. Jill, 16, a bright Black girl, the youngest of five in a middle-class family with high aspirations, was failing in school, cutting classes, fooling around with drugs, and while still very tied to mother, hated her father intensely. She appeared to be making a predominantly masculine identification and showed little evidence of femininity. We suspected from the beginning that she was also quite depressed, but overtly she only showed an almost paranoid suspiciousness of adults, coupled with a hostile flippancy. Rose, white, Roman Catholic, and at 15, the youngest in the group, was precariously close to dropping out of school; she also was having serious problems with her foster parents. When approached with an offer of help, Rose rejected individual contact but reluctantly accepted the idea of the group. Phyllis, 17 ½ , white, Protestant, and a gifted musician, was an only child living with her disturbed single mother. She became depressed during her senior year in school and asked the guidance counselor for a referral to a treatment setting. Janet, 16, a white Roman Catholic, living with her parents and several siblings, was intensely hostile to her mother and very jealous of a younger sibling. She had taken to cutting school and was failing in her subjects. Elaine, nearly 17, a lovely looking Black Protestant girl of clearly above average intelligence, had been seen briefly in family therapy focused on problems with her mother. Out of that experience Elaine had indicated an interest in getting further help, admitting that she was truanting; she also had some history of stealing and was underachieving at school. The latecomers were Kathy, 16, Protestant, shy and depressed, prone to excessive involvement with school work and no social life, and Lola, an attractive, sophisticated 17–year–old, who was doing extraordinarily well at school, but already was quite promiscuous sexually and experimenting heavily with drugs.

The girls had each met Mrs. Jones, the group therapist, several times prior to that first group meeting, and in fact, had also seen the observation and group therapy rooms. While they were all "willing to give the group a try," which was what was asked of them, Ann and Janet were clearly very reluctant. Phyllis and Elaine seemed quite interested, while Jill was suspicious. In the preceding individual sessions and the first group meeting, the group therapist told the girls that they shared common concerns, that she felt they could help each other, that she, too, would like to be helpful, and that they were likely to experience anxiety which was to be expected in a new situation. From the outset, the girls joked about similar experiences which they had read about, such as marathon groups or nude groups, describing these as places where "everyone tells all" and where promiscuity abounds. They clearly were asking the group therapist, "What will happen here?" The anxiety level was high and very much connected with the adult's presence. Before the first session, one girl, who eventually dropped out, telephoned the worker four times, each time to change her mind about whether or not she was coming to the meeting. Several girls kiddingly "locked" the group therapist out when she briefly left the room to show some latecomers in. Ann and Jill were quite open in agreeing that the girls shouldn't tell anyone they're coming to this place because "if other people know you're coming here, they will think you're crazy or something." As already noted, another common fear early, in therapy is that the group therapist can read minds. Thus, one girl who dropped out after one session told Mrs. Jones, in front of the others, that while she might have a problem, "You mean some place down in my deep, dark unconscious — if I do, I'm really not going to be able to find it and I don't think anyone here is going to get that far either." The other girls agreed completely. They also concluded, while briefly chatting about drugs, that adults could never understand anything about this subject. The girls spoke indirectly about their fears of Mrs. Jones when they described their expectations or experiences with other adults: Ann was critical of her mother for "inspecting her work"; Jill's mother screams, demands, and criticizes; Elaine's mother worries constantly, talks a blue streak, will not listen, and thus Elaine clams up. Will Mrs. Jones be like any of these people?

The word "problem" was initially out of bounds for this group; to them it meant that they were either out of control or crazy. Thus, Jill told the girls that it was too hard for them to talk about problems since they all had different ones and came from different backgrounds. She suggested that they instead talk about "something else," and if something came up naturally, they could discuss it "without concentrating on problems." At times the girls relieved their anxiety by giggling at everything the group therapist said. When a girl found a session too stressful, she sometimes would miss the following week's session, offering as an excuse her need to study or a minor somatic complaint. The girls, in general, used the early sessions to identify themselves as to where they go to school, what their interests are, whether they have boyfriends, and very superficially, about why they were in treatment. By Session 4, the separateness which was marked from the outset had changed, and was supplanted by a chummy friendliness among the girls. They drank the Cokes without any hesitation and asked for a follow-up about something one of the girls had discussed the prior week. On the other hand, these superficial facts having been shared, the girls were also prone to anxious silences, as they were not yet sure whether or what to share. The big issue was "Can we trust each other?" but also and most particularly, "Can we trust her?", meaning Mrs. Jones. The group therapist offered constant support, noting how hard it was to talk, especially with her there, and reassured them that all groups go through this.

When no one offered a subject for discussion, the therapist usually introduced a theme, as in the following illustration. (This was because the girls could not tolerate silences and were always ready to run from them.) Phyllis, wanting badly to please Mrs. Jones and really in need of nurturance from her peers, reached out to the group with the first "problem" concerning a boy she was interested in. The others grasped at this straw; Jill, who was vying with Mrs. Jones for the group's leadership, quickly offered a pat solution in a domineering way, leaving no place for opposition; Elaine, intrigued with the problem, asked a few questions, and then there was silence. Mrs. Jones picked up Jill's comment, remarked on it as an interesting possible solution, noting also that Elaine seemed to be pursuing another idea, and asked if she or anyone else wanted to take it further. As the girls appeared to have gone as far as they could with this, the therapist touched on Jill's comment, and soon the others, led by Janet and Ann (both hostile to their mothers) began contemptuously to speak of mothers in general: they're ignorant, jump to conclusions and blame teenagers for everything. The group therapist was sympathetic and did not question their reasoning, but at the same time did not agree with it. As might be expected, problems with mothers represented the first subject that all of the girls were willing to talk about.

Speaking about mothers (but more likely about her anxiety as to whether the group therapist could be trusted), Elaine stated in this group that she would never tell her mother if she were ill. Lola remarked that she kept almost everything from her mother, who she felt really did not want to know anyway; Lola did voice a not uncommon concern that her mother might be upset about Lola's sharing in the group what she wouldn't ever share at home.

Often, in the midst of this kind of discussion, Jill in her role of peer leader, would accuse Mrs. Jones of wanting to force the girls to talk too fast. She would then order another girl to talk and when the latter, often Elaine or Janet, actually began a story, Jill would stop them with, "that's enough," clearly demonstrating her own as well as the group's ambivalence about moving ahead. Although Jill's behavior seemed almost overwhelming to the other girls, Mrs. Jones had to avoid direct intervention. To do so with Jill would have set Mrs. Jones up as an unduly threatening adult, something which could have jeopardized the further progress of the group. It was also apparent that Jill was actually terrified of Mrs. Jones, and was doing most of her attacking or intervening with the other girls because of this fear. Mrs. Jones became especially attuned to the possible danger of premature attempts to limit Jill, when the following week, after she in fact gently stopped her from taking over on a few occasions, the whole group became utterly silent. They thus again betrayed their anger and fear of Mrs. Jones. When they next spoke, Janet was the first to warn Mrs. Jones indirectly by telling the others that it took her a long time to make friends because she'd been hurt so often. Others in the group, most particularly Jill and Phyllis, wanted Mrs. Jones to tell them what she thought of them, demonstrating a sharp, though temporary increase in their anxiety about the adult. It was only when Jill, the girl who was most fearful of Mrs. Jones, became eventually more relaxed, that they could coalesce into a group. Subsequently, she did not need to take over so much and the others became comfortable enough to limit her, when necessary.

Although this group was not beset with many absences (which

often occurs in teen groups), it did lose two of its members, which was felt keenly. They subsequently had to deal with the late admission of two replacements. This was timed at the point when the participants were beginning to feel comfortable with one another, so that they could accept the newcomers and help them get oriented. The few early absences which did occur were very much noticed by those present, and served as sources of disturbance as the girls moved toward group cohesiveness. Thus, Janet and Jill questioned whether Rose's absence was for a good reason, and in another session Ann was told outright that she should not make a date on a group night. Underlying these expressions of concern seemed to be a beginning commitment to each other. During this early period, probably commencing with the fourth or fifth session, the girls were also acutely attuned to whether a story sounded honest, though they accepted anything that was shared and rarely asked personal questions of one another. In fact, when Lola gave some information on birth control to the girls (which made it fairly obvious that she had had sexual experiences while failing to describe these experiences), the others dropped the subject, agreeing that they had no basis on which to discuss it. Not only were they not yet sure what they could ask Lola, but they were also not ready to discuss sex in front of Mrs. Jones. Of great help at this stage of struggle with how much they might ask of other members, were comments from Mrs. Jones on their interest and wish to help one another, while recognizing their simultaneous reluctance to push too hard. They also raised the question of whether sharing can help, and whenever this theme came up, Mrs. Jones encouraged the girls to think about it. The group continued to be concerned about how self-disclosure to Mrs. Jones would be received. Thus, in Session 7, when Mrs. Jones made a comment to Kathy that the latter clearly did not want to pick up on and about which she might have felt awkward, Mrs. Jones' reassurance that "it's okay to take your time," was the most encouraging response. Such remarks, plus careful, sensitive handling of Jill resulted in the latter's approaching Mrs. Jones individually for help; this in turn led to sharing significant data regarding her depression. The girls subsequently moved from this state of insecurity into a truly cohesive entity, a step which usually signals the termination of the first phase in the group's life.

An All Boys' Group

An all boys' group may discuss different issues, but is actually likely to go through the same initial struggles around trusting the adult that was characteristic of the girls' group described above.

Thus, a group of seven 13½- to 14½-year-old boys, led by a female therapist, met for a period of about two years during which time there were only two dropouts. There were five white boys (one Puerto Rican), and two Black ones. Problems for the most part related to rather serious school difficulties and some delinquency. One member seemed to be developing along homosexual lines, while another was felt to be very disturbed and possibly in need of more intensive therapy. Most of the boys were seen in some individual treatment prior to admission to the group, and a few of them continued with it during the life of the group. (As discussed in Chapter 11, the use of combined treatment is not unusual, and in fact applied to a few of the girls who attended the group described earlier.) The boys were initially very shy and awkward and not able to talk too much, needing considerable help from the group therapist to involve them. When they were able to speak, their complaints were very similar to the girls', involving hostility to teachers and school and their general feeling that "adults pick on kids and don't like children." The boys, unlike the girls, however, also went into graphic detail describing all of the mischievous adventures in and outside of the school setting, and participated in some rather dramatic physical acrobatics in the group therapy room. (We found it characteristic of adolescent boys that they used their bodies to express feelings much more so than did girls who, while restless, nevertheless tended to remain in their seats.) One youngster, when describing a serious event which almost led to his expulsion from the school, said it was important for him to talk in the group because "at least people can hear my misery." This was a youth prone to acting out and not used to articulating his feelings.

The group's early sessions were monopolized by talk of dramatic adventures, seemingly to test how the group therapist would react. They described shop classes where people cut their fingers off, and such outside behaviors as purse snatchings or truancy. They then went on to talk about girls and what they liked to do with them, but this kind of discourse did not go too far. What they found easiest to reveal was their totally negative attitude toward school. Nowhere in the early sessions of this boys' group were there really serious complaints about parents; instead, almost all of the anger was displaced onto the school setting. They seemed to admire all types of conflict and giggled as they described dramatic fights and near fights. When the group therapist asked if they could say in words what their giggling meant, they laughed more, as they were unaccustomed to using words to the extent to which adolescent girls were. It took a while for them to get down to talking openly about whether they could trust each other, something which the girls did much more quickly. But interestingly enough, after they talked about this, they seemed to move more readily into closeness, and related to one another earlier than did the girls' group.

The attendance in this particular boys' group was very good as they appeared to have "a ball" during the sessions, and following the meetings they enjoyed running down 19 flights of stairs together. They were in fact so active that the agency personnel utilizing nearby offices had to be fairly tolerant. When the boys came early they kidded around some, flirted with the secretaries, and occasionally tried to peek in to see their therapist or some other people whom they had met. They at times also followed some girls whom they had seen in the waiting room, and in general caused much more stir than did the adolescent girls' group. The boys also said quite openly that "outside teachers and counselors spoil the fun." What will the therapist do? Does she believe in fun? (With a female therapist such bragging and flirting is to be expected.)

Socially deprived youths share the psychological struggles of their more advantaged peers, but have the additional burden of their reality deprivation and of their not uncommon verbal poverty. Unused to expressions of feeling through language, these youngsters tend to resort to action, sometimes of a destructive nature. MacLennan and Felsenfeld (1968) underscored the special difficulty such teenagers have in utilizing the group initially; they find it difficult to trust, much more than the average middle–class children, and cannot readily identify with the therapist whose background is likely to be different from theirs; and they have no faith in goals for the future for they have seen little success around them. Practitioners working with these youngsters generally agree that a much longer period of testing can be expected, and that the group therapist may need to involve himself with the group in an activity or even go outside to help these youngsters individually with their pressing reality concerns.

John, age 14, fits this description. A Black boy from a broken family on welfare, John was not only beset with emotional problems that at times resembled a schizophrenic picture, but also by the reality of not having proper clothing or food, and of almost never having had stable family members within the household. His father, when he saw him, was frequently drunk. Most often, he was absent, almost never working. An older sister, who was fooling around with drugs and quite promiscuous, was threatening to leave the house. His mother was either angry and drinking, or depressed and unavailable. She alternately leaned on John and rejected him, seeing him as representative of the men who had used her.

When John came to the group he was caustic and hostile, openly suspicious, and raised questions about how the white group therapist could possibly understand him since he was Black. He wondered from the beginning about the issue of racial prejudice, and also told the adult in another session that what was on his mind was that he was poor. It appeared for a very long time that John never felt that talking would solve his reality problems, and one wondered what held him in the group altogether. It undoubtedly was the relationship which the group therapist was able to establish with him by reaching out and by consistently offering herself as a nurturing object. She would not push herself on the boy but was available for crises; was not critical of him when he described some of his semi-delinquent activities, but also did not encourage him to follow that direction; and in fact showed him new constructive possibilities for the future. It took much longer for John than his more advantaged peers to learn how to utilize the group setting. The type of activity the group therapist undertook with this boy is clearly different from the traditional psychoanalytic group psychotherapy offered to middle-class teenagers. For example, there were a number of individual contacts outside the group which were not psychotherapy per se, but rather counseling sessions to solve concrete problems which threatened to overwhelm this boy and his family. There were also many school visits and contacts, calls to the YMCA and to job placement settings, and brief "chats" in the hall several times a week as the boy turned up unexpectedly when anxiety threatened to overwhelm him or he just couldn't bear school that week.

Magary and Elder (1970), in describing a group of inner-city girls, observed that the lower-class Black girl with an absent father is unable to "play" out her conflict in the usual way. She lacks the reality of the stable masculine figure against which to correct her shifting fantasies. Unlike the middle-class girl, she cannot choose to be close to or aloof from the father — since she has no opportunity to be in contact with him at all. Achieving independence from the mother is complicated by the long overdependence on her as (frequently) the sole important adult, and also by the fact that the mother's way of life is often precisely what the adolescent consciously rejects. Therefore, there may be no adequate adult models, in contrast to the middle-class patterns of a "mother with whom I identify" in order to win "father-as-a-good husband" (p. 41). They went on to note that school achievement does not serve the same function for the lower–class Black girls because their fantasies of succeeding cannot be supported by their observation of successful people in their environment, so that under the slightest pressure these fantasies crumble and the goals are given up.

Although all adolescent groups in the beginning phase can cause the new group therapist great anxiety, it is certainly true that a group of disadvantaged youths can be even more taxing. These often hostile and suspicious teenagers may act out considerably, absent themselves for weeks on end and then turn up unexpectedly in serious trouble, requiring dramatic intervention. Once the group therapist is able to hold such a youngster in the group initially, this is likely to change; the first 10 to 15 weeks in the group's life are crucial, however, often determining the very outcome of the treatment.

Hurst and Gladieux (1980) have outlined the prerequisite characteristics of a successful leader of adolescent treatment groups. Generally speaking, the aim of group therapy with adolescents is to support the ego in its struggle to cope with instinctual pressures and external reality. Within this framework, adolescent groups have in common specific themes characterizing the beginning, middle, and end of treatment, which reflect the adolescent's own basic conflicts during these years. We have already seen how the initial struggle within the group is likely to revolve around trust of the adult and of each other. The content usually centers on the members' common hostility toward and contempt for parents, the unfairness and incompetence of school authorities, and the external, superficial facts about each of their life situations. One sees the clearly emerging dependent–independent struggle fought out at home, at school, and with the group therapist. Once this major issue of trust is resolved, the individual member invariably moves into the group, while the group as a whole moves into the middle phase within which more intensive treatment can occur.

Fried, in her article "Ego Emancipation of Adolescents Through Group Psychotherapy" (1956), suggested that behavior of the adolescent is more related to the conscious and unconscious parental demands than it is to environmental reality. She described, for example, how an unconscious need on the part of a parent to have a particular boy reject his masculine identification might result in his actually doing so, or on the contrary, in his dramatically acting out to prove he is a boy. She observed that when two parents are united in their conscious or unconscious conviction, there is even more danger that their child will respond in a pattern connected with these covert parental wishes. It was already noted how the ego in adolescence has a limited capacity for organization and integration, so that very wide fluctuations in behavior, aims, and symptoms occur. Group treatment, while temporarily heightening the adolescent's tendency toward disorganization because of the presence of multiple stimuli and varied models for identification, may at the same time force the youth to examine what *he* wants and needs, in order that his gratification will be *self-determined* rather than "a parent-servicing ego" (p. 367). For many an adolescent, emancipation can mean a frightening desertion of parents, since he lacks certainty concerning his capacity to care for himself; thus, he often is conflicted about whether he should indeed attempt to ascertain his own wishes and feelings or follow through on parental demands without thinking. The group offers the teenager a chance to consider where his feelings are taking him, and where his behavior follows environmental reality versus where it diverges. Group members often ask each other such questions as: "Why are you truanting? How did it happen that you stole that purse? You were depressed last December and this May; what do those periods have in common, if anything?" In the middle phase, with a therapeutic alliance consolidated, the therapist can encourage the members to look at these issues, and when they fail to do so, periodically suggest that there's something going on within the group or within a particular member which is causing resistance. The group therapist can also explore more directly with any particular member the basis of some of the behavioral manifestations, either within the group or without.

An example of the middle phase of treatment in an all girls' group follows.

Middle Phase of an All Girls' Group

Margie, a 15-year-old in a group of five teenage girls, had been consistently failing since junior high school, and was involved in a chronic battle with her mother around this poor academic performance. She had been in this group just a few weeks when she came in one week reporting a grade of 85% on an examination. She then stated that her mother still was not satisfied and had not lifted any of the unfair restrictions imposed previously as a punishment for the girl's failure. Barbara and Lois picked up on this immediately and told Margie that she had done quite well and that she should be proud of herself. They were at the same time very sympathetic with her plight, as far as the maternal restrictions were concerned, and both indicated that Margie could do something about them. They thought that, above all, she shouldn't mess herself up in school, and that she could win her mother over eventually. They proceeded to list some ways whereby she might not antagonize her mother and still win out in the end. Lois, 17, said that her mother had been just as restrictive in the past, which seemed to make Margie feel much better.

On another occasion, this particular group was discussing "teenage rebellion" in a very intellectual fashion, all agreeing that it was normal, but not always necessary. One of the girls remarked that "some rebellion is silly—you should get educated." The two underachievers of the group exchanged glances and Margie remarked that she "was very hung up on this in the past year," but she was beginning to feel better. The group therapist noticed that Margie's tone of voice, usually very hostile when talking about her mother, was now calm. In another session, Barbara, 17, who was having a hard time separating from her mother, turned to the group therapist and asked her if she thought a child should stand up for her views or go along with her parent. When the adult threw this question back to the group, Lois remarked that she didn't have the strength to stand up to anything since she couldn't get along with her mother. Although nobody picked it up in this session, weeks later Barbara pointed out how competent Lois was, and that there was a consistent interest in the independent activities which the latter had demonstrated. She was given great credit when she was able to travel to the group by herself, something which had not been possible earlier in the year. Similarly, when the issue of independence was examined in relation to the question of job hunting, Margie, listening to Barbara's joking about her interest in taking a summer job in the country, remarked on the girl's anxiety about this, saying, "You were certainly scared of a job." This took the girls into a discussion about work, how one approaches it, and what people are worried about. While they kidded a lot, they were ultimately quite supportive and encouraging of each other, offering the suggestion that "when you earn your own money you're more your own person." One participant, who had been working for some time, shared a number of her positive experiences and recalled her own initial anxiety, noting that this was something everyone goes through and gets over. Later on within this group there was also an increasing ability to share important feelings. Thus, Barbara started a session by telling the girls that she had been extremely depressed after seeing her former boyfriend at a party the previous weekend. The boy had suddenly "dropped her" during the summer, and she had never really gotten over this or, in fact, the unexpected earlier divorce of her parents. The girls were extremely sympathetic, understanding why she would feel this bad, and then they began to ask some questions. The group therapist picked up on what Barbara said and remarked on her affect, suggesting that seeing the boy in a party situation and recalling all that had occurred was a serious blow to her self–esteem. Lois remarked on the inevitability of changing patterns of relationships in adolescence, and went on to describe her own severe depression the previous December, after she had broken up with her boyfriend. The girls moved from this subject to a discussion of their parents' relationships, especially those which were either unstable or had actually ended in divorce. They spoke about how their experiences of being left by adults often made them feel that there was something wrong with them. They considered whether their depressed moods meant they were crazy, but immediately reassured themselves, saying all teenagers get depressed and "kooky," and that they had good reason to feel sad sometimes. Although Barbara in particular reported that after "opening up" (telling the girls about how depressed she was), she had felt quite sad in the group, in later sessions she noted that she didn't quite feel the same about the experience and was not as depressed. We subsequently saw Barbara gradually move into activities which she had previously avoided, such as joining a sorority at school and attending dances on the outside as well. Her breaking the silence about a subject as frightening as depression, resulted in the other girls being able to grapple with the question of whether there was a hereditary predisposition to messing up one's relationships. Several members jokingly suggested that prostitution or out-of-wedlock relationships might be a better way to deal with men and sex, both subjects having been avoided in the early phase of the group.

In this second phase of the group's life, the girls tended to select seats, and to keep them; they came regularly and were furious when one of them cancelled for a minor reason; they were quick to respond to each other's feelings, and were capable of exploring problems and confronting a peer with her avoidance. Some of them even began to criticize the group therapist. There was a new feeling of solidarity here, which one could sense immediately upon entering the room. Individuals offered ready advice and seemed to feel a responsibility for each other's progress, an attitude which greatly influenced the group members' behavior. We also noted that verbal interventions were now generally more sensitive, well-timed and astute, and often dealt with self-defeating behavior either within or outside the group. At times, they were terribly moralistic, in fact, more demanding in their expectations than any adults.

In a mixed group (boys and girls), an additional issue is likely to emerge in this middle phase following the initial period of discomfort. It refers to the considerable flirting aimed at asserting sexual adequacy which not infrequently can lead to some dating of members outside of the group.

Although it is true that there is a significant lessening of kidding around in the middle phase of treatment, one does nevertheless see in almost every session short periods of chatter, giggling, or intellectual conversation interspersed with the work. The group therapist must have some tolerance for such recouping efforts which the chatter or discussion of world affairs represents. If, however, the main work of therapy is truly thwarted, the source of resistance must identified. For instance, the girls' group described above had to be transferred to a different therapist after about 15 sessions, due to the first therapist's leaving the agency. For months afterward, there were periods of depressed silence, interspersed with irrelevant chatter. Then, once the group was solidly reestablished but preparing for the summer break, the old pattern reappeared. When the group therapist questioned the basis of the blocking, one girl remarked that she felt sad that the group was going to break up for the summer. This eventually enabled other girls to voice what seemed to be a common fear: would the second group therapist also leave them? Any feelings such as these, are bound to lead to blocking.

Conjoint Individual Therapy

Individual sessions with group members are used selectively by most group therapists, but as discussed in Chapter 11, there is a wide diversity of opinion here. Some therapists always do combined individual and group psychotherapy, while others prefer using the group as a primary treatment modality.

Lois, a member of the second adolescent girls' group described above, was seen in combined individual and group treatment. The decision was made to offer her simultaneous individual treatment after a year within the group. Prior to this she had declined further individual contact after having had three sessions in preparation for entrance into the group. She was very tied to her mother and

seemed fearful that individual therapy would threaten this relationship. When Lois again became depressed and fearful that her
mother's second marriage might break up, she reached out to the
group therapist and requested individual sessions. She continued
to utilize the group effectively but needed much more at this particularly critical time, and recognized by herself that she was going to
have to work intensively on her fear about separating from her
mother. While the acute awareness of her core conflict added
markedly to the level of her anxiety and depression, it also made it
possible for her to recognize her need for the additional help.

Another girl in the group described above, Barbara, was also
offered individual treatment when it became clear that she was suffering from periodic depressions. Her work in school was suffering and
her outside relationships were very poor, but Barbara was extremely
reluctant to be more closely involved with the group therapist,
especially since she had been very attached to the first therapist who
had left her. It was only after a year and some months of group treatment with the second therapist, that Barbara was willing to enter into
a simultaneous time–limited and focused individual contact.

There are occasions, such as summer breaks or personal crises,
when these youths must be offered something supplemental to the
group. (This may be particularly true in once–a–week group psychotherapy.) By contrast, as in the case of Lisa, who had been seen
for two–and–one–half years in intensive individual treatment prior
to admission to the group, one aim of the group therapist was to utilize this experience to help the girl relinquish her need for individual
therapy. Since the group treatment was felt to be a crucial part of the
termination process, no individual appointments were offered Lisa
on a regular basis after the first few group therapy sessions; but when
she occasionally requested them, they were granted.

Termination of the Therapy Group

The final period of an adolescent therapy group tends to focus
on the working through of the sexual identification process. In the

girls' group there was great interest in relationships with boys, and a moving away from the special connection to father and hostility to mother characteristic of the earlier period. While the interest in the father was still there, as is love for him where he exists as a nurturing figure, the extrafamilial heterosexual object was firmly the choice at this point. In the last phase, girls and boys are apt to bring in vivid descriptions of their outside heterosexual relationships, and in mixed groups we also see use of one another to test out their facility in dealing with the opposite sex. Some of their fantasies about the opposite sex, including their fears, are aired, and the group is again used supportively to test out reality as far as sexuality is concerned. Although there is occasional acknowledged sexual experimentation within the group, members often encourage each other to avoid actual intercourse, pointing out the possible complications, i.e., pregnancy, depression, guilt.

The treatment group, in effect, is a substitute family enabling the members to utilize it as a transitional support while separation from the primary parental objects takes place, and to test themselves in a small, protected setting before venturing forth to a world outside. We understandably found that each member at times reacts to other group members and to the group therapist in part as he did to his own family. As a group member's perception of his reality is altered by his own growth and by others' observations and challenges, we would expect him to perceive the group members and the group therapist more as each really is. Slavson (1950) delineated this dissolution of the transference as the ultimate task in the life of the group.

Needless to say, as in all groups, the termination process also entails feelings of mourning and loss, including even short-lived relapses in behavior, which have to be understood and mastered.

Para-Therapeutic Groups for Adolescents

Traditional psychoanalytic group psychotherapeutic techniques must be altered in treating adolescent delinquents and addicts. Some of these groups are held in closed settings, such as hospitals, prisons or reform schools, and are not totally "voluntary," while others are taking place in environments not considered clinical in nature. These youngsters have something special in common which separates them from the professional group therapist and brings them into closer relationship with their peers. For this reason, addicts' groups, for example, often employ a former addict as leader, with the co-leader or consultant being a trained group therapist. This is due, in part at least, to the addicts' tendency to trick the unsophisticated professional who is not part of the addicts' world, into believing he is off drugs. Underlying this, too, must be the fact that the group therapist often has considerable anxiety about working with such clients, and may, on another level, be fascinated by drugs himself so that he could either unconsciously stimulate the use of drugs, or, as a reaction formation, act restrictively and critically with group members. Because of the special difficulty inherent in leading such a group, co-therapists are frequently utilized. (While there are many problems inherent in the co-therapy situation, as noted by Davis and Lohr [1971], including the very real issue of staff shortages, with this type of group there may be good reason to seriously consider such an approach.)

Groups for addicts and for seriously delinquent youths were initially utilized after fairly conclusive evidence showed that individual therapy was generally unsuccessful. Several short-term groups were offered institutionalized delinquents, often aimed at facilitating adjustment to the institution and motivating the boys for further (individual) therapy. Feder (1962) noted that both these aims were served. In the long-term treatment models, Epstein and Slavson (1962) and Schulman (1957) remarked on the necessity of altering techniques during the beginning phase of the group. This is primarily due to the absence of basic trust which the severe non-neurotic delinquent brings to the group experience. Schulman (1957) described the delinquent as grossly intolerant of anxiety, impulse-ridden, externalizing his conflicts often via physical aggressiveness, and as having considerable impairment in time perspective (so that past and future are meaningless — only the present counts). He further stated that group sessions with delinquents must be structured, or the group will indefinitely remain focused on sexual and aggressive activity and frequently scapegoat the therapist; on the other hand, the latter cannot be too powerful or even ask group members to confront each other — for they will view this as an attack. Instead, Schulman suggested that the group therapist point out how their silence is not helpful to their own aims, i.e., leaving the institution. He defined his ultimate therapeutic goal as character synthesis, not analysis. Epstein and Slavson (1962) described their first several months with a boys' group in a residential treatment center as similarly characterized by distrust, much physical movement (in and out of the group), and boasting of sexual and aggressive exploits. It appeared to be essential here that the group therapist be cued in to the boys' interests so that he could capitalize on some random comment made by one of them and get the rest of the boys curious. This particular group was ultimately able to progress in a more traditional fashion, but most of the groups reported in the literature have emphasized the long-term need for more controls and for special environmental manipulation, including the giving of food and presents. All have stressed the importance of attempting to help these boys become connected with their feelings insofar as they pertain to the need to continue delinquent behavior.

Blos (1961) saw treatment of the delinquent as aiming to transform the delinquency into a neurotic symptom, which can then be dealt with traditionally. Viewing delinquency as a symptom of ego pathology, Blos described the delinquent as suffering from a lack of basic trust, probably connected with his early sadomasochistic power struggles with the mother. In this configuration the delinquent fails to master his environment, and instead settles for control whereby the fantasied position of infantile omnipotence is maintained and the underlying feelings of helplessness and of dependency are very great. All conflict is externalized. In girls, this generally takes the form of sexual delinquency and/or drug addiction. Blos viewed female delinquency as often connected with one of two issues: intense clinging to the preoedipal mother, or, in the more mature girl (who does have a foothold on the oedipal level) an inability to give up the oedipal struggle; here, the delinquency is actually a continuous revenge on the mother. In both cases, a pseudo–heterosexuality may exist, but the preoedipal connection still strongly underlies it. In the boy, there usually is a continuation of intense castration anxiety, which may lead to considerable acting out in order to cope with the constant fear of damage.

The addicted young person appears to be seeking direct gratification of his oral needs; these have either never been adequately met, were prematurely disturbed or overly indulged, thereby providing the ego with little help in developing the capacity to tolerate tension. Very frequently a strong homosexual underpinning is seen in addicted young men, which they are fighting off by excessive heterosexual behavior, bragging, and other delinquency. Thus, these young men and women need the group milieu to offer the nurturance and support toward healthier adaptive patterns, before they can begin to tolerate the tension connected with relinquishing their behavior. This group experience would aim at enabling the young delinquent or addict to perceive reality differently from his usual perception of the environment as a hostile, ungiving, dangerous place, existing only for him to take advantage of and to desert.

FUTURE DEVELOPMENTS

Experience has shown the therapeutic group to be exceptionally promising for the treatment of children and adolescents. This fact, plus the tremendous upsurge in interest in all types of group approaches, has resulted in more professionals being trained to do group therapy, which ultimately will mean many more adolescent group programs. Whether true therapy groups for children will prosper as well remains an open question. In addition to the most common single–gender adolescent group, we anticipate an increase in mixed groups, since the few studies reported in the literature have not borne out the widely held concern that boys and girls together in a group invariably are stimulated to act out sexually (Ackerman, 1957; Kraft, 1968).

In addition to the long–term, intensive group treatment models described in this chapter, we expect to see many more short–term groups offered to persons who might benefit from a combined therapeutic–educative approach. One such short–term model is the multiple family group, a relatively new technique which combines theoretical concepts developed within the family therapy field with those of traditional group therapy. Kimbro, Jr. et al (1967) found that such a group was able to move, within 12 sessions, to examine destructive patterns of each family's interaction as well as to discuss the more universal intergenerational anxieties. The advantage of the multiple family group may lie in the greater likelihood of nonfamily members to cut through another family's strongly held defensive system. This technique does not pretend to replace separate therapy plans for individual family members where needed, but may loosen some destructive patterns and increase communication within the family. It is of paramount importance to evaluate these newer short–term methods in the face of the staggering need for mental health services and insufficient resources and staff to meet this need.

Part IV

Group Treatment of Adults

Introduction

The next section, Part IV of this book, contains two lengthy chapters on aspects of group psychotherapy with adults. The first, Chapter 10, depicts the course of treatment of a group of disadvantaged women with severe character disorders over a span of about 200 sessions. Since this work transpired about 25 years ago, it constitutes an interesting precursor of the field's contemporary preoccupation with the treatment of patients with primitive character pathology (Kernberg, 1980; Kohut, 1977).

In this connection, the reader might find it intriguing to compare the material in this chapter with Pine's (1980) recent summary of the following problems inherent in work with borderline patients: (1) Because of developmental arrests, such patients seek to merge with the therapist, with fellow patients, or with the group–as–a–whole. (2) People outside the group are perceived as "need-unsatisfying objects." (3) Marked fluctuations in mood, attitudes, and relationships are expected. (4) Ego states are not integrated, with a deficient observing ego standing out. (5) Due to faulty reality testing, stressful events and fantasies provoke regressive crises with periods of desperation and annihilation. (6) Because interpretations may fail to take hold, the therapeutic relationship must be specially maintained. (7) Treatment will be long and full of traumas. And (8) the therapist must not expect caring from the patients.

The three overlapping treatment phases in the women's group described here, i.e., ego strengthening, ego repair and integration, contain all of the above therapeutic challenges. What stands out especially is the crucial role of the fantasied "mother–group" as an ever–present source of support (see also Chapter 4 of this volume). In fact, contrary to the therapists' expectations, the heightened

189

anxiety occasioned by a projected change of group therapists, emerged as having been anchored in a fear of losing the group entity rather than the group therapist. The gratifying improvement in these women's ego functioning, brought about primarily through the last two phases (150 sessions) of exclusive group psychotherapy, is worth noting.

Chapter 11 constitutes an updated overview of the controversial issue of combined individual and group psychotherapy for adult patients. (The last such overview — Bieber, 1971 — had appeared a decade ago.) It is noteworthy that despite the actual widespread utilization of such combined psychotherapy by private practitioners, major authorities in the field continued to urge the sole reliance on group psychotherapy (Foulkes and Anthony, 1964; Ezriel, 1950; Yalom, 1970). Following a review of the literature, this chapter outlines the major assumed therapeutic factors in analytic group psychotherapy, including the planned, differential use of the two modalities by the therapist. A discussion of the clinical indications and contraindications for the use of combined and conjoint individual and group psychotherapy is followed by representative patient vignettes.

Chapter 10

GROUP THERAPY OF WOMEN WITH SEVERE CHARACTER DISORDERS IN A FAMILY SERVICE AGENCY

The special difficulties presented by adult clients with severe character disturbances are well known. These difficulties have been spelled out by workers concerned with so-called "multiproblem" or "hard-to-reach" families — families known to be breeding grounds for major social ills such as juvenile delinquency (Berman, 1959) and drug addiction. Kernberg (1976) has written about this subject more recently.

This chapter depicts the treatment process in a family service agency of an experimental group of eight Black women, each with three or more children. Diagnosed as having character disorders with early fixation levels, all of the women presented especially marked dependency problems. With but one exception they had had, prior to the commencement of group therapy, lengthy periods of individual treatment. For the most part, however, little significant change had occurred in their attitudes or functioning. While simultaneous individual contact with separate workers continued during the group's first phase (59 sessions), the final phase (sessions 50-205) was comprised of group therapy only.

Reprinted, in part, from *American Journal of Orthopsychiatry,* 31:776-785, 1961, by permission of the American Orthopsychiatric Association, Inc., and from *International Journal of Group Psychotherapy,* 16:174-189, 1966, by permission. The co-authors (of separate parts of the chapter) are Marjorie Pyrke and Marjorie A. Holden.

NATURE OF THE PROBLEMS

In assessing these women's common characteristics, it is note-worthy that all of them had experienced similar early deprivations. There was not a single instance of a gratifying child–mother relationship in their pasts. In three cases the father was also absent. Where fathers were present, they were overshadowed by depriving, narcissistic mothers. With such early traumatizations went marked ego pathology (Bellak, Hurwich, and Gediman, 1973). Thus, there were poor object relationships, and difficulties in impulse control and reality testing. These clients all suffered from feelings of worthlessness with underlying depression, and attempted to deal with their deep dependency needs by overeating and having a magical preoccupation with food. Narcissistic and self-absorbed, they engaged in repetitive, self-defeating behavior.

The initial treatment task was essentially one of ego strengthening. It was necessary, in this connection, to establish a therapeutic climate which would enable these women to shed some of their tenacious defensive maneuvers; to permit themselves to express and perceive their intense feelings; and, above all, to open a pathway for meaningful interpersonal relationships.

THE GROUP APPROACH

As the therapist followed the earliest group sessions it became increasingly clear that the usual group therapy techniques appropriate for less disturbed personalities would not be effective with these women. To meet their unique needs the therapist had to become active from the very beginning — she had to talk, intercede during silences, write individualized letters, and even telephone those who had been absent for a few consecutive meetings. In addition, the serving of coffee and cookies was introduced. The women repeatedly confirmed the impression that these activities were perceived by them as demonstrations that the therapist really cared, that she was a feeding and nurturing kind of person. One of them even confessed that she had stayed away from some sessions on purpose, so that she would get the therapist's letters. These stated that she had been missed — and "it was so nice to be missed."

During the sessions proper, the therapist would make frequent comments to break anxious silences or to demonstrate interest — for inactivity on her part seemed equated with not caring. This was particularly important in helping the more depressed and withdrawn members to feel involved. As the individuals became strengthened and the group-as-a-whole became more cohesive, such supportive comments were gradually supplanted by confrontations aimed at the recognition and tolerance of feelings.

Individual therapists have reported on the problem of irregularity of interviews with clients with character disorders (Reiner and Kaufman, 1959). Our experience was similar. For the first six months, the women were irresponsible about attending. They never phoned to explain an absence, nor did they give a reason upon returning to the group, unless specifically asked. It was amazing that at the same time they could talk of liking the meetings and even be overjoyed when there was a "full house" — that is, everyone present. When the therapist asked about enlarging the membership they agreed, so that "there will always be someone here to talk to when we come." Their reasons for absences, unlike those of neurotic clients, rarely appeared to be related directly to group developments. Instead they tended to coincide with recurring feelings of depression or exhaustion, or were tied up with conflicts at home. While characteristically late, they never wanted the meetings to end. After a session they were often noted to linger as a group in front of the building for as long as an hour!

Most striking at the outset was the relative ease with which these women were able to express their feelings. It was as though the fears of self-revelation and of verbalizing feelings, so characteristic of such clients in an individual relationship, were greatly diminished from the very start. Certainly there was also much watchfulness, isolation, and withdrawal. In their egocentricity, for a period of months, they could not even remember each other's names, referring to one another in such terms as "the lady with the five children" or "the woman that got deserted." With all this, however, feelings of intense hurt, of anger and rebellion, were blurted out. These were counterbalanced by "magical" visions of a better future and a rejuvenation. Furthermore, from the very beginning each woman, no matter how self-preoccupied or weak, listened to the others and offered support and concern. It was almost standard procedure for this group to give the floor to the individual who was most upset on the particular evening. Only after she had described her problems and expressed her feelings did the others come in with their reactions, ideas, and above all, with their sympathy. A surprising kind of tenderness toward one another emerged repeatedly, even at points where the context was one of rage or contempt toward people outside who had been hurting them. No matter how emotionally burdened themselves, there always seemed room for some empathic concern for another member (see Chapter 3 on the concept of empathy).

They were elated over the coffee and cookies served by the therapist, and said repeatedly that the coffee was the best they had ever tasted. Those with insomnia even found that it did not keep them awake. It was not until the 42nd session, at which point reality concerns were in ascendancy, that someone inquired about the brand of coffee used and was astounded to learn that it was the same brand she had been using in her own home.

There were other, more directly phrased, positive expressions about the meaning the group held for them. Considering their deep fears of relating, these were rather significant. The most common feeling was that one's own problems loomed less large when measured against those of others.

> Mrs. Davis spoke of gaining a new perspective through the group discussions; Mrs. Atkins said that she couldn't stay away because she was afraid of missing something. If people wanted to know how she felt about these meetings, the frequently depressed Mrs. Thomson exclaimed, "I jump over chairs to get here." Mrs. Burke talked of a "dizzy feeling at nine o'clock," when she stayed away from a session. In addition she claimed that the therapist's phoning her one

time prior to a meeting had saved her from "disaster," as she had been planning to resign. As if wanting to perpetuate the group experience, there was wishful talk at this same session of their all going together to the agency's summer camp. The enhanced group cohesiveness was also exemplified by a more responsible attitude toward attendance.

EARLY GROUP THEMES

The first few sessions contained outbursts of anger and feelings of contempt toward the husbands, with emphasis on the latter's irresponsible, pleasure-seeking behavior. In these women's search for vengeance there was an angry suggestion that the agency set up a group for men; this group was to be different from theirs—"a lecture group," which would tell the men what their responsibilities were! As for children, there were complaints about their being overdemanding, with teenagers in particular showing no appreciation or gratitude for a mother's heavy task. While underlying feelings of deprivation and of ungratified dependency needs were being verbalized, these were not recognized or felt as such. Their troubles were due to others—husbands, children, outside agencies. There was an almost paranoid tinge to their feeling disadvantaged and tied down. Simultaneous with these angry, demanding complaints went magical expectations for a better future. In this connection there was an unmistakable oral quality about the search for inspiration, for remedies and a single formula to solve the most complex problems. Their hopes centered at times on some miraculous intervention in their lives. Some thought that just by joining this group and getting out of their homes they would become more sociable and lose their depression. The group sessions became their "night out"; they spoke of each other as "the girls," and pondered how to develop "trim girlish figures" by sticking to a diet. A single piece of advice from the therapist or another member was sought like a "prescription."

All placed great faith in the value of food as a corrective for unhappiness, in some cases even as a cure for chronic physical ailments.

> Mrs. Atkins described how she cured her uncle's rheumatism by feeding him things behind his back. She used powdered liver and "Tiger Milk," a brew she made from yeast and pineapple juice. Mrs. Thomson offered here that she mixed kelp and bone marrow, adding fruit juice for taste. Mrs. Atkins thought that a foot cramp could be due to diet and recommended a special book for it. Through its help she cured herself of warts, and her husband, of falling hair.
>
> In a subsequent session, another woman gravely promoted a combined *anal* and *oral* prescription known as "cleaning out the pipe line." This diet cured colds and relieved depressions. Following a day of drinking only salt water — "to clean out the system" — she took quantities of orange juice to build the system up again. More realistically she confessed sadly that while such a regimen, or the overeating of sweets, might "soothe" her, it did not take away her unhappy moods. The group members who had a better reality orientation would invariably raise questions, or modify such extreme, fantasied notions. At a later point the therapist assumed a similar function.

Gradually, from rages at burdensome children and husbands, there was a shift toward compassion and toward some pleasure in responsibility. While husbands remained targets, there were reluctant admissions that they were rather good with the youngsters. This was, however, because men were so childish themselves. By virtue of bearing children, women were seen as possessing superior understanding of them. This led to a recognition, fostered by the therapist, that children had feelings. While they could not focus on their own needs and feelings, there was an obvious vicarious gratification and even flashes of self-understanding through the sensitive discussions of the needs and feelings of the young.

By identifying with their children they came to acknowledge that children need two parents. Thus, the recognition of the importance of feelings in children led to a modification of the rigid attitudes toward men. They now tried to figure out what made their husbands so childlike. The consensus was that being spoiled by possessive, overprotective mothers made them dependent, "rotten" husbands. While such a conclusion undoubtedly reflected these women's pathological perceptions of the maternal figure, it must also be noted that the husbands of most of them were in reality rather immature.

Through such discussions of children's early need for love, some of the women's own feelings about caring occasionally broke through the group's defensive wall. In small dosages, some personal feelings or "secrets" came to be acknowledged—usually with the accompanying defenses of denial, projection, and isolation held in readiness.

> Mrs. Burke could not quite understand how Mrs. Atkins could say that she "needed no love"; everyone needs to have a feeling of "being cared for." Mrs. Thomson said she couldn't get on at all unless she felt wanted. Mrs. Atkins repeated that she had given up caring; if she were to care she would feel she was just "floating in space." Yes, she cares about her children—that is her life. Pressed by Mrs. Burke, that one can't care for children as for a husband, Mrs. Atkins replied that she didn't remember about sex. It was no longer a part of her feelings. (Mrs. Atkins after many months revealed to the group that she had had no sex life with her husband for years. This "secret" had been covered up until then by a fantastic story of a wonderful contraceptive in her possession. Doctors had even taken it off the market because it was so foolproof.)

At this stage of the group's development there were even occasional excursions into the past, with attempts to tie such recollections up with current problems. This was illustrated by the following excerpt from a session:

> There was a silence after a discussion about children's feelings. Therapist: "Feeling kind of stuck?" There was further quiet and then Mrs. Atkins spoke up: "I'm not stuck, I'm thinking. I'm not here, I'm way, way back. I'm reliving seven to eight. I'm feeling like it was then." Mrs. Thomson: "The same thing is happening to me. Sometimes when I do not speak here, somebody has said something that reminds me of myself when I was little. I am thinking of how hushed I was, never speaking up."

Among other vividly recalled experiences have been those of childbirth. Here, the women could reveal such fears as complete loss of control, of death through pain, and even fantasies of damag-

ing the child during birth. Ambivalence toward having children
emerged together with confessions of attempted abortions. Their
major way of dealing with hateful feelings toward children was to
incorporate them psychologically — "the child is a part of you —
your own flesh and blood."

By the 50th session, which marks the end of the group's first
phase, these initially passive and suspicious women became out-
going and talkative. They were now remarkably free to express
feelings, and even to make direct demands of the therapist. What
they earlier regarded as impersonal stories from their fellow members, turned into definite themes and specific people. In addition,
the awareness of a connection between their current problems and
the childhood experiences with their mothers had been close to the
surface. The sessions became replete with mimicking or drama-
tizing for emphasis, and ready use of slang. The women sometimes
became hysterical with laughter, the latter being occasionally an
expression of elation, more often a cover-up of underlying sadness
and despair.

THE MIDDLE PHASE

During the middle phase, which began with the 51st session,
three of the original eight group members had dropped out due to
various reality reasons. With the remaining five, all individual
contact was discontinued, and group therapy became the only
treatment modality.

The major treatment task now centered on *ego repair* via an
enhanced sense of identity and awareness of self and others. During this phase, through the initiative of the group therapist, feelings
were no longer merely released and tolerated but were looked at
and examined. The tensions inherent in such an attempt, at facing
the feelings they had heretofore avoided, were made tolerable by
the group members' enhanced personal strength and by their trust
in the therapist. Of even greater potency in this connection was the
continued, unusually strong attachment to the group. As will be

developed at a later point, this group bond now appeared to include many realistic elements in addition to the primitive identifications to which it was anchored in the beginning stages of treatment.

Initially, in the course of this middle treatment phase, no new themes emerged. The women still talked about their children, about food, and about physical ailments. What stood out, however, was that these same subjects were now handled in a different manner. The theme of food serves as a good illustration since it was so very much a part of these deprived women's core problems. During the first treatment phase, which covered 50 sessions, orality was not only an omnipresent concern but also included these women's earnest belief that food was a cure for unhappiness and even for disease. In contrast, at this stage of the group experience, the coffee and cookies provided by the therapist seemed to lose their fantasied symbolic qualities. In fact, in their quest for more attractive, slimmer figures, the women had asked that the cookies be replaced with celery and carrot sticks. Furthermore, when Mrs. Thomson, the most oral of the group members, introduced the problem of diet and her love for candy, this was approached in a thoughtful and objective way by the others.

> Mrs. Thomson wailed, "But eating candy has such a soothing effect. How am I ever going to give it up?" The therapist interjected: "Let's understand this. What is so soothing?" Mrs. Olson blurted out: "Almost like you would soothe a baby." This led to a discussion of how childish oral desires persisted in adulthood. Mrs. Atkins brought up her efforts at reducing her smoking with the ultimate goal of giving it up entirely.

Along with beginning attempts to grasp cause and effect in behavior, the issues of values also emerged. At times this was stimulated by the therapist's conscious focusing on the women's goals for their children and for themselves. The perspectives of the past and of the future were part of these discussions. Not infrequently, universalizing about human emotional responses or about accepted principles of child–rearing led to a consideration of personal and societal values. Gradual changes of attitudes and incorporation of new values were a major part of this treatment phase. In this process of what could be termed "identity–building" (Erikson, 1959), the cognitive and experiential aspects were not readily distinguishable.

The forward movement of the group was brought to a standstill, if not reversed, by the necessity of a change in therapists. The group was prepared for this during session 76; the new therapist was introduced and sat in on the latter part of the meeting. At the subsequent session, the first with the new group therapist, not one of the women appeared! Considering that the attendance had consistently been above average, and that the need for changing therapists had been aired in advance for at least six sessions, this reaction highlighted these clients' extreme vulnerability to separation and object loss. The dread of being abandoned again, as they had been in childhood, was so pervasive that they could not face a full discussion of it. No matter how the therapist tried, this theme could be tackled by them only indirectly, for instance, via talking about Mrs. Thomson's problem with her son moving out of the home without prior notice. (It is noteworthy that more than two years later, when the group was to end, a similarly intense reaction to the theme of object loss was evoked. At that point, however, as will be seen later, these feelings were aired and handled in a more realistic manner.)

The setback due to the change of workers was of short duration. Within a month from the time of the new therapist's arrival, the group was back on its forward path. Considerable time was now spent on trying to distinguish between the frustrations and anger appropriate to their hard realities and the many "worn" feelings from the past which, like old clothing, were no longer appropriate to current circumstances. The magical air of hopefulness characteristic of the group's initial phase had given way to painful assessment of their reality circumstances. Mrs. Atkins, who had finally earned a practical nurse's diploma against almost insuperable odds, could not secure a good position; racial prejudice was at least partly responsible. Mrs. Dayton, who had taken her immature husband back, following his promise that he would reform, found him again having affairs with other women. Mrs. Thomson discovered her oldest son smoking marijuana; she did not know how to handle this with him lest he revolt and leave the home. After years of denial and suppression, Mrs. Atkins "told all" about her husband's homosexuality and increasing personality deterioration.

Open and realistic discussion of feelings was gradually replacing the earlier, deeply ingrained patterns of relying almost exclusively on defensive denial, projection, and isolation. In this connection, Mrs. Atkins, who had previously also withheld the tragic story of her marriage from her grown children, revealed spontaneously "how much the air was cleared" when she was able to talk openly with her teenaged daughter about her father's homosexuality. It turned out that the girl had known about this for some time.

As the women began to deal with their underlying concerns as well as with their frustrating life circumstances, appropriate anxiety and depressive reactions came to the fore. Instead of running away from these feelings or resorting to magic, they now tried to understand and master them. Thus, Mrs. Olson, on her own, related her depression to anger with her husband and with herself for "having been such a fool." She described how these feelings tended to immobilize her and interfere with clear thinking and acting. She credited the group with making it possible for her to approach these situations differently from the way she had in the past.

Session 92 was a high point in the women's efforts to supplant their earlier defensive maneuvers with a genuine search for understanding of their underlying motivations. At the end of this session they seemed surprised to realize that it was possible for part of one's self to retain enough objectivity and detachment to observe the experiencing, subjective part.

It would be misleading not to keep in mind that introspective deliberations of this nature had to give way frequently to emotional upsets brought on by the many realistic crises in these women's lives. Much time was accordingly spent in trying to find ways of dealing with these crises before the work of uncovering and self–

understanding could be resumed. Even so, not all of them were able to maintain the pace. For example, after a particularly meaningful session, Mrs. Thomson reacted violently to what she had felt to be an intentional slight by the others: when they were making plans to go for coffee after the meeting, her name was not called specifically. She left angrily, deciding not to return to the group. When she came back with the encouragement of the therapist, this incident was used to generalize about her patterns on the outside, where she also was overly prone to see rejection where none was intended.

As might be expected, incidents with children were repeatedly brought up for group consideration. In this phase there was a minimum of complaining or of advice–giving. Children's needs were kept in the foreground, but the discussions inevitably led to the women's own feelings when they were young. Connections between their parents' behavior and their own current attitudes were sought.

Confrontations and clarifications were most effective when offered by other group members. For example, when Mrs. Thomson described an interchange between herself and her son, most of the women detected the resentment in her voice. She had heretofore not been aware of her suppressed anger, which she later explained was due to her son's failure to pay for his maintenance. This led to a consideration of Mrs. Thomson's most thorny problem, her treatment of her two older sons as children, when in actuality they were grown men. When Mrs. Thomson fell into a stance of helpless dependency, asking what exactly she should say to her son, a touching development occurred. Mrs. Atkins and Mrs. Olson proceeded in all seriousness to stage a dramatic interchange between a mother and her grown son. In the midst of all this, Mrs. Thomson interrupted with an anxious laugh, saying that Mrs. Olson sounded exactly like her son Joshua. This spontaneous use of role–playing in the group is of particular interest in view of the strong advocacy of this technique by Riessman et al. (1964) as being especially useful with socially disadvantaged clients who are devoid of social skills.

During this phase, humor was utilized with great frequency. As a rule, this was to ease the pain and anxiety evoked by enhanced self-awareness. General laughter with vigorous nodding followed the discovery that it was easier to perceive undesirable patterns in the other person than in oneself. This had been stimulated by Mrs. Atkins' difficulty in acknowledging her resentment over her daughter's having a steady boyfriend.

Elements of uncovering as well as of "working through" were repeatedly in evidence, especially during the latter part of this treatment phase. Talking about outside events gave way to increasing preoccupation with their developing personalities. The group therapist utilized every opportunity to help each woman evolve a coherent image of herself, an ego identity anchored in a past and moving toward a meaningful future. The women now talked less of coming to their "club" and more about needing and wanting treatment. They were alert to the therapist's interventions, as when Mrs. Olson remarked about the therapist's questions as "helping us to think about what is under the surface." This led to a thoughtful consideration of the use they were making of their physical complaints and of their depressions. One woman blurted out: "You know, I think I do everything possible to hold on to this instrument of depression. I don't know what I'd do if somebody really loved me. It is easier to have self-pity and moan nobody loves you, nobody cares. Sure, sometimes I get exuberant for a while, but it does not last very long because I think 'My God, what's going to happen?'"

Near the end of the middle phase, which encompassed roughly 100 sessions, there were umistakable signs of healthier attitudes and of improved ego functioning in all of the women. A new sense of self-confidence and inner strength was evident in Mrs. Atkins' reply to Mrs. Thomson's remark that she didn't have the strength of a man to also be a father to her children: "Look, don't keep saying that; you've got a different kind of strength. You have to stand on your own two feet, and it is not a matter of being a man or a woman or a mother or a father. You've got a job to do and that is what you have to do." Mrs. Atkins was not giving an inspirational talk. She had in fact managed in the course of the group experience to secure permanent work as a practical nurse, to separate from her psychotic husband, to send her daughter to college, and even to think of buying a little house, away from her slum neighborhood. As for Mrs. Olson, after repeated earlier trials, she succeeded in finally separating from her childish, unreliable husband; her functioning as a mother and at work was greatly improved. Mrs. Ramos learned to function more independently of her husband and of her children. After years of fearful hesitation and of resistance, Mrs. Thomson was finally able to move to a new apartment, to the delight of the others.

The new look of this group was dramatically illustrated when Mrs. Burke, a former member who had had to drop out after the 50th session, returned for a visit, 18 months later. At first they all reminisced about the olden times in a superficial, casual tone. However, when they began to bring Mrs. Burke up-to-date on where they now were in regard to the understanding of their problems, she became like a friendly stranger in a foreign country. Needless to say, she did not return to the group again.

The Final Phase

While this treatment phase, comprising about 50 sessions, abounded in elements of further "working through" and of ego repair, certain new and different aspects gained ascendancy. These could be subsumed under the concept of *integration* (i.e., the ego's attempts to assimilate and synthesize experiences of the past with those of the present), as well as happenings within the group with those on the outside. In their effort to fathom the totality of the treatment experience with the agency, the members did much reminiscing about earlier contact with caseworkers. These contacts were seen in retrospect as frequently unsuccessful because they had been unable to establish a close, trusting relationship. There was emphasis on how the group helped each of them to face their real problems and then to act rationally in relation to them. Mrs. Olson and Mrs. Atkins credited the group experience with making them see how "sick" their respective marriages had been. Mrs. Olson doubted whether she had been involved in "real" treatment prior to two years ago. Until then, she had not wanted "to see myself; I wanted to solve my problems without even feeling anything." Mrs. Atkins spoke of how a male caseworker had once "cornered me when I was too busy protecting my innermost thoughts. I didn't think it was anyone's business to know what I was feeling, so I tried to divert his attention." When she finally got another caseworker whom she trusted, the worker left the agency. She described how she accepted an invitation to join the group as a way out. She preferred a group to a new caseworker, feeling that she had to cooperate in some way, lest her son's treatment be discontinued.

The women's retrospective view of the start of the group, three years earlier, is significant. Mrs. Atkins described how she was very cagey at first, "talking about everything under the sun." As the others nodded agreement, she added that being evasive in this way soon became too difficult. A "group bond" had developed which permitted them to be themselves. Mrs. Ramos said that with her linguistic handicap (she was Hispanic), she got a great deal from merely listening. She didn't always fully grasp the others' problems as she was happily married; nevertheless, she felt the "common bond" and wanted to attend. Mrs. Olson and Mrs. Atkins related how readily it emerged that the therapist and the other group members were there to help them, not to pry into their lives.

This review of the group experience was followed by a recital of how each had been helped personally. Mrs. Olson spoke of how much more secure she felt now. She did not get into panics, the way she used to. She also was more tolerant with herself. She was more able to think through some things, although she still had a way to go. She felt that she was able to handle the relationship to her new boyfriend better than before. She was confident that she could never get involved again with anyone as disturbed as her second husband. The other women talked of their progress in a similar vein.

Interestingly, during this final period of treatment, heterosexual and oedipal themes emerged with considerable frequency. It was as if the women had moved, as part of their development, from pregenital to more mature psychosexual orientations. It is noteworthy that Kaplan and Roman (1963) view this kind of preoccupation with heterosexual concerns as characteristic of all treatment groups in their final developmental phase. The discussions were sparked by Mrs. Olson's reports about her relationship to her new male friend, as well as Mrs. Atkins' account of a few flirtatious adventures. Mrs. Thomson openly admitted being jealous, since she felt herself ready to try a new experience with the "right kind" of man. She revealed that she was going to dances and other social gatherings, which she seemed to enjoy.

The group's reaction to the idea of termination was striking, though not altogether surprising. As if in response to some extrasensory cue, no one showed up for the meeting at which the therapist was planning to bring up the subject. A special letter was necessary to urge that everyone attend the following session. The first response to the discussion of termination was disbelief, followed by anger. Mrs. Atkins seemed most agitated; turning to the others, she said: "You better speak up too; you see what this woman [the therapist] is trying to do — she is trying to end this group." Following Mrs. Atkins' instigation, the women began to recount remaining problems for which they needed the group to continue. Contrary to her recent pattern, Mrs. Atkins was eating the refreshments rapidly. She caught herself, saying, "I don't know why I'm eating all this food tonight, but it's like I'm eating the Last Supper." In their initial shock, they found it hard to believe that it was not a superior, but the therapist herself who had made the decision about termination.

It is theoretically significant that in this regressive reaction, the major separation anxiety was expressed in regard to the threatened loss of the group as an entity, not the loss of the therapist. For example, Mrs. Olson said that "The group is like someone to turn to, as though all the people make up someone." Mrs. Atkins spoke of how it was easy to go through a week because of the knowledge that there was the group on Thursday, that "somehow or other there is a sense of security, there's a value in the group." In the course of the first wave of anger, Mrs. Olson suggested that they ought to picket the agency with big placards reading, "CSS is unfair. It will not permit this group to continue" (see also Chapter 4 on the concept of the "mother–group").

It did not take long to help the women understand the meaning of their short–lived regressive reaction to termination. They could see how the thought of ending the group touched off intense earlier feelings about discontinuing meaningful relationships. While acknowledging that everyone could use some further treatment, the therapist pointed out how their wish to continue the group was, in effect, a denial of their newly gained capacities for independence and self–direction. Even Mrs. Atkins, who appeared most frightened at the prospect of terminating contact, had to acknowledge that despite her claims of needing more help, she had made significant gains. All of the women were assured of the worker's availability should there be a need for it in the future. Since the group's termination, however, only one woman has required an interview. Two others have telephoned the worker that they have been able to manage remarkably well on their own.

Case Illustrations

Space limitations make a detailed presentation of individual material on each of the women impossible. Therefore, developmental sketches of only two of them, Mrs. Atkins and Mrs. Thomson, are offered. Both of these had been adjudged prior to the group experience as clinically the most disturbed, and as having very poor prognoses.

Case # 1

Mrs. Atkins, age 43, never knew a mother, her mother having died in childbirth. Her father died soon thereafter, and she had to

stay with a great-aunt. Placed in a series of foster homes, she felt
mistreated and exploited. Even though she could be with her only
on weekends, the great-aunt kept the child when she finally ran
away from a foster home. Mrs. Atkins spoke in the group of how
she had to stifle her fears at being alone lest the authorities again
place her. The great-aunt died when Mrs. Atkins was 16, and
from that time on she had to support herself. She told the others
with much bravado how rearing herself had caused her to become
"uppity" and bellicose. She would talk back to people in authority if
they took advantage of her. She once hit her son's teacher, and she
had to be restrained from using a knife against another woman.

An illegitimate pregnancy forced her marriage to an ineffectual
younger man. She relegated him to the role of a child as she evolved
into a mother for all the surrounding children, including three of
her own. She even took various neighborhood youngsters into her
home to live. Much earlier, when she had been pregnant with her
first child, she had thought of placement. However, she changed
her plan when the doctors predicted that the infant was going to
die. Defying the medical verdict, she "rescued" this helpless child,
nursing her to health. In her ensuing symbiotic tie to this girl, she
was still all but eating and breathing for her, when the child was ten
years of age.

At the time the group therapy began, Mrs. Atkins' strong preoccupation with mothering continued. She was, in fact, acting out
her "rescue fantasies" by seeking out neglected children, one of
whom she adopted. The others would stay in her home for various
periods, causing marked resentment in her own children.

During the first group treatment phase, Mrs. Atkins vied for
control of the group, monopolizing discussions. Near the end of
this period, she moved from a manic-type state in which she
pretended that love and peace reigned in her home, to a beginning
acknowledgment of how things were in actuality. (It was mentioned
earlier that she eventually revealed during the middle phase the
whole sad story of her marriage to an active homosexual male; in
the group's first few months she had claimed a normal sex life,

including a fantastic story of a wonderful contraceptive which doctors had withheld from the public because it was so foolproof.) As she began to face the stark truth of her present life, her euphoric states gave way to more appropriate periods of depression coupled with complaints of severe headaches. At the time individual treatment was discontinued (50th group session), Mrs. Atkins was beginning to respond to the therapeutic efforts to help her separate her own needs from those of her children.

In the course of the group's middle phase, Mrs. Atkins was enabled to supplant her defensive fantasies and feelings of omnipotence by more reality–oriented perceptions and actions. With her newly gained self–awareness, she could also mobilize herself to break with her husband and to get training as a practical nurse. This work apparently allowed for a kind of sublimation of her "rescue fantasies." In addition, with her son now married and supporting himself, Mrs. Atkins not only was able to send her daughter to college, but also to care for her adopted son, while working full–time. Near the end of the treatment, Mrs. Atkins had managed to purchase a modest house in a middle–class neighborhood.

The dramatic improvement in Mrs. Atkins' ego functioning does not gainsay this woman's remaining areas of weakness. Considering the almost complete absence of mothering in her early years, her vulnerability is not surprising. Her remaining sensitivity clusters around her sexual identification, her orality, as well as the primitive sphere of object loss which was highlighted by her extreme reaction to the group's termination. It must be noted, in this connection, that she was able, to an extent at least, to face the feelings engendered by the separation and to view it in the broader perspective of earlier upsets in which object loss was involved.

Case # 2

As for Mrs. Thomson, references have already been made to her difficulty in keeping up with the group's progress, especially during the middle phase with its emphasis on fostering self–awareness. The background history on Mrs. Thomson is rather scanty. She was born in a small mining town, where her father owned a fruit stand. She wanted to become a beautician or dressmaker but, due to discrimination against Blacks, could only secure sporadic domestic employment. Her parents were so rigid and controlling that she was not permitted any contact with boys until she was 20 years old. When her older sister married and moved away, Mrs. Thomson went to live with her, hoping to improve her social life. She had always felt that her parents favored the youngest brother, a "hunchback." Much to her dismay, Mrs. Thomson found that her sister was as strict as her parents.

Through a "Lonely Hearts Club," Mrs. Thomson corresponded for two years with a man in a large city. She subsequently met the man and married him. She soon found out that he was a peddler of stolen goods. He was frequently in jail, and her married life was characterized by much discord and physical abuse. Eventually, her husband had to be committed to a mental institution. When referred to the agency, Mrs. Thomson complained of severe depressions, insomnia, and a variety of aches and pains. She felt that her children, her co-workers, and almost all of her acquaintances, were rejecting. She had an insatiable need for support and reassurance. On the positive side, she was able to prepare herself for a clerical position which helped her to care for herself and for her four sons after she had separated from her husband.

Mrs. Thomson's initial reaction to the group experience was a positive one. She related to it in an inspirational manner and was surprised that she continued to like it, since she had never been able to belong to a group before. She drew much commendation from the other members when she joined a gym class at the "Y" and vowed to go on a diet. Coupled with these positive feelings, Mrs. Thomson had many jealous and hostile reactions as well, but she found it extremely difficult to reveal these openly. Instead, she would simply stop attending the meetings, as she did when she felt that two of the women were feeling closer to one another than to her.

Mrs. Thomson's greatest upsets emerged when her older sons broke away from her. She had an intense need to hold on to her children, which she had rationalized in terms of her terrible loneliness. She vowed to move to a larger, more attractive apartment so that her sons would prefer to live with her. As already mentioned, it took her over a year, with much pressure from the group, to mobilize herself to make this move.

Mrs. Thomson's need to be loved by her children was so intense that she even resented her sons being close to each other. She was especially hurt when her "little one," aged 19, supported his older brother's wish to get an apartment of his own. Of all the women, Mrs. Thomson was the slowest in relinquishing her oral cravings and her magical rituals. She spoke openly of needing sweets to soothe her during periods of depression. At such times, "when down in the dumps," as she put it, she would also resort to reading psalms or to exercises in "positive thinking." On one occasion, she complained of leg cramps during a group meeting and asked the therapist for some hot coffee, in the expectation that the heat would penetrate to her legs and ease the pain.

In general, however, near the end of the first treatment phase (50th session), Mrs. Thomson spoke more consistently of feeling better physically and mentally. She had fewer difficulties with her co-workers on the job, but continued to be very sensitive to imagined rejection. This same sensitivity also emerged at times in relation to the other group members, assuming on occasion almost paranoid proportions. Mrs. Thomson gave repeated indications of a strong need to feel mistreated, to feel "no one loves me." Even with her caseworker, she would assume a hurt, hostile air, coupled with self-pity when she felt her dependency needs were not being completely met. (Individual treatment had been discontinued at this point because of Mrs. Thomson's inability to gain more from it.)

There were moments in the group when Mrs. Thomson responded constructively to confrontations offered by the other women. She even once volunteered the thought that perhaps she felt so hurt at her sons' trying to separate from her "because I've felt all my life no one loved me." On other occasions, Mrs. Thomson seemed to want only support and reassurance.

While she undoubtedly moved at a slower pace than the others, Mrs. Thomson nevertheless made specific gains in ego functioning. Her self-image was enhanced, as evidenced by her greater sense of hopefulness and her more attractive appearance. Not only was she able to move to a larger and better apartment, but she also had a firmer grasp on reality, coupled with better control over her deep-seated defensive reactions. She became more involved in social activities. To what extent any basic changes in her character structure were effected remains to be seen. There is no doubt that her deep-seated, oral-sadistic and provocative orientation to people, interfered with her ability to make the fullest possible use of the group experience.

Conclusions and Implications

The process involved in the group treatment of socially disadvantaged Black women with severe character disorders was depicted. There appears to be no doubt that when appropriate techniques are employed, such clients can sustain a group approach utilizing confrontation and clarification, with the aim of developing self-awareness. (The term "clarification," as employed here, is directed at psychological content residing in the preconscious level of the personality, some of which is not accessible to the client's awareness without the intervention of the therapist. Sands and Fischman [1963] have used this term in a similar manner to make a distinction between it and the psychoanalytic concept of interpreting unconscious content.)

The following three overlapping treatment phases were distinguished: (1) ego strengthening; (2) ego repair through self-awareness, and identity development; (3) integration.

When compared to the individual therapy of such clients, as depicted by Reiner and Kaufman (1959), it appears that the group approach contains certain unique advantages. To begin with, the well-known supportive nature of the group experience facilitated a speedy and less complicated establishment of an initial treatment relationship. These same supportive elements played a major role in minimizing the anxiety and depression evoked in the course of uncovering warded-off feelings and underlying concerns.

As has been developed in another context (Scheidlinger, 1964), the group experience also enhanced the possibilities for ego support because it allowed for realistic and symbolic identifications with the therapist, with the group entity, and with peers. Primitive identification with a fantasied "mother-group" (as discussed in Chapter 4), was especially noticeable during the initial treatment phase, as well as being apparent during later periods (i.e., change of therapists; discussion of termination) when anxiety regarding object loss was reactivated. In this connection, our observations underscore the residual scarring of individuals who have experienced early maternal deprivation and their consequent extreme vulnerability to subsequent threats of separation or object loss.

Among the additional advantages of group therapy for such clients are the greater opportunity for social and emotional distance, and the availability of peers who can offer confrontations and interpretations. These "peer" interventions are likely to be perceived in a less threatening vein than if originating with the authoritative parental figure of the therapist. Besides being in itself a carrier of values, the group also contains identification models in the persons of the therapist and of the other members.

It should be noted that, because of its experimental character and the intent to observe the treatment process in great detail, this group lasted considerably longer than would otherwise have been necessary. It is very likely that satisfactory results could have been obtained within a span of 150 sessions, and perhaps even fewer.

Such a group approach for socially disadvantaged and ego-disturbed clients can be readily adopted by human service agencies equipped to offer group treatment. In addition, in this period of growing concern for meeting the mental health needs of the multitudes of poor people in urban centers, it should have particular applicability for the field of community mental health (Peck, 1963).

Chapter 11

GROUP THERAPY COMBINED WITH INDIVIDUAL PSYCHOTHERAPY

The group psychotherapy field distinguishes between two distinct patterns of utilizing group psychotherapy for a patient who is concurrently receiving individual treatment. The first pattern, employed with the greatest frequency, involves the "combined" use of individual and group treatment by the same therapist. The second, termed "conjoint" therapy, calls for the cooperative utilization of the two treatment modalities for a given patient by two different therapists. The respective technical issues posed by these two similar, yet distinct, approaches will be delineated at a later point.

While we share the belief of most clinicians that both individual and group psychotherapy have their respective places in the clinical realm, and that there are many specific circumstances where individual psychotherapy alone is not enough for certain kinds of patients, this view is not necesssarily shared by others. In fact, as we will note in the review of the literature, there are a number of authorities in the group psychotherapy field, especially from the so-called "British School," who conversely advocate the *exclusive* use of group treatment for most patients, and are principally opposed to simultaneous dyadic interventions in any form. These latter group therapists frequently view the introduction of individual

---

Reprinted from a chapter coauthored by Kenneth Porter, M.D., in *Specialized Techniques in Individual Psychotherapy*, ed. T. B. Karasu and L. Bellak. New York: Brunner/Mazel, 1980, by permission.

sessions as a dilution of the potent group transference and as a resistance to the group treatment medium.

While combined therapy has been also employed with children and adolescents, as noted in Chapter 9, our chosen focus here will be on the treatment of adults only.

REVIEW OF THE LITERATURE

It is noteworthy that well over 50 contributions dealing with combined individual and group psychotherapy appeared during the 1950's and 1960's. The virtual absence of more recent publications on this subject is probably due to the fact that, like group psychotherapy employed exclusively, these once new and controversial modalities have by now become an accepted part of the mental health scene.

Beginning with a paper by Wender and Stein in 1949, there were a number of articles during the decade of the fifties dealing with the general subject of combined psychotherapy (Fried, 1954; Papanek, 1954; Lipschutz, 1957; Sager, 1959). The emphasis was on how the two approaches could be afforded equal importance in an overall treatment strategy or, in Wilder's (1974) case, how he utilized the group sessions to facilitate his primary reliance on dyadic psychoanalysis. The most recent comprehensive review of the entire subject of combined therapy is that of Bieber (1971).

There were many publications which depicted the use of combined therapy for patients with specific diagnostic categories. These range from an early paper by Baruch and Miller (1946) on the treatment of allergic conditions, through the use of combined therapy in inpatient settings (Klapman, 1950; Hill and Armitage, 1954), to a number of articles on the advantage of such treatment for oral characters (Jackson and Grotjahn, 1958; Rosenbaum, 1960; and Tabachnick, 1965). Wolberg (1960) discussed the use of combined therapy for borderline patients, while Glatzer (1960) and Durkin (1964), among many others, emphasized the special value of such an approach for narcissistic and other preoedipal character disorders. Some authors, among them Graham (1964), employed combined therapy successfully with psychoneurotic patients.

As might be expected, the technical questions pertaining to the differential uses of individual and group sessions raised by Sager (1959) and Spotnitz (1954), as well as to transference and resistance in these concurrently used modalities, evoked much interest and controversy in the literature. Thus, Stein (1964) subjected the broader issue of transference in combined therapy to special scrutiny, while Beukenkamp (1955) depicted the ways in which this approach could facilitate the resolution of transference problems. Berger (1960), among others, paid particular attention to the subject of resistance.

Other technical issues such as the handling of confidentiality, when and how to introduce the group medium, and countertransference in combined individual and group treatment were discussed by Aronson (1964) and Sager (1964). Some authors, such as Ormont (1964) and Teicher (1962), reviewed the relative advantages of combined versus conjoint group psychotherapy.

As we mentioned earlier, some authorities in the group therapy field view combined group therapy with disfavor, advocating instead an exclusive emphasis on group therapy alone. Wolf and Schwartz (1962), for example, asserted that individual therapy would interfere with the establishment and resolution of the transference neurosis characteristic of what they termed "group psychoanalysis." Whitaker and Lieberman (1964), Foulkes and Anthony (1957), and Ezriel (1957) are also against the use of combined therapy, claiming that the group medium is markedly powerful in its own right and that individual interventions would be counterproductive.

The Unique Potential of the Psychoanalytic Therapy Group

When a clinician decides to add group therapy to the individual treatment of his patients, he is likely to be influenced by certain assumptions regarding the special therapeutic ingredients inherent in the therapeutic group process. These have been spelled out in much detail in the voluminous group therapy literature and will accordingly be reviewed here in brief outline only.

The Group as a Real Social Experience

The co–presence of a number of people fosters multiple inter-personal relationships revealing to everyone's full view each indi-vidual's coping and defensive patterns. As a group member's char-acteristic ways of relating emerge and evoke reactions from others, the stage is thus set for both nonverbal and verbal interventions by other group members as well as the therapist. This is especially ad-vantageous for those patients, who in their massive employment of denial, projection, silences, and withdrawal, are difficult to engage in the one–to–one setting.

Multiple Transferences

In addition to the above–noted largely conscious interpersonal relationships, the unconscious group level is characterized by transference manifestations to other members and to the therapist, as well as to the group as an entity. These transferences frequently assume the representations of siblings, of parental figures, and of the family as a whole. The shifting character of these "neurotic" transferences — coupled with the emergence of more primitive, de-fensive transference manifestations such as "splitting," identifica-tions, and part–object relationships — allow for significant diagnos-tic observations and for appropriate therapeutic interventions both in the group and in the individual sessions.

In this connection, the group psychotherapy literature is replete with discussions of the regressive perceptions and relationships which characterize the unconscious levels of group processes. As was noted in Chapter 2, these primitive emotional themes are believed by some writers, such as Bion (1959), to be of even greater "depth" than those elicited in the dyadic psychoanalytic setting. Such fleeting group manifestations pertaining to the reactivation of early relationship patterns, and especially of primitive perceptions of the therapist, other members, and the group entity, can be subjected to a more planned and controlled scrutiny in the context of combined therapy. Breen (1977) provided a poignant illustration of some of the differences in the unconscious object relationship themes evoked by the group therapy and individual analytic settings, respectively.

Opportunity for Reality Testing

In contrast to the relatively unstructured dyadic setting which tends to promote only a regressive climate, the group, with its accompanying reality component of an open circle and the co-presence of a number of people, facilitates the testing of reality. Imagined fears, hurts, and retaliations, as well as transference distortions, are thus subject to easier exploration and correction.

Support of Peers

While ego support offered in the context of individual psychotherapy is likely to reinforce dependency on the therapist, this is more readily avoided in the supportive climate of the group. Here, the frequently disheartened and demoralized patient is soon helped to realize that he is not alone nor necessarily the worst off. Furthermore, vivid examples of change for the better on the part of others promote hope for one's own improvement. The group's code of acceptance and of honesty, which is consciously fostered, tends to reduce irrational feelings of shame and guilt, to correct biases and cultural misinformation. Being afforded the role of helper to others enhances each patient's self-esteem besides serving as a motivation to take personal risks on the road to new behaviors.

MAXIMIZING THE EFFECTS OF INDIVIDUAL THERAPY

The above-noted unique motivational factors for change and growth inherent in the group setting tend to enhance the effectiveness of the patient's simultaneous one-to-one treatment. In addition, other more experienced group members can serve as role models in the acceptance of irrational feelings and anxiety, as well as of the need for self-exploration as a necessary ingredient of therapy. Furthermore, confrontations and interpretations by peers are often more readily accepted than those from the authority figure. The motivational reinforcement of the group's commitment to work toward therapeutic progress also helps to overcome resistances. While the earlier-mentioned regressive group transactions are likely to facilitate the expression of deeply repressed ideations, the necessary lengthy, detailed and individualized working through of such material is usually not possible in a group because the coexisting needs of so many others interfere with this process. It is here, as noted by Scheidlinger (1968b), that the individual sessions serve to complement the group situation, allowing for the repetitive and necessarily slow process of "working through" to occur. The patient's observing ego is thus enabled to master the new insights at its own pace, with due regard to the inevitable resistance reinforced by early traumas.

SPECIFIC INDICATIONS FOR COMBINED THERAPY

There is considerable agreement in the literature that combined therapy, while potentially useful with most ambulatory patients, is the treatment of choice for character disorders and borderline personalities. The integrated use of the two modalities lends itself especially well to working with primitive, preoedipal transferences and related rigid character defenses which, as noted by Kernberg (1976), are frequently coupled with schizoid behavior and deep fears of intimacy. (Some of these same problems are encountered in severe psychoneuroses.)

As mentioned earlier, the group's aid in the evocation and resolution of complex transferences and resistances is likely to hasten the pace of individual treatment and its reconstructive nature. This is especially true under prevailing conditions of practice where financial limitations constrain many patients to a less intensive schedule of individual therapy than is clinically indicated. Under such circumstances, a single group session can often be combined with even a single individual session to marked advantage.

Following are some of the major therapeutic problems of patients with character pathology, including "borderline" conditions, which were found to be specially responsive to combined individual and group treatment.

Difficult Transferences

The varied complexities in the resolution of primitive transference themes encountered in preoedipal character problems in the dyadic treatment context are well known, and do not require repetition. By introducing simultaneous group treatment, the patient's rigid narcissistic, paranoid, withdrawing or dependent transference patterns become subject to the group's scrutiny and confrontations. The therapist may at first need to use the individual sessions to support the patient in view of the group's undermining of his tenaciously defended perceptions. Subsequently, the inevitable negative transference reactions to other group members (siblings) are likely to be displaced onto the therapist, where they belong. At the same time, the positive transference ties to some of the group peers and the perception of the group entity in a positive maternal vein can serve as support on the painful road to the analysis of the patient's distorted angry perceptions of early objects, in both the individual and group encounters. Individual sessions can be used flexibly — at times to offer ego support when the group's confrontations promote too much anxiety, at other times for analytic exploration and working through. Group meetings, as well, are likely to serve varied functions at different stages of treatment. These include experiential frustrations or gratifications of transference wishes, and direct verbal expressions and confrontations of transference feelings coupled with reality testing and resolution.

Analysis of Rigid Character Defenses

We referred earlier to the unequaled value of the group setting for portraying interpersonal behavior patterns and defenses. In fact, group therapists have often noted with amazement how different their patients appear in the group when compared to their behavior in the dyadic session. Thus, when the new group member's narcissistic defenses of grandiosity, aloofness, and arrogance persist over a period of time, the other members are bound to confront the unacceptable conduct and later undertake concerted efforts to demand relevant self-scrutiny and modification. Similarly, a cohesive therapy group, imbued with a spirit of self-examination coupled with genuine emotional support, will not tolerate persistent patterns of projection, denial, withdrawal, withholding, or intellectualization. The frequently painful sequelae of such transactions are likely to involve the therapist, both in group and individual sessions, as supporter, confronter, and interpreter, according to the demands of the situation.

Clinical reports are unanimous about the special value of a group setting as a way station for patients to work through problems of relating to members of the opposite sex, or overcoming schizoid withdrawal. Somehow, these issues are better *lived* out in at least a microcosm of the real world — the group — rather than being merely talked about in the individual session.

The Differential Uses of Individual and Group Sessions

During combined therapy, group sessions tend to be generally used to elicit and resolve resistances and to promote the expression of the earlier-noted deep affects and fantasies. The individual sessions can then serve as the calmer "laboratory" to analyze in greater detail and comprehensiveness these therapeutic productions, especially the primitive transference perceptions. In either type of session, the emphasis occasionally may need to be placed on the provision of ego support. As part of the working through process, group meetings are more likely to offer opportunities for experimenting with new behaviors, while the individual sessions would stress the integration of deeper intrapsychic themes.

Needless to say, all therapists do not necessarily operate in accordance with this scheme. The unique needs of different patients, the variability in the character of therapy groups, and the therapist style may dictate different ways in which the two media are harmonized to enhance the task of therapy. (The patients depicted in the preceding Chapter 10 did decidedly better when treated through group therapy alone during the later treatment phases.)

Technical Issues in the Initiation and Scheduling of Combined Therapy

It is an almost universal practice among therapists employing combined therapy to initiate treatment with a period of individual psychotherapy, and to add group therapy at a later point. A common view is that group therapy may be introduced once the patient has developed a strong working alliance with the therapist, and after a transference has been clearly established and at least partially understood. If the patient is introduced to group therapy too soon, transference patterns may become confused or repressed and therapeutic progress halted. In fact, some patients may flee treatment altogether, should they fail to be fully prepared for the group, and feel that they are being "thrown to the wolves" or abandoned.

Similarly, patients in individual treatment should probably not be brought into a group until the acute problems that led to the treatment have been at least partially resolved and the patient's self-esteem is sufficiently strong to withstand the inevitable stresses entailed in group belonging.

In practice, there is considerable variation in the timing of combined therapy, ranging from the introduction of the group after only a few weeks, at one extreme, to a preceding stretch of several years of individual psychotherapy, at the other.

Although the pattern of commencing treatment with individual psychotherapy and later adding group therapy is the most common approach, there is no reason why the reverse procedure cannot be employed. Thus, some clinicians begin combined therapy with exclusive group psychotherapy, and only after a period of months or years do they add individual sessions. This scheme may be best suited to patients with previous psychoanalytic experience or those who are extremely frightened of their transference reactions in the individual treatment setting.

As for the composition of therapy groups in combined therapy, these may consist of a mixture of patients, including some in exclusive group therapy and others in combined or in conjoint therapy. While this might seem to create formidable problems of transference complexity and rivalry reactions within the psychotherapy group, most clinicians have actually found such an approach quite workable. Given sufficient sensitivity and experience in the employment of combined therapy on the part of the therapist, the use of a flexible approach permits a truly rich variety of therapeutic transactions.

As can be expected, raising the issue of joining a group with a patient in individual treatment is likely to provoke a number of concerns. Most common are feelings of rejection, narcissistic injury, separation anxiety, and sibling rivalry. These feelings invariably provide significant themes for the ongoing treatment program.

Combined treatment is usually initiated either by adding a group therapy session to the patient's preexisting schedule of individual sessions or by substituting a group meeting for an individual session. The decision is made on clinical grounds, depending on the optimal intensity of individual psychotherapy sessions and the availability of time and of financial resources. Naturally, the issues posed by the planning for combined therapy will differ in the two circumstances and the therapist must be prepared to deal with the relevant therapeutic material which is bound to arise.

The most common pattern of combined therapy appears to be: one group therapy session per week, combined with one or two individual sessions. Fewer therapists employ a twice-weekly group therapy schedule.

Whether it is feasible to combine a more intensive individual psychoanalytic schedule of sessions with group therapy has been extensively debated. Some writers maintain that the deep regressive transference of a classical individual psychoanalysis is incompatible with concurrent group therapy, while others believe that a schedule of three, four, or even five times a week for individual psychoanalytic sessions, including the use of the couch, can go hand–in–hand with group therapy. These therapists report that patients exhibit a variety of transference reactions in both group and individual sessions. Although the anonymity of the clinician is obviously not preserved, the essential nature of the analytic development and resolution of the transference is believed not to be disturbed.

The most prevalent point of view at this time among practitioners of combined therapy is that intensive, three to five times weekly individual psychoanalytic sessions may be combined with group therapy. While this probably alters the nature of the transference relationship within the individual analytic treatment, the total process of this type of combined therapy is nevertheless considered as being compatible with the overall reconstructive goals of the psychoanalytic approach.

Confidentiality in Combined Therapy

Concurrent individual and group psychoanalytic sessions offer the therapist a range of possibilities in exploiting therapeutic material which exceeds what is possible through the use of either therapeutic modality alone. To restrict the utilization of themes that emerge in either modality to subsequent sessions within the same modality only, would deprive combined therapy of some of its greatest potential. For example, individual meetings may be utilized to permit the patient to discuss the defensive or transference patterns of fellow group members. These discussions may lead to considerable insight for the patient, and often facilitate his deeper understanding of similar aspects of his own psychopathology. Similarly, with the patient's permission, material from individual sessions may be productively employed to further understanding of this topic within the group transactions.

Considerations of clinical judgment and personal tact are, of course, critical in the flexible use of therapeutic data emanating from combined therapy.

COMBINED THERAPY AND CONJOINT THERAPY

As noted at the outset, "conjoint therapy" refers to combined treatment in which group and individual therapy of a patient are conducted by two different therapists. It is similar to traditional shared treatment in most respects, and offers most of the same advantages.

The main issue that distinguishes combined from conjoint therapy is the effect of such a divided treatment structure on the working alliance and transference. Conjoint therapy fosters the development of multiple transferences and of transference splitting even more than the use of combined group and individual therapy. Some clinicians have claimed that this allows for clearer delineation, and hence for easier resolution, of some patients' transference patterns. Many others believe that the use of two therapists unnecessarily confuses the picture and invites complicated countertransference issues; it may also foster the conscious and unconscious manipulation of the treatment situation by the patient to such a degree as to inhibit the successful resolution of basic pathology.

At this time, it is probably fair to say that both treatment approaches appear to be effective, that their uses are similar, and that a clear preference for one or the other is up to the therapist. However, the fact that conjoint therapy is much less frequently employed suggests doubt among clinicians regarding its efficacy in deeper, reconstructive psychotherapy. Further experimentation will reveal the specific ways in which combined and conjoint therapy, respectively, have their proper place in the therapeutic armamentarium according to the varying needs of different patients, psychopathologies, and treatment situations.

Contraindications to Combined Therapy

There was a time when both group therapists and individual psychotherapists were wary of combined therapy. Individual therapists felt that the addition of group therapy to dyadic treatment would dilute it to the point where the attainment of analytic goals would be made more difficult, if not impossible. Alternatively, clinicians who employed group therapy as the treatment of choice for most patients feared that the addition of individual sessions would drain off energy and material from the group.

It is our belief that to date neither side in this dialogue has been proven correct. We think that individual psychoanalytic treatment can essentially proceed with the attainment of its goals when group therapy sessions are added to the treatment regimen, and that, if anything, the work of character reconstruction may occur with greater alacrity and depth. Similarly, psychoanalytic group therapy is most often enhanced by the addition of individual sessions as patients are provided with the opportunity to work through issues in greater genetic and intrapsychic depth. The only two major clinical contraindications for combined therapy appear to be:

1. *Classical psychoneuroses*, which probably are still best treated with the technique of intensive individual psychoanalysis. For these patients, the addition of group therapy is probably unnecessary, since the latter's virtue is to facilitate the resolution of the character problems and severe transference patterns which are not characteristic of the neuroses.

2. *Some borderline, psychotic and masochistic patients,* whose ego structure is such that they respond to the addition of group therapy with enhanced anxiety, regressed behavior, or depression, when exposed to the group's psychological forces of regression and contagion.

Case Illustrations

Case #1

Joe is a 32-year-old public utility repairman with a poor working-class background. He spends his free time as part of a group of motorcycle riders who use a variety of nonaddictive drugs. He is bright, upwardly mobile and committed to psychotherapy. His childhood was characterized by a very domineering mother and the almost total absence of a father. He is overweight, fierce-looking, and filled with rage toward women, coupled with a strong desire to overcome it. He was married for five years to a woman he described as in many ways a carbon copy of his mother. He said that he did not love her, but nevertheless could not get himself to leave her and his five-year-old daughter.

Joe began once-weekly individual psychotherapy and a year later was invited to join a psychoanalytic therapy group led by the same male therapist. At first the therapeutic work in individual sessions was largely supportive, aiming to help Joe deal more competently with his wife and child as well as with a variety of work-related, practical conflicts. Joe related to the therapist in a friendly and submissive fashion.

In the group Joe was initially withdrawn and silent, and was often depressed. His occasional talk consisted of sarcastic comments to the women members and deferentially friendly remarks to the males. He usually came dressed in his torn, greasy work clothes.

Over a period of two years, the other group members at first gently, then more firmly, confronted Joe with his tendency to withdraw into depressions instead of dealing with his problems. The defensive aspects of his "macho" denial of dependency, of his dress, appearance and aggressiveness, were repeatedly emphasized.

In time, several significant changes were noted. Joe began to talk spontaneously during every session, emerging also as being concerned and involved with all group members. He could now acknowledge pain, inadequacy, and vulnerability in front of the others, including the women. In fact, he began to use the group to practice new ways of relating to women as equals whom he might care about. In addition, there were the beginnings of a kind of transference rage toward women, as well as, for the first time, toward his male group therapist.

At this point, the nature of Joe's individual therapy sessions gradually also underwent change. Dreams began to appear and the sessions became less reality-oriented and supportive, and more concerned with genetic and intrapsychic material. The heart of this work settled for a time on homosexual fears and wishes involving male friends, Joe's father, and the therapist.

After three years of combined therapy, Joe was enabled to separate from his wife, to lose a significant amount of weight, to alter his style of dress, reduce his involvement with motorcycles and drugs, and begin to date women for the first time in his adult life.

This case illustrates the following points concerning combined therapy: (1) the value of the group to reveal and resolve character defenses; (2) the use of the group to explore and begin to resolve patterns of transference rage; (3) the group's availability as a testing-ground for more adaptive behavior during the working-through process; (4) the opportunity to focus in the individual sessions on genuine reconstructive psychotherapy.

Case #2

Rose is a 28-year-old nurse who is married and has a nine-month-old son. Rose's mother is schizophrenic; one of her psychotic episodes followed Rose's birth. Her father beat the patient when she was young. Rose was in individual psychoanalytically oriented psychotherapy for five years with a female therapist whom she described as "very supportive and maternal." She felt that she had benefited greatly from this period of treatment, but she and her therapist believed that an added span of analytic group therapy accompanying the individual work would be helpful to deal with issues related to her anger and need to be more self–assertive.

Rose entered a therapy group led by a male therapist. At first, she was quiet and shy. She rarely spoke, even when she appeared to be obviously upset. The group therapist suggested that she perhaps experienced the entire group as her schizophrenic mother and felt that if she asserted herself by asking for help, the group would not be emotionally available to her, just as her own mother had not been. Subsequently, with continued encouragement from the others, she began to verbalize her feelings, requests, and needs to an ever greater extent.

Following this, the other members began to consider Rose's shyness, hesitancy, and soft voice as relating to difficulties with self–assertion and anger. Her timidity and marked friendliness were repeatedly interpreted as reaction formations to underlying feelings of anger. Soon, Rose began to oppose others in the group, starting with the females but then going on to challenge also the male members and the therapist. She reported a concurrent increased ability to confront her husband when she felt he was treating her unfairly. Recently, she gave birth to a girl and went through the postpartum and infancy periods without significant symptomatology. She is now making plans to return to part–time work over the mild objections of her husband. Needless to say, the two therapists communicated with each other on occasion, with Rose's knowledge.

This case illustrates the following: (1) the conjoint use of individual and group therapy sessions with differing therapists, in which the individual sessions served a mixed supportive–reconstructive function, and the group sessions came to take on a primarily reconstructive quality; (2) the resolution of transference patterns in the group; (3) the use of group sessions to reveal and resolve character defenses; (4) the opportunity offered by the group to serve as an arena for the practice of new, adaptive patterns of behavior.

Part V

Group Psychotherapy in the 1980's

Chapter 12

A GLIMPSE AT THE FUTURE

Predicting tomorrow in the realm of human services is hazardous at best, even within a period of relative societal stability. Given the current unprecedented rate of socioeconomic changes, heralded by the sudden reversal in the country's national policies, such predictions might well seem foolhardy. And yet, since some sense of the future is preferable — no matter how imprecise — to a total lack of orientation, I will venture some guesses about likely developments in group psychotherapy during this decade. These projections will of necessity be offered in the broadest of strokes.

Despite the clouded future generally predicted for the human services, I believe that the phenomenal rise and acceptance which group psychotherapy has experienced during the last 30 years is likely to continue, if only at a slightly reduced pace. Its recognition as a major treatment form is evidenced by the fact that the large majority of training programs for the core mental health professions, i.e., psychiatry, psychology, social work, and psychiatric nursing, have by now incorporated group psychotherapy into their basic curriculum.

An earlier need to clamor for recognition from various governmental bodies and professional organizations has been supplanted by an assured knowledge that our field has become a firmly entrenched and respected intervention modality within the realm of mental health. It is noteworthy, in this connection, that two interdisciplinary bodies of the American Psychiatric Association have recently approached the American Group Psychotherapy Association, the movement's professional arm, to participate in two major and separate collaborative ventures: the development of a DSM–III volume on treatment planning and a Psychiatric Treatment

Manual, the latter to be sponsored by a special Commission on Psychiatric Therapies. As for the American Psychological Association, its Division on Psychotherapy decided this year to form a special Section on Group Psychotherapy.

Such favorable signs of the mainstreaming of group psychotherapy must not be taken as an indication, however, that mental health professionals and consumers are now clear about the precise nature of group treatment when compared with the other group intervention modalities, discussed in Chapter 1 of this volume. However, the charting of more exact boundaries between the varied "people–helping" groups is likely to be hastened by the current push for specificity and accountability from the third party payers of mental health services.

The Mental Health Delivery System

Given the current low priority accorded the mental health services in the United States, coupled with an absence of a comprehensive health or insurance program, the public delivery system is expected to become even more fragmented and specialized under the promised move from federal to state control. This could be at least partially mitigated, should some liberal states choose to preserve the current model of neighborhood–based community mental health centers. They could accordingly continue with their multi–faceted task of meeting the mental health needs of the majority of people who lack the resources to obtain services from the private sector (Scharfstein, 1978). As I noted in Chapter 1 of this volume, these federally funded community mental health centers (780 centers serviced about 50% of the U.S. population in 1980) had been in the forefront since the early 1960's in sponsoring a great variety of group treatment measures and in–service training ventures. The growing number of Health Maintenance Organizations (total of 246 in 1980) had been playing a similar role in their sections devoted to psychotherapy.

Any retrenchment in public funding and in meaningful planning for comprehensive services will probably lead to an even more dysfunctional mental health service system than we have today. The chronically ill (about 15%–20% of the population), as well as the less disturbed psychiatric patients who are devoid of insurance coverage, are bound to suffer the most. For them, the "revolving door" practice of state hospitalization will be revived. Furthermore, with the expected continued growth of the financially more viable, acute psychiatric treatment programs in general hospitals (municipal and voluntary), the reimbursable short-term treatment episodes are likely to be fostered, over the more costly, but preferable, partial hospitalization and outpatient treatment (Tarail, 1980).

What about the role of group psychotherapy in the context of this, hopefully overly pessimistic, scenario? It is ironically very likely that, because of their relative cost-effectiveness, group treatment services will be the last to go when other programs face curtailment. However, the increased pressure for all services, with staffing reduced, is bound to affect the quality of group treatment. With it will inevitably go a disproportionate emphasis on the short-term and the more superficial group modalities. The currently prevalent mode of long-term, psychoanalytic group psychotherapy will need to be reserved for the independent private practitioners and for the few advantaged free-standing clinics and private institutions — all geared to serving the well-to-do patients.

It is important to note here that we do at present have much (if not all) of the knowledge and skills required for the effective operation of an integrated and comprehensive mental health service system in each community. Such a system would include a wide array of interventions including group modalities to provide intensive treatment for short-term and long-term inpatients and outpatients. The critical question is whether the federal and state governments will provide the funds required to support such publicly sponsored programs, geared primarily to serving the lower classes and the poor.

SPECIAL POPULATIONS AND CLINICAL CATEGORIES

It can be said that in the human services, and particularly in the health services, demography is destiny. Accordingly, our mushrooming aged population, with its estimated 15%–25% of individuals with significant mental health problems, will be in dire need of increased services during the 1980's and beyond. Is group psychotherapy prepared for this development? It is my impression that despite the general recognition that group approaches are probably the treatment of choice for the elderly, whether in outpatient or in nursing home settings (Group for the Advancement of Psychiatry, 1971; Ingersoll and Silverman, 1978), clinical professionals have been regrettably slow in entering this area of practice. I was surprised to note, for example, that the 1979 review of the group psychotherapy literature (Silver, Lubin, Silver, and Dobson, 1979), contained less than 3% of publications on group treatment of the elderly. An interesting suggestion by M. Lakin, K. Mooney and S. Havasy (1977)—that their study of naturally occurring modes of interaction among the elderly could be used to develop appropriate group treatment models—was totally ignored. It is my hope that the growing number of post–graduate gerontology training programs will serve to redress this lack. Otherwise, we can expect the much less desirable crash training programs, which are likely to attract people with inadequate motivation and experience levels.

My earlier-noted observation (Chapter 9 of this volume) regarding the paucity of group treatment programs for children will hold true for this decade as well. The solution to this problem will depend on the interest and commitment of the administrators of public and voluntary psychiatric children's services. This is so because of the complexity involved in organizing workable children's groups in private practice settings.

I can predict a much surer future for the continued sponsorship of groups for medical patients (Cunningham, Strassberg, and Roback, 1978). Such homogeneous groups, generally focused on symptom relief and enhanced adaptation to chronic or even terminal illnesses (Yalom and Grieves, 1977), have received gratifyingly positive responses from the medical profession. This is due, in part at least, to the demonstrated good results; Rahe, Ward, and Hayes

(1979), for example, found that myocardial infarction patients in group treatment had significantly less follow–up coronary morbidity and mortality than an untreated control group. Another likely factor is the increasing recognition in the field of medicine generally of the intimate relation between body and mind, even in ailments not generally viewed as psychosomatic.

With group approaches having emerged during the last two decades as a valuable modality for the multi–faceted treatment of alcoholism and substance abuse, one can expect further work in this direction (Kornblith and Kaplan, 1981). Needless to say, the prognosis for these conditions continues to be quite guarded, except for instances where the patient is truly motivated to remain in treatment (Hill and Blane, 1967). As part of a continuing trend toward professional administration of drug treatment programs, cost–effectiveness studies will probably be conducted with increasing frequency, using substitutes for post–treatment outcomes (Des Jarlais, Deren, and Lipton, 1981).

Among the inpatient psychosocial treatments for schizophrenia, psychoanalytic group psychotherapy, with its emphasis on the promotion of insight, has been increasingly supplanted in recent years by the "therapeutic" group approaches (see Chapter 1 of this volume). These modalities have proven themselves useful when oriented toward providing support, developing social skills and self–esteem. Since group treatment is rarely offered alone in inpatient settings it is difficult to assess its specific effectiveness (Scheidlinger, 1978). Although selected outcome studies of group treatment as the sole modality suggested some beneficial effects, questionable design methodologies nevertheless precluded any definitive conclusions (Parloff and Dies, 1977). However, group therapy combined with other interventions (i.e., drugs, videotape, social interaction) was found to be superior to single treatment forms. These mildly promising results with inpatients notwithstanding, it is my belief that the major thrust in the future will lie in the use of community–based group treatment with chronic schizophrenic patients. As noted by Mosher and Gunderson (1979), such treatment is likely to be offered in tandem with other therapies, as part of a broader, total rehabilitation effort directed at deinstitutionalized patients in the public sector. The desired therapeutic factors in these group interventions will stress group acceptance, mutual support and interpersonal relationships.

The growing preoccupation of psychoanalytic group practitioners with the outpatient treatment of patients with borderline and narcissistic conditions has already been touched on in Part III of this volume. This trend is accelerating and should lead to further theoretical and research endeavors in the future.

Theoretical Advances

There has been a marked discontent in recent years with the dominant, rigidly held and circumscribed theoretical orientations in both dyadic and group psychotherapy. From an earlier, almost chauvinistic adherence to competing ideological camps, seasoned clinicians of all persuasions have begun to move toward a new pragmatism, eclecticism, and search for commonalities among the varied psychotherapies. I would accordingly venture a guess that most group clinicians would nowadays probably accept the 12 curative factors which Yalom (1975) has postulated as underlying the group psychotherapy process. Differences are likely to emerge only with respect to which of these factors should be considered as primary in role. Freudian group psychotherapists, for example, would probably take issue with Yalom's (1975) belief that "interpersonal learning," rather than transference interpretations leading to insight and to "working through," is fundamental (Weiner, 1974).

Frank (1973), who is well versed in both dyadic and group psychotherapy, has been a leading proponent of the idea that certain common features are shared by all psychotherapeutic approaches. In this same vein, Lazarus (1977), an authority in behavioral psychotherapy, asserted that instead of the advancement of delimited ideologies, there be "...an advancement in the understanding of human interaction, in the alleviation of suffering, and in the know-how of therapeutic intervention" (p. 553).

I foresee a continuation of this trend toward pragmatism and eclecticism in group psychotherapy theorizing, including the experimental borrowing by psychoanalytic practitioners of such "foreign" techniques as role playing, direct feedback, marathon sessions, and hypnotic suggestion. I hope that such introduction of new techniques will follow Parloff's (1979) admonition and pursue the question of "what kinds of changes are effected by what kind of techniques, applied to what kinds of patients, by what kind of therapists under what kind of conditions" (p. 303).

The greatly needed elucidation of therapeutic factors unique to group psychotherapy is hampered by the continued lack of clear and consensual definitions of basic concepts (Scheidlinger, 1967). A case in point is "cohesiveness," a notion vitally relevant for both social psychologists and group therapy practitioners. Social psychologists have studied cohesiveness in its connotation as a condition for change, i.e., the attractiveness of a group for its members. Group psychotherapists are interested in cohesiveness as a therapeutic factor pertaining to a group's acceptance of individual members, and more generally, with reference to the varied meanings entailed in group involvement. It is thus regrettable that Frank's (1957) early inquiry into group cohesiveness and Scheidlinger's (1964) further exploration of identification as an underlying process in group belonging have not been followed up by others. We are left with the recent conclusion by Bloch, Grouch, and Reibstein (1981) that there is need for much further work in group psychotherapy regarding cohesiveness as a therapeutic factor, with emphasis on member acceptance, on its promotion of behavioral change, and more generally, on its influence on outcome.

It is my hope that in this further study of group cohesiveness, an earlier-stated question of how covert, individual perceptions and fantasies become shared group-level manifestations (Scheidlinger, 1980) will be pursued. With it might go a renewed investigation of the development and meaning of a person's self and identity in group belonging, following the earlier conceptualizations of an individual and group identity by Erikson (1959) and Klein's (1976) "I" and "We" aspects of the self-concept. Anthony's (1980) more recent discussion of the family as a child's internal object, as well as Stechler and Kaplan's (1980) reexamination of psychoanalytic ideas pertaining to the self in its autonomous and affiliative dimensions, represent promising steps in this direction. Such inquiry might even offer us some leads into the still unanswered question of whether human gregariousness is an inborn characteristic (Buirski, 1980).

With respect to the broader issues in the development of group psychotherapy theory, the recent interesting efforts of some writers notwithstanding (Kellerman, 1979; Cooper and Gustafson, 1979; Durkin, 1981), I continue to doubt that, given the complexity of the field, there can be an acceptable global group psychotherapy theory in the near future. I continue to believe that "limited-domain" theorizing, as exemplified by my own contributions in Part II of this volume, and by such papers as those of Aronson (1967), Kauff (1977), as well as Grunebaum and Solomon (1980), where the focus is on specific concepts or on mini-models, will lead to connecting links which might serve as foundations for the eventual development of a general theory of group psychotherapy (Scheidlinger, 1975).

Research

In his overview of three decades of group psychotherapy research, Dies (1979) reported on the marked recent increase in the number of contributions to the literature. And yet, despite this growing volume of work, the greater methodological sophistication and readiness of clinicians for research input, we still lack conclusive evidence about the precise factors in group psychotherapy efficacy. Bloch et al. (1981) are somewhat more optimistic, suggesting that empirical research on the therapeutic factors in group psychotherapy, such as self-disclosure, insight, interaction, acceptance, catharsis, and guidance, has in fact produced practical knowledge directly applicable to the clinical situation. They decry the failure of clinicians to address themselves to these findings.

There is general agreement that group psychotherapy process research needs to focus on the delineation of the therapeutic features unique to this method, including the specific circumstances under which they can be optimized for the promotion of the desired behavioral changes in patients. This will require more focused attention to issues of basic conceptualizations as well as of research design (Bednar and Paul, 1978).

All psychotherapies, group psychotherapy included, are under current pressure, by third-party payers and by consumers, for greater precision regarding the differential choice of therapy for a given patient, with a given problem, at a given time. With it goes a demand for documentation of treatment effectiveness (Frances and Clarkin, 1981). The ongoing projects for a DSM-III Treatment Planning Book and for a Psychiatric Treatment Manual, noted earlier in this chapter, are part of this movement.

This push toward therapeutic specificity as well as toward outcome and cost-effectiveness is bound to spark new group psychotherapy efficacy studies, more circumscribed with regard to specific patient categories, intervention models, patient-therapist match, and especially, session frequency and duration (Parloff and Dies, 1977). I would envision in this connection a marked expansion in the literature on short-term, group psychotherapy (Bernard and Klein, 1977; Waxer, 1977; Imber, Lewis, and Loiselle, 1979).

As Dies (1979) has observed, the climate is currently more favorable than ever for improved process and outcome research endeavors in group psychotherapy. The sponsorship of a group therapy outcome instrument (Parloff and Dies, 1978) and of a special research member category by the American Group Psychotherapy Association augurs well for the future. There is a clear danger, however, that the avowed lack of interest of the Reagan administration in supporting any research which smacks of social science will serve as a serious deterrent. Perhaps some private sources of funding will fill the gap.

SUMMARY

Gazing into my crystal ball has revealed that group psychotherapy will continue to flourish in this decade as a respected modality in mental health. It will find particular application in the outpatient treatment of the growing number of patients suffering from severe character pathology, i.e., borderline and narcissistic conditions, as well as schizophrenia, where the absence of satisfying interpersonal relationships is a major complaint.

The expected drastic changes in the public mental health delivery system fostered by the new national administration are likely to affect the kinds of groups employed and the patient categories served, rather than the volume of group psychotherapy practice. Special emphasis will in fact be required in regard to the increased use of group treatment for the elderly, for children, for medical patients, and for substance abusers.

The push of the marketplace will impinge on all psychotherapy in a similar fashion. Group psychotherapy's catchwords will accordingly be pragmatism, eclecticism, and clarification. Reimbursable clinical practice will move toward greater professionalization, codification, specificity, cost–effectiveness, and the employment of combined therapies, including pharmacology. Long–term group psychotherapy will be reserved for patients in the more affluent private sector, with emphasis on character reorganization, problems of living, and existential concerns.

The positive side of these broader developments might well lead to a speedier interdisciplinary elaboration of group psychotherapy's scientific base, coupled with a more precise delineation of its unique motivational forces for change and growth. Testing the validity of existing techniques might be accompanied by the development of new and improved ones. Whether there will be sufficient funding sources to support such endeavors remains to be seen. Nonetheless, the unprecedented nature and rate of societal change forecasts that group psychotherapy will be uniquely suited to play a vital role in alleviating some of the serious problems — alienation, depersonalization, and generalized anxiety — characteristic of our day.

References

Abraham, A. (1973), A model for exploring intra- and inter-individual process in groups. *Internat. J. Group Psychother.*, 23:3–22.

Abrahams, J. (1958), Correlations in combined treatment by group and individual psychoanalysis. *Internat. J. Group Psychother.*, 8:126–128.

Ackerman, N. W. (1957), Group psychotherapy with a mixed group of adolescents. *Internat. J. Group Psychother.*, 2:249–260.

Adorno, T. W., Frenkel-Brunswik, E., Levinson, D. J., & Sanford, R. N. (1950), *The Authoritarian Personality.* New York: Harper.

Alexander, F. (1942), *Our Age of Unreason.* Philadelphia: Lippincott.

Allport, G. W. (1954), *The Nature of Prejudice.* Cambridge, Mass.: Addison-Wesley.

Alpert, A. (1957), A special therapeutic technique for certain developmental disorders in prelatency children. *Amer. J. Orthopsychiat.*, 27:256–270.

Anthony, E. J. (1980), The family and the psychoanalytic process in children. *The Psychoanalytic Study of the Child,* 35:3–34. New Haven: Yale University Press.

Aronson, M. L. (1964), Technical problems in combined therapy. *Internat. J. Group Psychother.*, 14:403–412.

———— (1967), Resistance in individual and group psychotherapy. *Amer. J. Psychother.*, 21:86–95.

Arsenian, J., Semrad., E. V., & Shapiro, D. (1962), An analysis of integral functions in small groups. *Internat. J. Group Psychother.*, 12:421–434.

Axline, V. (1947), *Play Therapy.* Boston: Houghton Mifflin.

Bach, G. (1954), *Intensive Group Psychotherapy.* New York: Ronald.

Back, K. (1951), Influence through social communication. *J. Abnorm. Soc. Psychol.*, 46:9–23.

Bales, R. F. (1950), *Interaction Process Analysis.* Reading, Mass.: Addison-Wesley.

Barcai, A. & Robinson, E. H. (1969), Conventional group therapy with preadolescent children. *Internat. J. Group Psychother.*, 19:334–345.

Baruch, D. & Miller, H. (1946), Group and individual psychotherapy as an adjunct in the treatment of allergy. *J. Consult. Psychol.*, 10:281–284.

Bass, B. M. (1960), *Leadership, Psychology and Organizational Behavior.* New York: Harper.

Beck, A. P. & Peters, L. (1981), The research evidence for distributed leadership in therapy groups. *Internat. J. Group Psychother.*, 31:43–71.

Bednar, R. L. & Paul, T. J. (1978), Experiential group research: Current perspectives. In: *Handbook of Psychotherapy and Behavior Change*, ed. S. L. Garfield & A. E. Bergin. New York: Wiley, pp. 769–815.

Bellak, L. (1954), *The TAT and CAT in Clinical Use*. New York: Grune & Stratton.

_____, Hurvich, M., & Gediman, H. K. (1973), *Ego Functions in Schizophrenics, Neurotics and Normals*. New York: Wiley Interscience.

_____ & Small, L. (1965), *Emergency Psychotherapy and Brief Psychotherapy*. New York: Grune & Stratton.

Bennis, W. G. (1958), On a genetic theory of group development. Presented at the Annual Conference of American Psychological Association, New York.

_____ (1959), Leadership theory and administrative behavior. *Admin. Sci. Quart.*, 4:259–260.

Berger, I. L. (1960), Modifications of the transference as observed in combined individual and group psychotherapy. *Internat. J. Group Psychother.*, 10:456–470.

Berger, M. M. (1964), Some implications of nonverbal communication in psychotherapy. *J. Soc. Psychiat.*, 19:31–39.

Berman, L. (1950), Psychoanalysis and group psychotherapy. *Psychoanal. Rev.*, 37:156–163.

_____ (1959), Antisocial character disorder: Its etiology and relationship to delinquency. *Amer. J. Psychother.*, 29:612–621.

Bernard, H. & Klein, R. (1977), Some perspectives on time limited group psychotherapy. *Compr. Psychiat.*, 18:579–584.

Berne, E. (1966), *Principles of Group Treatment*. New York: Oxford University Press.

Beukenkamp, C. (1955), The multi-dimensional orientation in analytic group therapy. *Amer. J. Psychother.*, 9:477–483.

Bibring, E. (1947), The so-called English school of psychoanalysis. *Psychoanal. Quart.*, 16:69–93.

Bieber, T. B. (1971), Combined individual and group psychotherapy. In: *Comprehensive Group Psychotherapy*, ed. H. I. Kaplan & B. J. Sadock. Baltimore: Williams & Wilkins, pp. 518–533.

Bion, W. R. (1948–1951), Experiences in groups. *Human Rel.*, 1:314–320, 487–496; 2:13–22, 295–303; 3:3–14, 395–402; 4:221–227.

_____ (1952), Group dynamics—a review. *Internat. J. Psycho-Anal.*, 33:235–247.

_____ (1955), Group dynamics—a review. In: *New Directions in Psychoanalysis*, ed. M. Klein, P. Heimann & R. Money-Kyrle. New York: Basic Books.

_____ (1959), *Experiences in Groups and Other Papers*. New York: Basic Books.

Bloch, S., Grouch, E., & Reibstein, J. (1981), Therapeutic factors in group psychotherapy. *Arch. Gen. Psychiat.*, 38:519–526.

Blos, P. (1961), Delinquency. In: *Adolescence: Psychoanalytic Approach to Problems in Therapy*, ed. S. Lorand & H. I. Schneer, New York: Harper-Hoeber.

_____ (1962), *On Adolescence: A Psychoanalytic Interpretation*. New York: Free Press.

_____ (1979), *The Adolescent Passage*. New York: International Universities Press.

Borgatta, E. R. (1954), Analysis of social interaction and sociometric perception. *Sociometry*, 17:7–32.

Bornstein, B. (1951), On latency. *The Psychoanalytic Study of the Child*, 6:279–285. New York: International Universities Press.

_____ (1953), Masturbation in the latency period. *The Psychoanalytic Study of the Child*, 8:65–78. New York: International Universities Press.

Bradford, L. P., Gibb, J. R., & Benne, K. D., eds. (1964), *T-Group Theory and Laboratory Method*. New York: Wiley.

Breen, D. (1977), Some differences between group and individual therapy in connection with the therapist's pregnancy. *Internat. J. Group Psychother.*, 27:499–510.

Brown, J. F. (1936), *Psychology and the Social Order*. New York: McGraw Hill.

Buirski, P. (1980), Toward a theory of adaptation in analytic group psychotherapy. *Internat. J. Group Psychother.*, 30:447–459.

Buxbaum, E. (1954), Techniques of child therapy: A critical evaluation. *The Psychoanalytic Study of the Child*, 9:297–333. New York: International Universities Press.

Bychowski, G. (1948), *Dictators and Disciples from Caesar to Stalin*. New York: International Universities Press.

Campbell, R. J. (1965), Psychotherapy in a community mental health center. *Amer. J. Psychiat.*, 122:143–147.

Caplan, G. (1974), *Support Systems and Community Mental Health*. New York: Behavioral Publications.

_____ & Killilea, M., eds. (1976), *Support Systems and Mutual Help*. New York: Grune & Stratton.

Cartwright, D. & Zander, A., eds. (1953), *Group Dynamics, Research and Theory*. Evanston, Ill.: Row, Peterson.

Cattell, R. B. (1951), New concepts for measuring leadership in terms of group syntality. *Human Rel.*, 4:161–184.

Churchill, S. R. (1965), Social group work: A diagnostic tool in child guidance. *Amer. J. Orthopsychiat.*, 35:135–140.

Coolidge, J. C. & Grunebaum, M. G. (1964), Individual and group therapy of a latency-age child. *Internat. J. Group Psychother.*, 14:84–96.

Cooper, L. & Gustafson, J. P. (1979), Toward a general theory of group therapy. *Human Rel.*, 32:967–981.

Corsini, R., ed. (1973), *Current Psychotherapies*. Itasca, Ill.: F. E. Peacock.

Couch, A. S. (1961), The psychological determinants of interpersonal behavior. In: *Proceedings of the Fourteenth International Congress of Applied Psychology*. Copenhagen: Munksgaard.

Cunningham, J., Strassberg, D. & Roback, H. (1978), Group psychotherapy for medical patients. *Compr., Psychiatr.*, 19:135–140.

Davis, F. B. & Lohr, N. E. (1971), Special problems with the use of co-therapists in group psychotherapy. *Internat. J. Group Psychother.*, 21:943–958.

Des Jarlais, D. C., Deren, S., & Lipton, D. S. (1981), Cost effectiveness studies in the evaluation of substance abuse treatment. In: *Substance Abuse: Clinical Problems and Perspectives*, ed. J. H. Lowinson & P. Ruiz. Baltimore: Williams & Wilkins.

Dies, R. R. (1977), Group therapist transparency: A critique of theory and research. *Internat. J. Group Psychother.*, 27:177–200.

————— (1979), Group psychotherapy: Reflections on three decades of research. *J. Applied Behav. Sci.*, 15:361–374.

Dumont, M. P. (1974), Self-help treatment programs. *Amer. J. Psychiat.*, 131:631–635.

Durkin, H. (1964), *The Group in Depth*. New York: International Universities Press.

————— & Glatzer, H. T. (1973), Transference neurosis in group psychotherapy. In: *Group Therapy 1973*, ed. L. Wolberg & E. K. Schwartz. New York: Stratton Intercontinental.

Durkin, J. E., ed. (1981), *Living Groups: Group Psychotherapy and General Systems Theory*. New York: Brunner/Mazel.

Edgecumbe, R. & Burgner, M. (1972), Some problems in the conceptualization of early object relationships. *The Psychoanalytic Study of the Child*, 27:283–314. New York: Quadrangle.

Ekstein, R., Bryant, K., & Friedman, S. W. (1958), Childhood schizophrenia and allied conditions. In: *Schizophrenia*, ed. L. Bellak. New York: Logos.

English, D. S. & Pearson, G. H. J. (1945), *Emotional Problems of Living*. New York: Norton.

English, M. B. & English, A. C. (1958), *A Comprehensive Dictionary of Psychological and Psychoanalytical Terms*. New York: Longmans Green.

Epstein, N. & Altman, S. (1972), Experiences in converting an activity group into verbal group therapy. *Internat. J. Group Psychother.*, 22:93–102.

————— & Slavson, S. R. (1962), Further observations on group psychotherapy with adolescent delinquent boys. *Internat. J. Psychother.*, 2:199–210.

Erikson, E. H. (1948), Hitler's imagery and German youth. In: *Personality in Nature, Society and Culture*, ed. C. Kluckhorn & H. A. Murray. New York: Knopf, pp. 485–510.

————— (1959), *Identity and the Life Cycle*. New York: International Universities Press.

Ezriel, H. (1950), A psychoanalytic approach to group treatment. *Brit. J. Med. Psychol.*, 23:59–74.

————— (1957), The role of transference in psychoanalytical and other approaches to group treatment. *Acta Psychotherapeutica*, 7:101–116.

Fairbairn, W. R. D. (1952), Theoretical and experimental aspects of psychoanalysis. *Brit. J. Med. Psychol.*, 25:122–127.

Feder, B. (1962), Limited goals in short-term group psychotherapy with institutionalized delinquent boys. *Internat. J. Group Psychother.*, 4:503–518.

Fenichel, O. (1945), *The Psychoanalytic Theory of Neurosis*. New York: Norton.

Ferreira, A. J. (1961), Empathy and the bridge function of the ego. *Internat. J.*

Psycho-Anal., 9:91–105.

Festinger, L. (1951). Architecture and group membership. *J. Soc. Issues,* 7: 152–163.

_____, Schacter, S. & Back, K. (1950), *Social Pressures in Informal Groups.* New York: Harper.

Fidler, J. W. & Fidler, G. S. (1963), *Occupational Therapy.* New York: Macmillan.

Fleischl, M. (1962), The understanding and utilization of social and adjunctive therapies. *Amer. J. Psychother.,* 26:255–265.

Foulkes, S. H. (1980), Psychodynamic processes in the light of psychoanalysis and group analysis. In: *Psychoanalytic Group Dynamics — Basic Readings,* ed. S. Scheidlinger. New York: International Universities Press, pp. 147–162.

_____ & Anthony, E. J. (1957 & 1964), *Group Psychotherapy: The Psychoanalytic Approach,* 1st & 2nd Ed. London: Penguin.

Frances A. & Clarkin, J. (1981), Differential therapeutics: A guide to treatment selection. *Hosp. Commun. Psychiat.,* 32:537–546.

Frank, J. D. (1957), Some determinants, manifestations and effects of cohesiveness in therapy groups. *Internat. J. Group Psychother.,* 7:53–63.

_____ (1973), *Persuasion and Healing.* Baltimore: Johns Hopkins University Press.

Frank, M. G. & Zilbach, J. (1968), Current trends in group therapy with children. *Internat. J. Group Psychother.,* 18:447–460.

Frazer, J. G. (1922), *The Golden Bough.* New York: Macmillan.

Freedman, M. B. & Sweet, B. S. (1954), Some specific features of group psychotherapy and their implications for the selection of patients. *Internat. J. Group Psychother.,* 4:355–368.

Freud, A. (1949), Certain types and stages of social maladjustment. In: *Searchlights on Delinquency,* ed. K. R. Eissler. New York: International Universities Press.

_____ (1965), *Normality and Pathology in Childhood.* New York: International Universities Press.

Freud, S. (1921), Group psychology and the analysis of the ego. *Standard Edition,* 18:67–145. London: Hogarth Press, 1955.

_____ (1931), Libidinal types. *Standard Edition,* 21:215–220. London: Hogarth Press, 1961.

Fried, E. (1954), The effect of combined therapy on the productivity of patients. *Internat. J. Group Psychother.,* 4:42–55.

_____ (1955), Combined group and individual therapy with passive narcissistic patients. *Internat. J. Group Psychother.,* 5:194–203.

_____ (1956), Ego emancipation of adolescents through group psychotherapy. *Internat. J. Group Psychother.,* 6:358–373.

Fries, M. E. (1958), Review of the literature on the latency period. *J. Hillside Hosp.,* 7:3–16.

_____ & Lewi, B. (1938), Interrelated factors in development. *Amer. J. Orthopsychiat.,* 8:726–752.

Ganter, G., Yeakel, M., & Polansky, N. (1967), *Retrieved from Limbo.* New York:

Child Welfare League of America.

Gibb, C. A. (1958), An interactional view of the emergence of leadership. *Austral. J. Psychol.*, 10:101–110.

Gibbard, G. S. & Hartman, J. J. (1973), The significance of utopian fantasies in small groups. *Internat. J. Group Psychother.*, 23:125–147.

————, ———— & Mann, R. D., eds. (1974), *Analysis of Groups.* San Francisco: Jossey-Bass.

Ginnott, C. (1961), *Group Psychotherapy with Children.* New York: McGraw Hill.

Glatzer, H. T. (1960), Discussion of symposium on combined individual and group psychoanalysis. *Amer. J. Orthopsychiat.*, 30:243–246.

———— (1962), Narcissistic problems in group psychotherapy. *Internat. J. Group Psychother.*, 12:448–455.

———— (1975), The leader as supervisor and supervisee. In: *The Leader in the Group,* ed. Z. A. Liff. New York: Aronson, pp. 138–145.

Golembiewski, R. T. & Blumberg, A. (1970), *Sensitivity Training and the Laboratory Approach.* Itasca, Ill.: Peacock.

Goodstein, L. D. & Dovico, M. (1979), The decline and fall of the small group. *J. Appl. Behav. Sci.*, 15:320–329.

Goulding, R. (1972), New directions in transactional analysis: Creating an environment for redecision and change. In: *Progress in Group and Family Therapy,* ed. C. J. Sager & H. S. Kaplan. New York: Brunner/Mazel, pp. 105–134.

Graham, E. W. (1964), A case treated by psychoanalysis and analytic group psychotherapy. *Internat. J. Group Psychother.*, 14:267–290.

Greenacre, P. (1972), Crowds and crisis. *The Psychoanalytic Study of the Child,* 27:136–154. New York: Quadrangle.

Greenson, R. R. (1959), The classic psychoanalytic approach. In: *American Handbook of Psychiatry,* ed. S. Arieti. New York: Basic Books.

Grotjahn, M. (1953), Aspects of countertransference in analytic group psychotherapy. *Internat. J. Group Psychother.*, 3:407–416.

———— (1972), Learning from dropout patients. *Internat. J. Group Psychother.*, 22:306–319.

Group Dynamics and Group Psychotherapy (1957), *Internat. J. Group Psychother.*, 7:3–154.

Group for the Advancement of Psychiatry (1971), The aged and community mental health: A guide to program development. 8:(No. 81).

Gruen, W. (1977), The effects of executive and cognitive control of the therapist on the work climate in group therapy. *Internat. J. Group Psychother.*, 27:139–152.

Grunebaum, H. & Solomon, L. (1980), Toward a peer theory of group psychotherapy. *Internat. J. Group Psychother.*, 30:23–49.

Guntrip, H. (1961), *Personality Structure and Human Interaction.* New York: International Universities Press.

Hall, C. S. & Lindzey, G. (1954), Psychoanalytic theory and its application in the social sciences. In: *Handbook of Social Psychology,* ed. G. Lindzey. Cambridge, Mass: Addison-Wesley, pp. 143–180.

Hamilton, G. (1947), *Psychotherapy in Child Guidance.* New York: Columbia University Press.

Hare, A. P., Borgatta, E. F., & Bales, R. F., eds. (1955), *Small Group Studies in Social Interaction.* New York: Knopf.

Harrington, M. (1962), *The Other America.* New York: Macmillan.

Hartford, M. E. (1972), *Groups in Social Work.* New York: Columbia University Press.

Hartmann, H. (1958), *Ego Psychology and the Problem of Adaptation.* New York: International Universities Press.

Hill, G. & Armitage, S. (1954), Analysis of combined therapy in patients with schizoid, obsessive–compulsive, or aggressive defenses. *J. Neurol. Ment. Dis.,* 119:113–134.

Hill, M. & Blane, H. (1967), Evaluation of psychotherapy with alcoholics: A critical review. *Quart. J. Study Alcohol,* 28:76–104.

Homans, G. C. (1950), *The Human Group.* New York: Harcourt.

Hoover, K. H., Raulinaitis, V. B., & Spaner, F. E. (1965), Therapeutic democracy: Group process as a corrective emotional experience. *Internat. J. Soc. Psychiat.,* 11:26–36.

Hurst, A. G. & Gladieux, J. D. (1980), Guidelines for leading an adolescent therapy group. In: *Group and Family Therapy 1980,* ed. M. Aronson & L. R. Wolberg. New York: Brunner/Mazel, pp. 151–165.

Imber, S. D., Lewis, P. M., & Loiselle, R. H. (1979), Uses and abuses of the brief intervention group. *Internat. J. Group Psychother.,* 29:39–49.

Ingersoll, B. & Silverman, A. (1978), Comparative group psychotherapy for the aged. *Gerontology,* 18:201–206.

Jackson, J. & Grotjahn, M. (1958), The treatment of oral defenses by combined individual and group psychotherapy. *Internat. J. Group Psychother.,* 8:373–382.

Jacobson, E. (1964), *The Self and the Object World.* New York: International Universities Press.

Janis, I. L. (1963), Group identification under conditions of external danger. *Brit. J. Med. Psychol.,* 36:227–238.

Jaques, E. (1955), Social systems as a defense against persecutory and depressive anxiety. In: *New Directions in Psychoanalysis,* ed. M. Klein, P. Heimann & R. Money-Kyrle. New York: Basic Books, pp. 478–498.

_____ (1970), *Work, Creativity and Social Justice.* New York: International Universities Press.

Jennings, H. H. (1943), *Leadership and Isolation.* New York: Longmans.

Journal of Applied Behavioral Science (1976), 12:261–463.

Kaplan, H. I. (1972), *The Origins of Group Psychoanalysis.* New York: Dutton.

_____ & Sadock, B. T. (1971), *Comprehensive Group Psychotherapy.* Baltimore: Williams & Wilkins.

Kaplan, S. R. & Roman, M. (1963), Phases of development in adult therapy groups. *Internat. J. Group Psychother.,* 13:10–26.

Katz, R. L. (1963), *Empathy: Its Nature and Uses.* New York: Free Press.

Kauff, P. (1977), The termination process. *Internat. J. Group Psychother.*, 27:3–18.

——— (1979), Diversity in analytic group psychotherapy. *Internat. J. Group Psychother.*, 29:51–66.

Kellerman, H. (1979), *Group Psychotherapy and Personality.* New York: Grune & Stratton.

Kernberg, O. F. (1976), *Object Relations Theory and Clinical Psychoanalysis.* New York: Aronson.

——— (1979), Regression in organizational leadership. *Psychiat.*, 42:24–38.

——— (1980), *Internal World and External Reality: Object Relations Theory Applied.* New York: Aronson.

Kimbro, E. L. Jr., Taschman, H. A., Wylie, H. W. Jr. & MacLennan, B. W. (1967), A multiple family group approach to some problems of adolescence. *Internat. J. Group Psychother.*, 17:18–24.

King, B. L. (1970), Diagnostic activity groups for latency age children. In: *Dynamic Approaches to Serving Families.* New York: Community Service Society.

King, C. H. (1959), Activity group therapy with a schizophrenic boy. *Internat. J. Group Psychother.*, 9:184–194.

Klapman, J. W. (1950), Observations on the "shuttle" process in individual-group psychotherapy. *Psychiat. Quart.*, 23:124–129.

Klein, G. S. (1976), *Psychoanalytic Theory: An Exploration of Essentials.* New York: International Universities Press.

Klein, M., Heimann, P., & Money-Kyrle, R., eds. (1955), *New Directions in Psychoanalysis.* New York: Basic Books.

Kohut, H. (1976), Creativeness, charisma, group psychology. In: *Freud: The usion of Science and Humanism*, ed. J. E. Gedo & G. H. Pollock. New York: International Universities Press.

——— (1977), *The Restoration of the Self.* New York: International Universities Press.

Konopka, G. (1970), *Group Work in the Institution.* New York: Association Press.

Kornblith, A. B. & Kaplan, S. R. (1981), Group approaches in drug treatment programs. In: *Substance Abuse: Clinical Problems and Perspectives*, ed. J. H. Lowinson & P. Ruiz. Baltimore: Williams & Wilkins.

Kraft, I. A. (1968), An overview of group therapy with adolescents. *Internat. J. Group Psychother.*, 4:461–480.

Kraupl-Taylor, F. & Rey, T. H. (1953), The scapegoat motif in society and its manifestations in a therapeutic group. *Internat. J. Psycho-Anal.*, 34:253–264.

Kris, E. (1943), Some problems of war propaganda. *Psychoanal. Quart.*, 12:390–399.

——— & Leites, N. (1947), Trends in twentieth century propaganda. In: *Psychoanalysis and the Social Sciences*, ed. G. Róheim. New York: International Universities Press, pp. 393–409.

Lakin, M., Mooney, K. & Havasy, S. (1977), Interaction among aged and group therapy intervention. *Gerontologist*, 17:85–90.

Lazarus, A. A. (1977), Has behavior therapy outlived its usefulness? *Amer. Psy-*

chol., 32:550-554.

Le Bon, G. (1903), *The Psychology of the Crowd.* London: Unwin.

Leviticus, 16:8-10. The holy scriptures. Philadelphia: Jewish Publication Society of America.

Lewin, K. (1947), Group decision and social change. In: *Readings in Social Psychology,* ed. T. Newcomb & E. Hartley. New York: Holt, pp. 330-344.

_____, Lippitt, R., & White, R. K. (1939), Patterns of aggressive behavior in experimentally created "social climates." *J. Social Psychol.,* 10:271-299.

Lieberman, M. A. (1977), Problems in integrating traditional group therapies with new group forms. *Internat. J. Group Psychother.,* 27:19-32.

_____, Yalom, I., & Miles, M. (1973), *Encounter Groups: First Facts.* New York: Basic Books.

Lindt, H. & Pennal, H. A. (1962), On the defensive quality of groups. *Internat. J. Group Psychother.,* 12:171-179.

Lippitt, R., Polansky, N., Redl, F. & Rosen, S. (1952), The dynamics of power. *Human Rel.,* 5:37-64.

Lipschutz, D. M. (1957), Combined group and individual psychotherapy. *Amer. J. Psychother.,* 11:336-344.

Lockwood, J. L. (1981), Treatment of disturbed children in verbal and experiential group psychotherapy, *Internat. J. Group Psychother.,* 31:355-366.

Loeser, L. H. & Bry, T. (1953), The position of the group therapist in transference and countertransference. *Internat. J. Group Psychother.,* 3:389-406.

Lowrey, L. G. (1944), Group treatment for mothers. *Amer. J. Orthopsychiat.,* 14:589-592.

Luborsky, L., Singer, B., & Luborsky, L. (1975), Comparative studies of psychotherapy. *Arch. Gen. Psychiat.,* 32:995-1008.

MacLennan, B. W. & Felsenfeld, N. (1968), *Group Counseling and Psychotherapy with Adolescents.* New York: Columbia University Press.

_____ & Levy, N. (1969), The group psychotherapy literature 1968. *Internat. J. Group Psychother.,* 19:382-408.

Magary, L. & Elder, V. (1970), Group therapy with adolescent girls: Two models. In: *Dynamic Approaches to Serving Families.* New York: Community Service Society.

Mahler, M. S. (1952), On child psychosis and schizophrenia. *The Psychoanalytic Study of the Child,* 7:286-305. New York: International Universities Press.

_____, Pine, F., & Bergman, A. (1975), *The Psychological Birth of the Human Infant.* New York: Basic Books.

Main, T. F. (1946), The hospital as a therapeutic institution. *Bull. Menninger Clinic,* 10:66-70.

Malan, D. H., Balfour, F. H. G., Hood, V. G., & Shooter, A. (1976), Group Psychotherapy: A long-term follow-up study. *Arch. Gen. Psychiat.,* 33:1303-1315.

Mandelbrote, B. (1979), The therapeutic community. *Brit. ·J. Psychiat.,* 135:369-371.

Mann, R. D. (1959), A review of the relationship between personality and performance in small groups. *Psychol. Bull.*, 56:211–270.

McCall, M. W. & Lombardo, M. M., eds. (1978), *Leadership — Where Else Can We Go?* Durham, N.C.: Duke University Press.

McDougall, W. (1920), *The Group Mind.* New York: Putnam.

Meerloo, J. A. M. (1950), *Patterns of Panic.* New York: International Universities Press.

Modell, A. H. (1978), The conceptualization of the therapeutic action in psychoanalysis. *Bull. Menninger Clinic,* 42:493–504.

Money-Kyrle, R. (1950), Varieties of group formation. In: *Psychoanalysis and the Social Sciences,* ed. G. Róheim. New York: International Universities Press, pp. 313–329.

Moore, B. E. (1979), Panel on psychoanalytic knowledge of group processes. *J. Amer. Psychoanal. Assn.,* 27:145–156.

Moreno, J. L., ed. (1945), *Group Psychotherapy: A Symposium.* New York: Beacon House.

Mosher, L. R. & Gunderson, J. G. (1979), Group, family, milieu and community support systems treatment of schizophrenia. In: *Disorders of the Schizophrenic Syndrome,* ed. L. Bellak. New York: Basic Books., pp. 399–452.

Moustakas, C. (1967), *Creativity and Conformity.* Princeton, N.J.: Van Nostrand.

Mowrer, D. H. (1964), *The New Group Therapy.* Princeton, N.J.: Van Nostrand.

Mulder, M. & Stemerding, A. (1963), Threat, attraction to groups, and need for strong leadership. *Human Rel.,* 16:317–334.

Munzer, J. & Greenwald, H. (1957), Interaction process analysis of a therapy group. *Internat. J. Group Psychother.,* 7:175–190.

Murphy, A. J. (1941), A study of the leadership process. *Amer. Sociol. Rev.,* 6:674–687.

Ogden, T. H. (1979), On projective identification. *Internat. J. Psycho-Anal.,* 60:357–373.

Ormont, L. (1964), The resolution of resistance by conjoint psychoanalysis. *Psychoanal. Rev.* 51:425–437.

Papanek, H. (1954), Combined group and individual therapy in private practice. *Amer. J. Psychother.,* 8:679–686.

Parloff, M. B. (1970), Group therapy and the small group field: An encounter. *Internat. J. Group Psychother.,* 20:267–304.

———— (1978), Group psychotherapy outcome instrument: Guidelines for conducting research. *Small Group Behav.,* 9:243–285.

———— (1979), Can psychotherapy research guide the policy maker? *Amer. Psychol.,* 34:296–306.

———— & Dies, R. R. (1977), Group psychotherapy outcome research 1966–1975. *Internat. J. Group Psychother.,* 27:281–319.

Peck, H. B. (1963), Some relationships between group process and mental health phenomena in theory and practice. *Internat. J. Group Psychother.,* 13:269–289.

Pigors, P. (1935), *Leadership or Domination.* Boston: Houghton Mifflin.

Pines, M. (1980), What to expect in the psychotherapy of borderline patients.

Group Analysis, 13:168-177.

Powdermaker, F. & Frank, J. D. (1953), *Group Psychotherapy.* Cambridge, Mass.: Harvard University Press.

Quarantelli, E. L. (1954), The nature and condition of panic. *Amer. J. Sociol.,* 60:267-275.

Rabin, H. M. (1970), Preparing patients for group psychotherapy. *Internat. J. Group Psychother.,* 20:135-145.

Rahe, R., Ward, H., & Hayes, V. (1979), Brief group therapy in myocardial infarction rehabilitation. *Psychosom. Med.,* 41:229-242.

Redl, F. (1942), Group emotion and leadership. *Psychiat.,* 5:573-596.

_____ (1944), Diagnostic group work. *Amer. J. Orthopsychiat.,* 14:53-67.

_____ & Wineman, D. (1952), *Controls from Within.* New York: Free Press.

Reik, T. (1949), *Listening with the Third Ear.* New York: Farrar, Strauss.

Reiner, B. S. & Kaufman, I. (1959), *Character Disorders in Parents of Delinquents.* New York: Family Service Association of America.

Rice, A. K. (1965), *Learning for Leadership.* London: Tavistock.

Riessman, F. (1965), The helper therapy principle. *Social Work,* 10:27-32.

_____, Cohen, J., & Pearl, A., eds. (1964), *Mental Health of the Poor.* Glencoe, Ill.: Free Press.

Rioch, M. J. (1970), Group relations conferences: Rationale and technique. *Internat. J. Group Psychother.,* 20:340-355.

Rogers, C. (1967), The process of the basic encounter group. In: *Challenges of Humanistic Psychology,* ed. J. F. T. Bugenthal. New York: McGraw Hill.

Rose, S. (1953), Applications of Horney's theories to group analysis. *Internat. J. Group Psychother.,* 3:270-279.

Rose, S. D. (1972), *Treating Children in Groups.* San Francisco: Jossey-Bass.

Rosenbaum, M. (1960), What is the place of combined psychotherapy? *Topic Probl. Psychother.,* 2:86-96.

Rostov, B. W. (1965), Group work in the psychiatric hospital. *Social Work,* 10:23-31.

Roth, B. E. (1980), Understanding the development of a homogeneous identity—impaired group through countertransference phenomena. *Internat. J. Group Psychother.,* 30:405-426.

Ruesch, J. & Bateson, G. (1951), *Communication: The social matrix of psychiatry.* New York: Norton.

Ruiz, P. (1972), On the perception of the "mother group" in T-groups. *Internat. J. Group Psychother.,* 22:488-491.

Sager, C. J. (1959), The effects of group psychotherapy on individual psychoanalysis. *Internat. J. Group Psychother.,* 9:403-419.

_____ (1964), Insight and interaction in combined therapy. *Internat. J. Group Psychother.,* 14:403-412.

Sands, R. M. & Fishman, M. S. (1963), Experimentation with group techniques with ego-disturbed mothers. *Internat. J. Group Psychother.,* 13:187-195.

Sanford, N. (1953), Clinical methods: Psychotherapy. In: *Annual Review of Psychology,* ed. C. P. Stone & D. W. Taylor. Stanford, Calif.: Stanford Annual

Reviews, pp. 322–341.

Saravay, S. M. (1975), Group psychology and the structural theory, *J. Amer. Psychoanal. Assn.*, 23:69–81.

———— (1978), A psychoanalytic theory of group development. *Internat. J. Group Psychother.*, 28:481–507.

Sarnoff, C. (1976), *Latency.* New York: Aronson.

Schafer, R. (1958), Regression in the service of the ego. In: *Assessment of Human Motives*, ed. G. Lindzey. New York: Rinehart, pp. 119–148.

Schamess, G. (1976), Group treatment modalities for latency-age children. *Internat. J. Group Psychother.*, 26:455–474.

Scharfstein, S. S. (1978), Will community mental health survive in the 1980's? *Amer. J. Psychiat.*, 134:1363–1365.

Scheidlinger, S. (1952a), *Psychoanalysis and Group Behavior.* New York: Norton.

———— (1952b), Freudian group psychology and group psychotherapy. *Amer. J. Orthopsychiat.*, 22:710–717.

———— (1955), Should teachers be group psychotherapists? *Progressive Educ.*, 14:70–75.

———— (1964), Identification, the sense of identity and of belonging in small groups. *Internat. J. Group Psychother.*, 14:291–306.

———— (1965), Three group approaches with socially deprived latency–age children. *Internat. J. Group Psychother.*, 15:434–445.

———— (1967), Current conceptual and methodological issues in group psychotherapy research. *Internat. J. Group Psychother.*, 17:53–56.

———— (1968a), Therapeutic group approaches in community mental health. *Social Work*, 13:87–95.

———— (1968b), The concept of regression in group psychotherapy. *Internat. J. Group Psychother.*, 18:3–20.

———— (1975), Editor's introduction. *Internat. J. Group Psychother.*, 25:123–125.

———— (1978), Inpatient group therapy: Some current perspectives. *Internat. J. Group Psychother.*, 28:319–340.

———— (1980), *Psychoanalytic Group Dynamics — Basic Readings.* New York: International Universities Press.

Scheidlinger, S., Douville, M., Harrahill, C., King, C., & Minor, J. (1959), Activity group therapy in a family service agency. *Social Casework*, 40:193–201.

Scheidlinger, S. & Freeman, H. (1956), Group therapy in family services. In: *The Fields of Group Psychotherapy*, ed. S. R. Slavson. New York: International Universities Press.

Scheler, M. (1954), *The Nature of Sympathy.* New Haven: Yale University Press.

Schiffer, M. (1969), *The Therapeutic Play Group.* New York: Grune & Stratton.

———— (1977), Activity–interview group psychotherapy. *Internat. J. Group Psychother.*, 27:377–388.

Schilder, P. (1936), An analysis of ideologies as a psychotherapeutic method, especially in group treatment. *Amer. J. Psychiat.*, 93:601–617.

Schindler, W. (1951), Family pattern in group formation and therapy. *Internat. J.*

Group Psychother., 1:100–105.

_____ (1952), The group personality concept. *Internat. J. Group Psychother.* 2:311–315.

_____ (1966), The role of the mother in group psychotherapy. *Internat. J. Group Psychother.*, 16:198–200.

Schulman, I. (1957), Modifications in group psychotherapy with antisocial delinquents. *Internat. J. Group Psychother.*, 3:310–317.

Schutz, W. C. (1955), What makes groups productive? *Human Rel.*, 8:429–465.

Schwartz, E. K. & Wolf, A. (1957), Psychoanalysis in groups: Three primary parameters. *Amer. Imago*, 14:281–297.

Semrad, E. V. (1958), Panel on a comparison of individual and group psychology. *J. Amer. Psychoanal. Assn.*, 6:121–130.

_____, Kanter, S., Shapiro, D., & Arsenian, J. (1963), The field of group psychotherapy. *Internat. J. Group Psychother.*, 13:452–464.

Shaw, M. (1971), *Group Dynamics: The Psychology of Small Group Behavior.* New York: McGraw Hill.

Shepard, H. A. & Bennis, W. G. (1956), A theory of training by group methods. *Human Rel.*, 9:403–414.

Silver, R. J., Lubin, G., Silver, D. S., & Dobson, N. H. (1979), The group psychotherapy literature 1979. *Internat. J. Group Psychother.*, 29:491–538.

Slater, P. E. (1966), *Microcosm.* New York: Wiley.

Slavson, S. R. (1943), *An Introduction to Group Therapy.* New York: Commonwealth Fund.

_____ (1950), *Analytic Group Psychotherapy.* New York: Columbia University Press.

_____ (1952), *Child Psychotherapy.* New York: Columbia University Press.

_____ (1955), Criteria for selection and rejection of patients for various kinds of group psychotherapy. *Internat. J. Group Psychother.*, 5:3–30.

_____ (1964), *A Textbook in Analytic Group Psychotherapy.* New York: International Universities Press.

Solomon, L. N. & Berzon, B., eds., (1972), *New Perspectives on Encounter Groups.* San Francisco: Jossey–Bass.

Spitz, R. A. (1963), Life and the dialogue. In: *Counterpoint, Libidinal Object and Subject,* ed. H. S. Gaskill. New York: International Universities Press, pp. 154–176.

Spotnitz, H. (1954), Comments on combined therapy for the hostile patient. *Amer. J. Orthopsychiat.*, 24:535–537.

Stechler, G. & Kaplan, S. (1980), The development of the self: A psychoanalytic perspective. *The Psychoanalytic Study of the Child,* 35:85–106. New Haven: Yale University Press.

Stein, A. (1964), The nature of transference in combined therapy. *Internat. J. Group Psychother.*, 14:413–424.

Stewart, D. A. (1956), *Preface to Empathy.* New York: Philosophical Library.

Stogdill, R. M. (1950), Leadership, membership and organization. *Psychol. Bull.*, 47:1–14.

———— (1959), *Individual Behavior and Group Achievement.* New York: Oxford University Press.

———— (1974), *Handbook of Leadership.* New York: Free Press.

Stone, L. (1961), *The Psychoanalytic Situation.* New York: International Universities Press.

Strauss, G. (1970), Organizational behavior and personnel relations. In: *A Review of Industrial Relations Research.* Madison, Wisc.: Industrial Research Association, pp. 241–250.

Sullivan, H. S. (1953), *The Interpersonal Theory of Psychiatry.* New York: Norton.

Tabachnick, N. (1965), Isolation, transfer splitting and combined therapy. *Compr. Psychiat.,* 6:336–346.

Talland, G. A. (1957), Role and status structure in therapy groups. *J. Clin. Psychol.,* 13:27–33.

Tarail, M. (1980), Current and future issues in community mental health. *Psychiat. Quart.,* 52:27–38.

Teicher, A. (1962), The use of conflicting loyalties in combined group psychotherapy. *Internat. J. Group Psychother.,* 12:75–81.

Thelen, H. A. (1954), *Dynamics of Groups at Work.* Chicago: University of Chicago Press.

Toffler, A. (1970), Future shock. New York: Bantam Books.

Toker, E. (1972), The scapegoat as an essential group phenomenon. *Internat. J. Group Psychother.,* 22:320–332.

Torda, C. (1970), A therapeutic procedure for adolescents with emotional disorders. In: *Pathways in Child Guidance.* New York: Bureau of Child Guidance.

Trotter, W. (1916), *Instincts of the Herd in Peace and War.* London: Fisher Unwin.

Waxer, P. (1977), Short-term group psychotherapy: Some principles and techniques. *Internat. J. Group Psychother.,* 27:33–42.

Weil, A. P. (1953), Certain severe disturbances of ego development in childhood. *The Psychoanalytic Study of the Child,* 8:271–287. New York: International Universities Press.

Weiner, M. F. (1974), Genetic versus interpersonal insight. *Internat. J. Group Psychother.,* 24:230–237.

Wender, L. (1936), The dynamics of group psychotherapy and its application. *J. Neurol. Ment. Dis.,* 84:55–56.

———— & Stein A. (1949), Group psychotherapy as an aid to outpatient treatment in a psychiatric clinic. *Psychiat. Quart.,* 23:415–424.

Whitaker, D. S. & Lieberman, M. A. (1964), *Psychotherapy Through the Group Process.* New York: Atherton.

Wilder, J. (1974), Group analysis and the insights of the analyst. In: *The Challenge for Group Psychotherapy — Present and Future,* ed. S. De Schill. New York: International Universities Press, pp. 251–263.

Wilmer, H. A. (1981), Defining and understanding the therapeutic community. *Hosp. Commun. Psychiat.,* 32:95–99.

Wolberg, A. (1960), The psychoanalytic treatment of the borderline patient in the individual and group setting. *Topical Probl. Psychother.*, 2:174–197.

Wolf, A. (1950), The psychoanalysis of groups. *Amer. J. Psychother.*, 4:16–50.

_____ & Schwartz, E. K. (1962), *Psychoanalysis in Groups.* New York: Grune & Stratton.

Yalom, I. (1970 & 1975), *The Theory of Practice of Group Psychotherapy,* 1st & 2nd Ed. New York: Basic Books.

_____ & Grieves, C. (1977), Group therapy with the terminally ill. *Amer. J. Psychiat.*, 134:396–400.

Zetzel, E. R. (1956), An approach to the relation between concept and content in psychoanalytic theory. *The Psychoanalytic Study of the Child,* 11:99–124. New York: International Universities Press.

INDEX

259